J. D. Salinger
and the Critics

Wadsworth Guides to Literary Study

Maurice Beebe, General Editor

APPROACHES TO *WALDEN*
edited by Lauriat Lane, Jr., University of New Brunswick

CONRAD'S *HEART OF DARKNESS* AND THE CRITICS
edited by Bruce Harkness, University of Illinois

CONRAD'S *SECRET SHARER* AND THE CRITICS
edited by Bruce Harkness, University of Illinois

CRIME AND PUNISHMENT AND THE CRITICS
edited by Edward Wasiolek, University of Chicago

DARWIN AND HIS CRITICS: The Darwinian Revolution
edited by Bernard R. Kogan, University of Illinois, Chicago

J. D. SALINGER AND THE CRITICS
edited by William F. Belcher and James W. Lee, North Texas State University

THE *KING LEAR* PERPLEX
edited by Helmut Bonheim, University of California, Santa Barbara

LITERARY CENSORSHIP: Principles, Cases, Problems
edited by Kingsley Widmer, San Diego State College, and Eleanor Widmer

LITERARY SYMBOLISM: An Introduction to the Interpretation of Literature
edited by Maurice Beebe, Purdue University

MELVILLE'S *BILLY BUDD* AND THE CRITICS
edited by William T. Stafford, Purdue University

THE RIME OF THE ANCIENT MARINER: A HANDBOOK
edited by Royal A. Gettmann, University of Illinois

SATIRE: THEORY AND PRACTICE
edited by Charles A. Allen and George D. Stephens, Long Beach State College

A *SCARLET LETTER* HANDBOOK
edited by Seymour L. Gross, University of Notre Dame

VOLTAIRE'S *CANDIDE* AND THE CRITICS
edited by Milton P. Foster, Eastern Michigan University

WHITMAN THE POET: MATERIALS FOR STUDY
edited by John C. Broderick, Wake Forest College

J. D. Salinger
and the Critics

88

Edited by

William F. Belcher

and

James W. Lee

North Texas State University

Wadsworth Publishing Company, Inc.
Belmont, California   2

To Florence and Dorothea

PREFACE

After publication of *The Catcher in the Rye* in 1951, the fiction of J. D. Salinger acquired enormous significance for young people. A symposium in the March 9, 1957, issue of the *Nation* demonstrated that Salinger's work had become a major influence upon college students: Stanley Kunitz, of Queens College, reported that Salinger was the only novelist he had heard "praised vociferously." Salinger's appeal, however, has not been exclusively to the young. His craftsmanship and understanding of the adolescent mind have also made his novel and recent stories a delight to mature readers. *The Catcher in the Rye* still sells at the rate of a quarter of a million copies a year, and *Franny and Zooey*, which had been published earlier in the *New Yorker*, led the bestseller lists for ten months after its publication in 1961 in a single volume. In light of this popularity, the publication of a new Salinger story is a major literary event.

Students in composition and literature classes will enjoy working with a writer they have read and feel they understand. Moreover, because this volume contains diverse critical studies of a literary figure whose stature is only tentatively established and whose forthcoming work will continue to shape his reputation, it will also appeal to the general reader and to students in advanced classes in literary criticism. By examining the selections—which are arranged chronologically—in Part One, the reader may see how criticism, beginning with exploratory suggestions about the complexities of Salinger's work, gradually becomes comprehensive. The reader will be able to see how critics are indebted to their predecessors, even when they disagree. A further advantage to students and young critics is that Salinger's stories have not been so exhaustively analyzed as the novel. By applying to some of the stories the critical techniques that have been used successfully on the novel, they may enjoy the experience of doing independent criticism.

The introductory selection in this volume reviews the generally known facts about J. D. Salinger the man and provides an overview of his work as a writer of fiction. Part One includes studies confined to *The Catcher in the Rye*. These selections, arranged chronologically, were chosen to present as great a variety of critical views as possible in the space available. Part Two contains general studies covering both the stories and *The Catcher in the Rye*, as well as short studies of individual stories. These pieces have been arranged to point up contrasting critical views.

In using this book in the university, students may profitably confine themselves to *The Catcher in the Rye,* but it will require very little additional effort and expense for them to familiarize themselves with *Nine Stories, Franny and Zooey,* "Raise High the Roof Beam, Carpenters," and "Seymour: An Introduction," so that they can see the parallels and prevailing themes in the entire body of work. Some of these similarities are implied in Part Three, "Suggestions for Study and Writing," following the reprinted selections. These topics will suggest subjects for original critical essays for advanced classes as well as subjects for research papers for freshman and sophomore classes.

The original pagination of the articles is indicated by means of raised brackets in the text. The amount of material eliminated from any essay can be determined by checking the original pagination (indicated in brackets) against the complete bibliographical entry accompanying each selection. Unspaced ellipses (...) are those of the original author; spaced ellipses (. . .) are our own. In several selections, footnotes have been renumbered to make a sequence for this book.

CONTENTS

PART THREE

J. D. Salinger
and the Critics

JOHN SKOW and THE EDITORS OF *TIME*

From "Sonny: An Introduction," *Time*, LXXVIII (September 15, 1961), 84–90. Courtesy of TIME; copyright Time Inc. 1961.

. . . As nearly as is possible in an age in which all relations are public, J. D. Salinger lives the life of a recluse. He says that he needs this isolation to keep his creativity intact, that he must not be interrupted "during working years." But the effort of evading the world must by now be almost more tiring than a certain amount of normal sociability would be. One critic and fellow novelist, Harvey Swados, has in fact suggested, pettishly, that Salinger's reputation is in part a consequence of his "tantalizing physical inaccessibility."

He has only once answered a reporter's questions (she was a 16-year-old Windsor, Vt., high school girl who wrote an article for her school paper in 1953). He will turn and run if addressed on the street by a stranger, and his picture has not appeared on a dust jacket since the first two printings of *Catcher* (it was yanked off the third edition at his request). He has refused offers from at least three book clubs for *Franny and Zooey*, and has not sold anything to the movies since Hollywood made a Susan Hayward Kleenex-dampener of his *Uncle Wiggily in Connecticut* in 1949.

Salinger's family and friends respect his hermitage and protect him like Swiss pikemen. For some of them, the conspiracy of silence is wearying; Author Peter De Vries clams as loyally as anyone, but admits that knowing Salinger makes him feel like a TV gangster: "You go skulking around not talking."

Salinger fans have filled the resultant vacuum with splendid imagination. The author apparently listens now and then behind his locked door, because in *Seymour, an Introduction*, his fictional alter ego refers to "poignant get-well-soon notes from old readers of mine who have somewhere picked up the bogus information that I spend six months of the year in a Buddhist monastery and the other six in a mental institution." One source of bogus information is the author himself; in the jacket blurb for *Franny and Zooey*, which he wrote himself, he says with coy fraudulence that "I live in Westport with my dog." The dark facts are that he has not lived in Westport or had a dog for years. But to disprove such rumors and humors involves infiltrating a distant-early-warning system equipped to detect journalists half a continent away.

SEARCHING FOR SEYMOUR. Some of the Glass legend, of course, parallels fact. All the Glass brothers sometimes sound like Salinger—introspective, sensitive, obsessed with words, hating what seems phony, dabbling in mysticism—and incidents in the author's life turn up later in[87] his fiction. Like the Glass children, Salinger was born in New York to a Jewish father and a Christian mother (to soothe her in-laws-to-be, Scotch-Irish Marie Jillich changed her name to Miriam when she married Sol Salinger). But Sol was, and is, a prosperous importer of hams and cheeses, and any connection he or Miriam ever had with show business is well hidden by the Salinger counterintelligence apparatus.

Sonny, as he was then called, a solemn, polite child who liked to take long walks by himself, had no brothers and only one sister, Doris, who was eight years older than he. Salinger once said that Seymour and Holden were modeled after a dead school friend, so reporters and Ph.D. candidates are forever searching for him. At least two of the author's prep school acquaintances died young, one of them a boy of great brilliance. But intensive detective work shows that Salinger, like a lonely child inventing brothers and sisters, has drawn most of his characters out of his own rare imagination.

Unlike Zooey and the rest, Sonny was anything but a Quiz Kid. His grades at public schools in Manhattan's Upper West Side were mostly Bs, but arithmetic baffled him. His IQ test score was merely average at 104, and his deportment was sometimes poor. The tall, skinny boy had a better time of it at Camp Wigwam in Harrison, Me., where, at eleven, he played a fair game of tennis, made friends readily, and was voted "the most popular actor of 1930."

Concerned about his studies, Sonny's parents enrolled him in Manhattan's highly rated McBurney School when he was 13 (at the enrollment interview, he said he was interested in dramatics and tropical fish). He flunked out a year later. A friend who knew Sonny then recalled that "he wanted to do unconventional things. For hours, no one in the family knew where he was or what he was doing; he just showed up for meals. He was a nice boy, but he was the kind of kid who, if you wanted to have a card game, wouldn't join in."

UNHIDDEN TEARS. When he was 15, Sonny was banished to Valley Forge Military Academy, a seat of learning heavily fortified with boxwood hedges and Revolutionary War cannon against dangers lurking in the Pennsylvania hills. Although the school is a recognizable model for Pencey Prep, the neurosis farm in *Catcher,* young Salinger—who talked of grabbing the big loot as a Hollywood writer-producer—was no Holden Caulfield. Classmate Alton McCloskey, first sergeant in Corporal Salinger's B Company and now a retired milk dealer in Lock Haven, Pa., remembers crawling through the fence with Salinger after lights out to poach local beer taps, but he is sure that Salinger never went AWOL, as Holden did, and practiced only accepted sorts of non-conformism.

In June 1936 Valley Forge gave him his only diploma. As literary editor of the yearbook, Salinger presented to the school a damply magnificent floral arrangement, since set to music and still sung at Last Parade:

> *Hide not thy tears on this last day*
> *Your sorrow has no shame;*
> *To march no more midst lines of grey;*
> *No longer play the game.*
> *Four years have passed in joyful ways—*
> *Wouldst stay these old times dear?*
> *Then cherish now these fleeting days,*
> *The few while you are here ...*

OFF TO BYDGOSZCZ. At night, tenting a blanket over his head to hide his flashlight beam from the Valley Forge duty officer, Salinger (by now called Jerry) had written his first short stories. But if he told his family that he intended to be an author, he did not convince Papa Sol. In 1937, after Jerry spent a few unproductive weeks at New York University, the two Salingers set out for Vienna. "I was supposed to apprentice myself to the Polish ham business," Salinger wrote in a 1944 issue of *Story* Magazine. "They finally dragged me off to Bydgoszcz for a couple of months, where I slaughtered pigs, wagoned through the snow with the big slaughtermaster. Came back to America and tried college for half a semester, but quit like a quitter."

Salinger's last brush with institutional wisdom came at Columbia, where he signed up for a short-story course given by Whit Burnett, editor of *Story*. In 1942 the author was drafted and used his weekend passes to hole up in hotel rooms with his typewriter. Typical of his output then was an earnest piece for *Story*, and a weepy lament in the *Saturday Evening Post* about a sensitive young man who dies before he has time to finish the world's greatest novel, but whose brother, in penitence for his sins, abandons his own career as the world's greatest songwriter to finish the book.

By 1944 the author was stationed in Tiverton, Devonshire, training with a small counterintelligence detachment of the 4th Infantry Division—almost exactly the situation of Sergeant X, the tormented hero of the warmest and best of the *Nine Stories, For Esmé—With Love and Squalor* (the author, like Sergeant X, passed the time by listening to choir practice at a Methodist church in Tiverton). On June 6, five hours after the first assault forces hit Utah Beach, Salinger landed with the 4th in Normandy, stayed with the division through the Battle of the Bulge. He was an aloof, solitary soldier whose job was to discover Gestapo agents by interviewing French civilians and captured

Germans. In France, Staff Sergeant Salinger had an audience with War Correspondent Ernest Hemingway, who read Salinger's work and, possibly in appreciation of it ("Jesus, he has a helluva talent"), took out his Luger and shot the head off a chicken. Salinger used a similar incident in *Esmé*.

FOXHOLE WRITER. With a swagger, the prospering young author in 1944 sent Burnett a $200 check to help other young writers, and added: "Am still writing whenever I can find the time and an unoccupied foxhole." He carried a typewriter around in his Jeep, and an Army acquaintance remembers him typing away, crouching under a table, while his area was under attack. Salinger's stories were improving, although his dialogue still had the kind of workmanlike falsity taught in writing classes. In one of his *Post* stories, Salinger introduced Sergeant[88] Vincent Caulfield, who "has a kid brother in the Army who flunked out of a lot of schools" and who is apparently killed in action in the Pacific. The story shows Salinger's fictional preoccupation with dead brothers, and his bent for starting his legends by killing off his main character. (The Glass legend similarly began with Seymour's suicide, in *A Perfect Day for Bananafish*, in 1948.)

Salinger in 1946 was back in New York, rid not only of soldiering but of a brief, unsuccessful marriage to a European woman physician. Though the two were obviously incompatible, he later insisted that they had a telepathic link, were aware of the same events happening at the same time. He lived with his parents on Park Avenue and spent his nights in Greenwich Village. Gentle and humorous, he loved arguing about grammar and augmented his skinny frame with bar bells. Although this was years before Buddhism was peddled in supermarkets, he eagerly studied Zen, gave reading lists on the subject to his dates. He brought an astonishing collection of girls to the Village, bagged with unobtrusive efficiency at a drugstore in Manhattan's chaste Barbizon Hotel for Women. Friends could almost see him storing up dialogue. The Barrymore of Camp Wigwam fended off too-curious Barbizonians with elaborate legpulls; one girl returned to the real world convinced that he was a goalie for the Montreal Canadiens.

ACROSS THE RIVER. Soon Salinger was much too absorbed with writing to need the Village, and he began a series of withdrawals. The first took him to a cottage 24 miles away, in Tarrytown. Friends apparently found his address, because he hid out in a sweatbox near the Third Avenue el for his three-week push to finish *Catcher*. He decided to move again, and in one of the notable failures of Zen archery, hit on Westport. The artsy-ginsy exurb was no place for Salinger. "A writer's worst enemy is another writer," he remarked ungraciously and accurately somewhat later.

There were no writers in Cornish, N.H., and no plumbing or furnace in the gambrel-roofed cottage Salinger bought on a 90-acre hillside tract overlooking the Connecticut River. That winter he happily carried water from his stream and cut wood with a chain saw. For company he hiked across the river to Windsor, Vt., and passed the time with teen-agers in a juke joint called Nap's Lunch. The kids loved him, but mothers worried that the tall, solemn writer fellow from New York would put their children in a book.

THE BLUE SUITCASE. In 1953, at a party in Manchester, Vt., Salinger met Claire Douglas, an English-born Radcliffe student. She was unimpeachably right-looking, extraordinarily pretty, not too categorically cashmere sweater and flannel skirt. Claire was fascinated by the intense, 34-year-old author, and visited him several times in Cornish. She soothed her family with a story that showed close attention to the master's style: Salinger lived, she said, with his mother, sister, 15 Buddhist monks, and a yogi who stood on his head. The girl discovered mysticism. "She was hung on the Jesus Prayer," recalls her brother Gavin, a wandering movie photographer. "Jerry is very good at hanging people on things."

Abruptly, Claire broke off with Salinger and married a young blue-suit from the Harvard Business School. Just as abruptly, she ended the marriage after several months and returned to Cornish. She and Salinger were married in 1955. His wedding present to his bride was *Franny,* whose heroine has Claire's looks, mannerisms, and—the sort of private salute that amuses the author—Claire's blue suitcase.

Uncharacteristically, Salinger threw a party to celebrate his marriage—it was attended by his mother, his sister (a twice-divorced dress buyer at Bloomingdale's), and Claire's first husband. A little later, at the Cornish town meeting, pranksters elected Salinger Town Hargreave—an honorary office unseriously given to the most recently married man; he is supposed to round up pigs whenever they get loose. Salinger was unamused.

ARTISTIC BATTLE. He had begun another of his withdrawals; he no longer spoke to the teen-agers with whom he had talked for hours in Nap's Lunch, cut off his widely spaced visits with Cornish neighbors. Occasionally he was seen at work in the nearby Dartmouth library, wearing, as a friend described it at the time, a checked wool shirt and "Genghis Khan beard." His working habits have not changed; Salinger takes a packed lunch to his cement-block cell, and works from 8:30 A.M. to 5:30 P.M. He can be reached there by phone—but, says a relative, "the house had damn well better be burning down." When he is not working, Salinger watches TV as avidly as any Fat Lady.

The author's most recent withdrawal may mean merely that his social needs are met by a wife and two children (Matthew, 1½, and Peggy, a precociously bright five-year-old). But Salinger is at work on his first really large body of fiction. The Glass family story cycle is already far longer than *Catcher,* and clearly it is nowhere near completion (a friend reports that Salinger intends to write a Glass trilogy). Since his marriage, the author has exhausted himself, and his supply of sociability, in a protracted effort to give his legend structure and direction, to deal with characters who speak his own most shadowed thoughts, and to solve the snarls caused by piecemeal publication. His face, after six years of struggle, shows the pain of an artistic battle whose outcome still cannot be seen. The battle almost certainly involves the matter of Seymour's sainthood and suicide.

INTO THE ESSENCE. Once there was a man (so goes an ancient Taoist legend) who was so expert at judging horses that he ignored such trivialities as color and sex, looking as he did into the very essence of the beasts. Such a man, gifted with the eye for the core of reality, was Seymour—at least in the estimation of his family. His oldest surviving brother, Buddy Glass, remarks: "I haven't been able to think of anybody whom I'd care to send out to look for horses in his stead."

The evolution of Seymour into this being of almost supersensory perception is one of the more fascinating parts of J. D. Salinger's history. Seymour first appeared in the limpid, shattering, 1948 short story, *A Perfect Day for Bananafish,* in which he goes swimming with a little girl on a Florida beach and, overcome by her innocence, swallows too much sublimity (or, one guesses later, too much despair). He returns to his hotel room, where his wife has been gabbling on the phone to her mother, and shoots himself through the head. Reasons for the cryptic suicide were suggested in a superb story written seven years later, *Raise High the Roof Beam, Carpenters,* in which Seymour's wedding day is recalled; it shows a sensitive, gentle, somewhat weak man about to tie himself to a mass of hair nets, deodorant bottles and parroted psychiatric untruths.

But not until Salinger's latest (1959), most convoluted and runic story, *Seymour, an Introduction,* in which the character is traced even farther back, does Seymour appear as a saint and major poet (although almost the only poetic evidence[89] given is a verse Seymour wrote when he was eight: "John Keats,/John Keats,/John,/Please put your scarf on"). The account was ostensibly set down by Buddy as a memorial, and the neurotically involved style, the endless self-conscious asides to the reader,* the masses of parentheses suggest brilliantly that

---

* Buddy's style reflects Salinger's own most delicate apostrophes, such as this dedication of *Franny and Zooey:* "As nearly as possible in the spirit of Matthew Salinger, age one, urging a luncheon companion to accept a cool lima bean, I urge my editor, mentor, and (heaven help him) closest friend, William Shawn, *genius domus* of *The New Yorker,* lover of the long shot, protector of the unprolific, defender of the hopelessly flamboyant, most un-

the narrator is cracking under the strain of having to live with the ever-growing memory of a loved but envied dead man. *Seymour, an Introduction* is one of the masterly seriocomic performances of recent literature. But in it, Seymour's suicide no longer makes sense. Saints may be martyred, but they do not shoot themselves. If the suicide in the hotel room was the act of a man weakened to insanity, then the whole legend is meaningless; Seymour supposedly was the sanest and strongest of men. If it was the departure of a holy man from an unworthy world, it was out of character; Seymour taught his six disciples not only to love and forgive the world but also, one judges from *Zooey*, to play their parts in the world wholeheartedly. The suicide was wrong, and, as Buddy now explains him, Seymour was not capable of a wrong act.

LOVE & DEATH. Can Salinger write his way back to the suicide and make his myth whole? If he brings it off, what he will have is anybody's guess. But it is certain that the Glass legend's landscape will be largely interior; there will be little of the panoramic sweep of the social novel. But whatever its form, it will express the essence of Salinger's time, embodied in the only theme Salinger has ever written about— the predicament of the good, sensitive man in a private world of love and death. It is his rare skill to make even goodness credible. He is a sentimentalist, but his sentiment is counterweighted by a colloquial, ironic style, and it has not impaired his judgment. More important, he is one of today's few serious authors who write about their characters—about man—with hope.

Salinger is clearly an original, the kind whose shadow is seen not in the writers who precede him but in those who follow. If he were to stop writing now, *The Catcher in the Rye* would be judged a small masterpiece—say about the size of *The Red Badge of Courage*—the *Nine Stories* a collection unmatched since Hemingway's *In Our Time*, and *Franny and Zooey* a glowing minor work. This much is a certainty: there is no one writing now who could be sent to look for horses in his stead.[90]

---

reasonably modest of born great artist-editors, to accept this pretty skimpy-looking book." Shawn, graciously bowing in reply, has ordered that *The New Yorker* give away 6,000 copies of the book this Christmas.

PART ONE

THE CATCHER IN THE RYE

From "Conservatism in Modern American Fiction," *College English, XV* (March 1954), 315–325. Reprinted with the permission of the National Council of Teachers of English and Hugh Maclean.

. . .

As Kirk [Russell Kirk, *The Conservative Mind*] points out, "conservatism" is not to be simply defined; it is too intricate to be condensed "to a few pretentious phrases." However, we may edit his catalogue of conservative characteristics, keeping in mind the purpose and limits of the present article, to suggest that four tenets are generally held by persons of "conservative" outlook. First, the watchword of the conservative is "order," as distinguished from that of[315] the radical, who swears by "natural rights." Classes, traditions, and prejudices are recognized as contributory (under moderating direction) to the order of society, which is paramount. The conservative maintains that bad government is more desirable than no government; he knows that "reform and change are not identical." Second, the conservative holds that "humanity has a natural proclivity toward violence and sin." He may call this "original sin," or "evil," or "the lees of things," or (like Milton) he may speak of human history as "a prolonged wandering from the way"; whatever his terminology, he knows that evil must be taken into account by us all. That "natural goodness" which the radical has often in the past assumed powerful enough, by its mere presence, to make nothing of evil, the conservative regards as relatively powerless. In this sense, Hawthorne and Melville were conservatives; Emerson a radical. Third, the conservative assumes limits to man's progressive possibilities; he does not believe that "education, positive legislation, and alteration of environment can produce men like gods." The dreary idea of the perfectibility of man (as D. H. Lawrence put it) repels the conservative, who regards man's limitations as an earnest of his dignity. Finally, the conservative puts his trust, not in that "reason" which too often means simply cold logic and which could inspire Bentham to call poetry "pushpin," but in "right reason," which S. L. Bethell has called "the total mind operating upon a complex and variable experience." The conservative knows the futility of erecting any such Goddess of Reason as the French revolutionists elevated; he has a tendency to substitute tradition as a guide to social organization, and (like Burke) he knows the value of healthy prejudice. To be sure, the conservative may exaggerate all these tenets, perverting their inten-

tions and subverting their application; in that case, he becomes a re-
actionary—a Tory, the radical would call him—and may no longer be
properly described as a conservative, whose course of action is ruled
by moderation. These four characteristics of conservatism look to one
central principle: the belief that man exists within a divine scheme of
things, and that a Purpose continues to evolve its grand Design of
which man is part. The limitations of man, in this view, become something not to be kicked against and regarded as overburdening by
"Faustian" man, who acknowledges no master; they are instead the
limits of that plan within which man may give expression, if he
chooses, to his nobler parts.[316]

. . .

Gatsby [F. Scott Fitzgerald, *The Great Gatsby*] trusted himself and
distrusted others; Pulham [John P. Marquand, *H. M. Pulham, Esq.*]
trusted others but distrusted himself; both discovered that they could
not hope by such means to find happiness in the world. Holden Caulfield, the adolescent hero of J. D. Salinger's *The Catcher in the Rye,*
knows almost from the first that any quest for happiness, in these
terms, is sure to fail. He distrusts others *and* himself. Pencey may have
a very good academic rating, but "it was a terrible school, no matter
how you looked at it." The headmaster is "a phony slob," the students
mostly repulsive, the school customs ridiculous: "The game with Saxon
Hall was a very big deal around Pencey....you were supposed to commit suicide or something if old Pencey didn't win." Hotels are
"crumby" and full of "perverts and morons." The band in the night
club is "putrid"; its female customers "witches" who can't make conversation and who keep looking for movie stars. Society is fully satirized
in the person of Sally Hayes; Holden suffers her for some time ("she
was so damn good-looking") but eventually repudiates the graces of
society in ringing terms: "You give me a[320] royal pain in the ass, if
you want to know the truth." Friends fail him too. Carl Luce ("one of
those intellectual guys"), whom Holden asks about the meaning of life,
turns out to be a tired sexual athlete, whose latest mistress is an
aging Oriental and whose ostentatious psychological jargon conceals a
jaded despair. Mr. Antolini, after a good deal of stimulating talk,
arouses Holden's suspicion and undoes even the measure of calm which
their conversation has produced in him. His family (save Phoebe, his
young sister) exists only in a disembodied way on the fringe of his consciousness. This distrust of the world without is balanced by an awareness of his own weakness. Stradlater masters him physically, with little
effort; his vocabulary, he admits, is "lousy"; his sexual essays abortive.
Even his moments of triumph are mocked by some blind force: the
repudiation of Pencey—"Sleep tight, ya morons!"—is followed by a
clownish tumble down the staircase; his evasion of the elevator boy

at home by another fall, this time over "about a million garbage cans."

These continual repudiations of the world, and of human life in all its forms, would be merely unpleasant if it were not that Holden Caulfield does like *some* things about the world. It is, however, significant that the thing he likes best is *not* in the world: his dead brother Allie, for whom, after Allie's death, Holden broke all the windows in the garage and as many as he could in the station wagon before they stopped him. In the actual world, Holden is drawn by beauty, imagination, art. He likes the swans in Central Park; the way his sister whirls round and round on the carousel; Ring Lardner, Hardy's *Return of the Native,* and a certain amount of other English literature; telling imaginative lies to Mrs. Morrow to make her proud of her son (actually one of the more repellent Pencey boys); and a dream-vision in which Holden imagines himself hovering round a group of children at play in a field of rye on the edge of a cliff and catching any child who strays unthinkingly near the brink. Holden Caulfield, in fact, is the defender of right reason—reason enlightened by the imagination and brought to bear upon the whole body of human experience—in a vicious world of materialistic rationalism; and the book describes his search for some assurance that his outlook is not altogether futile. This assurance is not forthcoming. Past, present, and future return a negative answer or remain silent. The ideal present—Jane Gallagher—never answers her phone. The ideal future—Phoebe—Holden sadly relinquishes, knowing he can't take her with him. The ideal past—the Egyptian mummy, entombed in the museum—is defaced by scribbled obscenities. Accordingly, Holden, who had already realized that "people are always ruining things for you," and who had found his only solace in the museum, where "the best thing...was that everything always stayed right where it was. Nobody'd change," is forced to the conclusion that "you can't ever find a place that's nice and peaceful, because there isn't any." The shock of this truth, which he had suspected (but hoped was a delusion), results at once in a physical collapse, and ultimately in confinement to a hospital, under the "care" of a psychoanalyst, the witch doctor of that world Holden cannot re-enter without bartering imagination for logic. *The Catcher in the Rye* is a conservative "No Exit." It reveals the "progressivist myth" clearly enough as ludicrous and obscene; it exposes with considerable force the shortcomings of reason and of the "natural man"; but it is entirely[321] negative, an "Everlasting No." Need this be the answer of conservatism?

It is certainly one answer, on the level common to the majority of conservatism's opponents; but Holden Caulfield's conclusions can hardly serve as a creed to live by. It remains for William Faulkner to provide men, through the medium of fiction, with a conservative scheme of belief. He is concerned not so much with "happiness" as with peace for the soul; and his outlook, though reflected in all the novels, is best exemplified by *The Bear*.[322]

. . .

ARTHUR HEISERMAN and JAMES E. MILLER, JR.

From "J. D. Salinger: Some Crazy Cliff," *The Western Humanities Review*, X (Spring 1956), 129–137. Reprinted by permission of *The Western Humanities Review*.

It is clear that J. D. Salinger's *The Catcher in the Rye* belongs to an ancient and honorable narrative tradition, perhaps the most profound in western fiction. The tradition is the central pattern of the epic and has been enriched by every tongue; for not only is it in itself exciting but also it provides the artist a framework upon which he may hang almost any fabric of events and characters.

It is, of course, the tradition of the Quest. We use the medieval term because it signifies a seeking after what is tremendous, greater than the love of a woman. The love of woman may be part of the seeking, part even of the object sought, for we have been told that the Grail has gender and Penelope did wait in Ithaca. But if the love of woman is essential to the seeking or to the object sought, we must call the search a romance. These two terms (quest and romance) distinguish thematic patterns, and have nothing to do with tragic or comic effects. Furthermore, the same plots, characters, and idioms might be employed inside either pattern. But somewhere upon the arc of the Quest, the love of woman must be eschewed or absorbed: the hero must bind himself to the mast, or must seek his Ducalinda because she is Virtue, not because she is Female.

There are at least two sorts of quests, depending upon the object sought. Stephen Dedalus sought a reality uncontaminated by home, country, church; for like Eugene Gant and Natty Bumppo he knew that social institutions tend to force what is ingenious in a man into their own channels. He sought the opposite of security, for security was a cataract of the eye. Bloom, on the other hand, was already an outcast and sought acceptance by an Ithaca and a Penelope which despised him. And, tragically enough, he also[129] sought an Icarian son who had fled the very maze which he, Bloom, desired to enter. So the two kinds of quests, the one seeking acceptance and stability, the other precisely the opposite, differ significantly, and can cross only briefly to the drunken wonder of both heroes. Bloom, the protagonist of *The Waste Land*, the Joads, Alyosha Karamazov, Aeneas, Ulysses, Gatsby— these heroes seek acceptance, stability, a life embosomed upon what is known and can be trusted. Dedalus, Huck Finn, Ishmael, Hans Castorp, Huxley's heroes, Dostoevski's Idiot—these protagonists place themselves outside the bounds of what is known and seek not stability but a Truth which is unwarped by stability.

American literature seems fascinated with the outcast, the person who defies traditions in order to arrive at some pristine knowledge, some personal integrity. Natty Bumppo maintains his integrity out-of-doors only, for upon the frontier a man must be a man or perish. For Huck Finn both sides of the Mississippi are lined with fraud and hatred; and because the great brown river acts as a kind of sewer, you're liable to find murderers and thieves afloat on it—even the father whom you fled might turn up dead in it, as though the river were a dream. But in the middle of the great natural river, when you're naked of civilization and in company with an outcast more untarnished and childlike than yourself—*there* is peace. And in northern Mississippi, in the ante-Snopes era, frontiersmen conquer the wilderness using only their courage and their fury; and they behave, even when civilization has almost extinguished them, with the kind of insane honor that drives Quentin Compson outside of society and into suicide. And the hunter, as he tracks the great mythic bear or the incredible whale, must leave behind whatever is unnatural or convenient. Similarly, when the bull charges, you are faced with the same compulsion for integrity as is required by the wilderness, the whale, the bear, the river; and very often, the world so botches things that you must "make a separate peace" in order to maintain your moral entity intact.

All the virtues of these American heroes are personal ones: they most often, as a matter of fact, are in conflict with home, family, church. The typical American hero must flee these institutions, become a tramp in the earth, cut himself off from Chicago, Winesburg, Hannibal, Cooperstown, New York, Asheville, Minneapolis. For only by flight can he find knowledge of what is real. And if he does not flee, he at least defies.

The protagonist of *The Catcher in the Rye*, Holden Caulfield, is one of these American heroes, but with a significant difference. He seems to be engaged in both sorts of quests at once; he needs to go home and he needs[130] to leave it. Unlike the other American knight errants, Holden seeks Virtue second to Love. He wants to be good. When the little children are playing in the rye-field on the clifftop,

Holden wants to be the one who catches them before they fall off the cliff. He is not driven toward honor or courage. He is not driven toward love of woman. Holden is driven toward love of his fellow-man, charity—virtues which were perhaps not quite virile enough for Natty Bumppo, Ishmael, Huck Finn, or Nick Adams. Holden is actually frightened by a frontier code of masculinity—a code which sometimes requires its adherents to behave in sentimental and bumptious fashions. But like these American heroes, Holden is a wanderer, for in order to be good he has to be more of a bad boy than the puritanical Huck could have imagined. Holden has had enough of both Hannibal, Missouri, *and* the Mississippi; and his tragedy is that when he starts back up the river, he has no place to go—save, of course, a California psychiatrist's couch.

So Salinger translates the old tradition into contemporary terms. The phoniness of society forces Holden Caulfield to leave it, but he is seeking nothing less than stability and love. He would like nothing better than a home, a life embosomed upon what is known and can be trusted; he is a very wise sheep forced into lone wolf's clothing; he is Stephen Dedalus and Leopold Bloom rolled into one crazy kid. And here is the point; for poor Holden, there is no Ithaca. Ithaca has not merely been defiled by a horde of suitors: it has sunk beneath waves of phoniness. He does, of course, have a Penelope who is still intact. She is his little sister Phoebe whom he must protect at all costs from the phantoms of lust, hypocrisy, conceit and fear—all of the attributes which Holden sees in society and which Huck Finn saw on the banks of the Mississippi and Dedalus saw in Dublin. So at the end, like the hero of *Antic Hay,* Holden delights in circles—a comforting, bounded figure which yet connotes hopelessness. He breaks down as he watches his beloved little Phoebe going round and round on a carousel; she is so *damned* happy. From that lunatic delight in a circle, he is shipped off to the psychiatrist. For Holden loves the world more than the world can bear.

Holden's Quest takes him outside society; yet the grail he seeks is the world and the grail is full of love. To be a catcher in the rye in this world is possible only at the price of leaving it. To be good is to be a "case," a "bad boy" who confounds the society of men. So Holden seeks the one role which would allow him to be a catcher, and that role is the role of the child. As a child, he would be condoned, for a child is a sort of savage and a pariah because he is innocent and good. But it is Holden's tragedy that[131] he is sixteen, and like Wordsworth he can never be less. In childhood he had what he is now seeking—non-phoniness, truth, innocence. He can find it now only in Phoebe and in his dead brother Allie's baseball mitt, in a red hunting cap and the tender little nuns. Still, unlike all of us, Holden refuses to compromise with adulthood and its necessary adulteries; and his heroism drives him berserk. Huck Finn had the Mississippi and at the end of the Mississippi he had the wild west beyond Arkansas. The hero of *The Waste Land* had Shantih, the peace which passes human understanding. Bloom had Molly and his own ignorance; Dedalus had Paris and Zurich. But for Holden, there is no place to go.[132]

. . .

CHARLES H. KEGEL

"Incommunicability in Salinger's *The Catcher in the Rye*," *The Western Humanities Review*, XI (Spring 1957), 188–190. Reprinted with permission of *The Western Humanities Review*.

Admirers of J. D. Salinger's *The Catcher in the Rye* ought to have welcomed the exciting analysis of that novel in the Spring, 1956, issue of *WHR*. One may not agree in every particular with Heiserman and Miller's "J. D. Salinger: Some Crazy Cliff," yet the article serves as a very convincing notice to students of recent American fiction that *The Catcher in the Rye* deserves careful, critical attention. Notwithstanding the rather insensitive and high-handed action of puritanical censorship groups like the Detroit Police Department, which removed the work from Detroit book stalls as "pornographic trash," many once-through-quickly readers have sensed in Salinger's novel a dignity which transcends the apprehension of prudish minds. Heiserman and Miller have gone still further and have shown that that dignity governs both the theme and the structure of the novel. By doing so, they have sent us back for a fresh and more serious look.

The Catcher in the Rye can certainly be read, as Heiserman and Miller suggest, as a double-barreled quest: first, for "acceptance, stability, a life embosomed upon what is known and can be trusted," second, for "a Truth which is unwarped by stability." Without contradicting this interpretation, however, the novel can also be read as Holden Caulfield's quest for communicability with his fellow man, and the hero's first person after-the-fact narration indicates, of course, that he has been successful in his quest.

Like Stephen Dedalus of *A Portrait of the Artist as a Young Man,*

Caulfield is in search of the Word. His problem is one of communication: as a teen-ager, he simply cannot get through to the adult world which surrounds him; as a *sensitive* teen-ager, he cannot even get through to others of his own age. The same impulse which caused Dedalus to contemplate subtle and slight differences in the meaning of words—"Canker is a disease of plants,/Cancer one of animals"— activates a comparable sensitivity in Caulfield, especially with word formulas. After his interview, for example, with Mr. Spencer, his history teacher at Pencey, Caulfield says, "He yelled something at me, but I couldn't exactly hear him. I'm pretty sure he yelled 'Good luck!' at me. I hope not. I hope to hell not. I'd never yell 'Good luck!' at anybody. It sounds terrible, when you think about it."

Caulfield places most of his attention, however, on the sympathetic rapport which must exist between communicators. He asks but one thing of those he talks with, sincerity; he asks only that they *mean* what they say. If they tell him, as does Maurice, the elevator operator, that the price of goods is "Five bucks a throw," Caulfield expects to pay only five dollars. If they ask, as did Mrs. Antolini, about the health of his mother, Caulfield expects sincere concern about his mother's health; he expects that the questioner[188] *actually* wants an answer to her question and will not interrupt him half way through it. Throughout the novel, he is troubled with people who are not listening to what he says, who are talking only to be polite, not because they want to communicate ideas. Like Hamlet, a "sad, screwed-up type guy" like himself, Caulfield is bothered by words and word formulas which only "seem," which are "phony." The honesty and sincerity which he cannot find in others, he attempts to maintain in himself. His repeated assertions that something he has said is *"really"* so demonstrate his attempt to keep faith with the Word. He is particularly distressed by the occasional realization that he too must be phony to exist in the adult world. With regard to the insincere "Glad to've met you" formula, he laments that "If you want to stay alive, you have to say that stuff, though."

As I have indicated, the main reason for Caulfield's communicative difficulty lies in his absolute hatred of phoniness. And he finds that phoniness, that hypocrisy, not only in the world of his personal contacts, but in the world of art as well. He detests phony books, phony music, phony movies and plays. He sees Hamlet as a "sad, screwed-up type guy" and wants him played that way instead of "like a goddam general." Likewise he is bothered by the way people "clap for the wrong things" and hence corrupt the promising artist. Very poignantly he understands the plight of Ernie, the piano player, or of brother D. B., once a sincere writer, but now "out in Hollywood...being a prostitute." He wants more Thomas Hardys—"old Thomas Hardy" Caulfield calls him endearingly—because he knows that the creator of "old Eustacia Vye" refused to prostitute himself, refused to be phony.

Holden Caulfield's inability to communicate satisfactorily with others represents itself symbolically in the uncompleted telephone calls and undelivered messages which permeate the novel. Seeing a phone booth is almost more than he can stand, for he almost constantly feels like "giving somebody a buzz." On fifteen separate occasions he gets the urge to communicate by phone, yet only four calls are completed, and those with unfortunate results. Usually the urge dies without his having even attempted to place the call; he seems fearful of what the results will be and rationalizes, "I wasn't in the mood." Likewise, none of the several verbal messages he asks others to deliver for him gets through to the intended receiver; he simply cannot succeed in making contact.

Growing logically out of this prolonged incommunicability is Caulfield's intention to become a deaf-mute. So repulsed is he by the phoniness around him that he despairs of communicating with any-body, and in a passage fraught with import, he contemplates a retreat within himself.

> I figured I could get a job at a filling station somewhere, putting gas and oil in people's cars. I didn't care what kind of a job it was, though. Just so people didn't know me[189] and I didn't know anybody. I thought what I'd do was, I'd pretend I was one of those deaf-mutes. That way I wouldn't have to have any goddam stupid useless conversa-tions with anybody. If anybody wanted to tell me something, they'd have to write it on a piece of paper and shove it over to me. They'd get bored as hell doing that after a while, and then I'd be through with having conversations for the rest of my life. Everybody'd think I was just a poor deaf-mute bastard and they'd leave me alone.... I'd cook all my own food, and later on, if I wanted to get married or some-thing, I'd meet this beautiful girl that was also a deaf-mute and we'd get married. She'd come and live in my cabin with me, and if she wanted to say anything to me, she'd have to write it on a goddam piece of paper, like everybody else.

Significantly, the fact that a message does get through to Phoebe— the only successful communication in the entire novel—leads toward the abandonment of the deaf-mute retreat. The Rousseauistic-Words-worthian theme of childhood innocence and sincerity which Salinger had played upon so effectively in "For Esmé—with Love and Squalor" works its magic again. It is Phoebe who furnishes the clue to the solu-tion of his problem, and when he refuses to ride the carrousel with her and thus gives up his idealistic attempts "to grab for the gold ring," he has initiated his transition from adolescence to adulthood. He does

not, of course, capitulate to the phoniness of life, but he attains an
attitude of tolerance, understanding, and love which will make it en-
durable. There can be no doubt but that when he returns to New
York—for he, unlike Dedalus, will return home—he will be in the mood
to give "old Jane a buzz."[190]

EDGAR BRANCH

"Mark Twain and J. D. Salinger: A Study in
Literary Continuity," *American Quarterly*, IX
(Summer 1957), 144–158. Reprinted by permis-
sion of *American Quarterly*, © Trustees of the
University of Pennsylvania.

In J. D. Salinger's *The Catcher in the Rye* Holden Caulfield reflects on Mr. Antolini, his former teacher, from whose homosexual
pettings he has just fled in panic: "I started thinking that even if he
was a flit he certainly'd been very nice to me. I thought how he hadn't
minded it when I'd called him up so late, and how he'd told me to
come right over... And how he went to all that trouble giving me that
advice about finding out the size of your mind and all..." Huckleberry
Finn, in his "close place" a century earlier, muses on his best teacher,
Jim: "I...got to thinking over our trip down the river; and I see
Jim...standing my watch on top of his'n,...so I could go on sleeping;
and see him how glad he was when I come back out of the fog...and
such-like times; and would always call me honey, and pet me and do
everything he could think of for me..." Huck can always depend on
Jim; their physical relationship is consciously innocent. But Mr. Antolini is Holden's last adult refuge in his disintegrating world. Huck,
resolving his inner conflict by a free moral decision, takes immediate
bold steps to help Jim. But Holden becomes "more depressed and
screwed up" than ever after fleeing Mr. Antolini. Ominously, as he
walks down Fifth Avenue, he feels he is disappearing. He retreats
to the Museum of Natural History, the "place where the mummies
were" and a favorite childhood haunt that he remembers as "so nice
and peaceful"—like Huck's raft. But even there life-obscenity intrudes
—Huck's raft has its Duke and Dauphin too—and he learns that "You

can't ever find a place that's nice and peaceful, because there isn't any."
Each of these experienced boys knows all about fraud[144] and violence but retains the charity of an innocent heart. Each is a measure
of the need and possibility for human love in his society.

Holden's society differs as dramatically from Huck's as does a
Broadway traffic jam from a raft drifting down the Mississippi a long
century ago. Yet a flight down the river and a flight through New
York streets turn out to be not so different after all. The pattern
of Holden's experience is essentially Huck's. Salinger's writing carries
familiar rhythms and attitudes. The creative imaginations of these
two authors who fuse given fact and boyish consciousness into expressive, dramatized narrative are strikingly similar. *The Catcher in the
Rye*, in fact, is a kind of *Huckleberry Finn* in modern dress. This paper
does not propose to reveal any direct, "real" or conscious "influences"—
if these exist at all—that *Huckleberry Finn* had upon Salinger's novel.
Nor is its purpose to compare the "then" and "now" of American
society through the illustrative use of these books. Rather, it attempts
to bare one nerve of cultural continuity in America by dissecting some
literary relationships between the two novels.

II

Consider first the narrative patterns and styles.

Huck initially flees conventionalities, constraint and terror. On the
river he meets murderous thieves, a treacherous fog, Negro-hunters and
a steamboat that rips through the raft and thrusts him among feuding
country gentility. He lives with professional crooks who fatten on
"greenhorns" and "flatheads." He sees a harmless drunk shot dead and
a Southern Colonel almost lynched, observes some theatrical obscenities
and at great personal risk saves the inheritance of three innocent girls.
Experience teaches Huck that truth is usually weak, trouble best
avoided and evil often inevitable. It confirms his love of beauty and
peaceful security. But notably in his greatest struggle, over Jim, he acts
spontaneously and defiantly for goodness. Huck eventually comes to the
Phelps plantation, the homelike place where Jim finds freedom and
where Huck will take leave of "sivilization" by going West.

Holden Caulfield, intensely troubled, escapes initially from the
stupid constraints and violence of his prep school life. Like Huck, he
enters a jungle world, New York City, where he knows his way around
but from which he is alienated. There for two hectic days and nights
he steers his course through battering adventures with fearsome
"dopes," "fakers," "morons" and sluggers. On this journey Holden's
Jim is primarily the recurring image of Jane Gallagher, an old friend
who needs love and whom he loves with strange unawareness. Holden's
Jim is also all little children, whom he would save from adult sexuality.
Like Huck, Holden has a conflict. His adolescent sexual urges are

somehow entangled with[145] what is predatory in the "mean guys" he hates. They befoul his sense of the fine and good. Although not as self-sufficient as Huck, Holden is usually as realistic, and he too loves beauty and peace. Yet he values goodness above know-how, sophistication, style, success. After a secret visit home, he plans to lead a hermit's life in the West, but is reconciled to the city by the love of his little sister Phoebe. Physically weakened and psychically wounded, he is last seen recuperating in a sanitarium. Clearly Mark Twain and Salinger present parallel myths of American youth confronting his world—Huck Finn over many months, when time was expendable; Holden over two days when, Salinger seems to imply, time is rapidly running out.

Each novel employs an appropriate first person vernacular. Holden has the more "educated" vocabulary, he speaks with a modern schoolboy's idiom and slang and he can spell. Also he can swear. Both boys observe accurately and swiftly. Both are artists of deadpan, yet can subtly convey the interplay of feeling and scene. Huck arrives at the Phelps farm: "When I got there it was all still and Sunday-like, and hot and sunshiny—the hands was gone to the fields; and there was them kind of faint dronings of bugs and flies in the air that makes it seem so lonesome and like everybody's dead and gone; and if a breeze fans along and quivers the leaves, it makes you feel mournful, because you feel like it's spirits whispering—spirits that's been dead ever so many years—and you always think they're talking about *you*. As a general thing it makes a body wish *he* was dead, too, and done with it all." Holden observes New York's streets from a taxicab: "What made it worse, it was so quiet and lonesome out, even though it was Saturday night. I didn't see hardly anybody on the street. Now and then you just saw a man and a girl crossing a street, with their arms around each other's waists and all, or a bunch of hoodlumy-looking guys and their dates, all of them laughing like hyenas at something you could just bet wasn't funny. New York's terrible when somebody laughs on the street very late at night. You can hear it for miles. It makes you feel so lonesome and depressed. I kept wishing I could go home."

Huck's speech, usually dispassionate and matter-of-fact, is relaxed and flexibly rhythmical. Holden, frequently conscious of the smothering omnipresence of sex, draws most things taut. Nervous, jerky reiteration often points up his emotional tensions. His speech is sometimes raucous and jarring. He tends to rail and condemn. Huck's direct apprehension gives us an objective recording rich in implication. His vision etches an open world, clear, solid, real, with living characters moving autonomously in it. Holden's tense outpouring is a convincing expression of his psychological unrest and of the release he is finding in psychiatric treatment. His speech carries hints of the frantic overtones of a Poe character speaking from a madhouse[146] (humanized by delightful comedy), and his world and its people, though violently alive, revolve in the whirlpool of his egocentricity. Both styles are effectively ironic and humorous.

Perhaps Huck's profoundest relation to life is an animal faith, an acceptance of reality that assimilates the irrational and cruel even while it condemns them through exposure. That acceptance promotes a classic simplicity of style, the more dignified for the dark undertones present. But Holden's rejection and disgust create a feverish modern dissonance. Alienation is expressed by obsessive revelation, sometimes more suggestive of Theodor Fischer in Mark Twain's *The Mysterious Stranger* than of Huck Finn. Holden's speech is indeed suited to his neurotic experience of the all-engulfing modern city. Huck's speech is equally well suited to his personality and to what Mark Twain had to say about a vanished era, a time permitting Huck's hard won victory over self and circumstance. Salinger's adaptation of the language to his hero's speech habits, character and times points up the stylistic continuity between the two books.

III

What experience brings Holden to the sanitarium? A brief answer to this question is required at this stage of the discussion.

Holden's parents are wealthy, seemingly happily married people. The father is a prominent corporation lawyer, the mother an able, tasteful woman. Phoebe, Holden's ten-year-old sister, is a staunch, wise little girl. Holden's younger brother, Allie, the "wizard" of the family, died of leukemia three years ago, and Holden is still guilt-stricken for the way he used to treat him. Allie used to write Emily Dickinson's poems on his fielder's mitt to have something to read when nobody was at bat. The night Allie died Holden "broke all the windows in the garage...with my fists, just for the hell of it." Huck also knew death at first hand, and when he looked down on Buck Grangerford's body, he felt guilty and sickened by life.

Holden himself is a rangy sixteen-year-old who is prematurely gray and has grown too fast. He is creative and intelligent but bewildered by strange impulses, a "madman." Girls are on his mind. "Sex," he admits, "is something I really don't understand too hot." If girls "like a boy, no matter how big a bastard he is, they'll say he has an inferiority complex, and if they *don't* like him, no matter how nice a guy he is, or how big an inferiority complex he has, they'll say he's conceited." Still, whenever girls "do something pretty," even if they're ugly or stupid, "you fall half in love with them." Whereas Huck is the sexless pre-adolescent, Holden is the sex-conscious boy who yearns for the uncomplicated state of Huck.

Pencey Prep is the third school Holden has flunked out of. All of them[147] cater to pocketbook snobs. At Pencey "they had this goddam secret fraternity that I was too yellow not to join." At Elton Hills School Holden had seen James Castle, an independent, stubborn, "skinny little weak-looking guy, with wrists about as big as pencils," lying dead, a gory mess on the sidewalk, after jumping out the window to escape the hazing of seven superior bullies.

Saturday evening Holden spends his last hours at Pencey with two dorm-mates. Unpopular Ackley, sullen and mean-minded, is an obvious slob—always squeezing his pimples and cutting his dirty fingernails where Holden will walk on them in his bare feet. Stradlater, Holden's roommate, is the handsome sexy egotist and *secret* slob. "He always *looked* all right, Stradlater, but for instance you should've seen the razor he shaved himself with. It was always rusty as hell and full of lather and hairs and crap..." To Holden's anguish it is Stradlater, with one idea in mind, who dates the visiting Jane Gallagher that very evening. After Stradlater is provoked into slugging him heavily, Holden packs up and clears out for New York.

There he seeks companionship in bar and night club, but feels only more depressed. Back at his hotel, a place "lousy with perverts," he pays Sunny, a prostitute, five dollars to talk with him and is then slugged by the tough pimp and shakedown artist, Maurice the elevator boy. He wants to jump out the window. "I probably would've done it, too, if I'd been sure somebody'd cover me up as soon as I landed. I didn't want a bunch of stupid rubbernecks looking at me when I was all gory"—the way they crowded around Boggs in Huck's story. But the next day Holden is off to a play and to the Radio City ice skating rink with his friend Sally Hayes, culture-hound and cute little "butt-twitcher." Then hours of desperate, lonely wandering through New York movies, bars and freezing streets leave Holden shivering and sick in body and spirit. He sneaks into his family's apartment after midnight to see Phoebe.

Phoebe gives Holden all her love and trust, but tells him: "You don't like *any*thing that's happening," and she challenges him to name one thing he would like to *be*. He recalls the joyful little kid he had heard that morning singing "Comin' Thro' the Rye," but he wrongly remembers the words as "If a body catch a body..." Holden answers: "I keep picturing all these little kids playing some game in this big field of rye and all....and nobody's around—nobody big, I mean—except me. And I'm standing on the edge of some crazy cliff. What I have to do, I have to catch everybody if they start to go over the cliff—I mean if they're running and they don't look where they're going I have to come out from somewhere and *catch* them. That's all I'd do all day. I'd just be the catcher in the rye and all.[148] I know it's crazy, but that's the only thing I'd really like to be." No comment from Phoebe.

In the early morning hours Holden visits Mr. Antolini, his Elton

Hills teacher. Mr. Antolini compassionately assures Holden that others also have been troubled morally and spiritually by human behavior, but warns him that he is heading for the kind of crack-up "designed for men who...were looking for something their own environment couldn't supply them with." Having fallen asleep on the couch, Holden wakes up minutes later to feel Mr. Antolini, next to him in the blackness, stroking his head. "Boy, I was shaking like a madman. I was sweating too.... That kind of stuff's happened to me about twenty times since I was a kid. I can't stand it." For the rest of the night he finds privacy in Grand Central Station.

Hardly able to walk the next morning, Holden plans to hitchhike west and live alone, but first says goodbye to Phoebe. Her sturdy refusal to let him go alone saves him from himself, and as the book ends he elatedly watches her ride the zoo merry-go-round. "I was damn near bawling. I felt so damn happy, if you want to know the truth. I don't know why. It was just that she looked so damn *nice*, the way she kept going around and around, in her blue coat and all."

The carrousel, bearing the beautiful child and playing the songs of Holden's childhood, goes round and round, going nowhere—a dynamic moment of happy, static immaturity eternalized in his mind. "Certain things," believes Holden, "they should stay the way they are." But he is unwilling to put this belief to the test for fear things will be different. He will not enter the Museum on his first trip there. And does he really want to talk with Jane Gallagher, whom he's always going to ring but never quite does? Will she be the same, or changed—like all the rest? Mr. Antolini sees Holden as a potential martyr, an idealist capable of "dying nobly...for some highly unworthy cause." Holden is imaginatively capable of feeling Maurice's horny fist bruising his flesh ("my old heart was damn near beating me out of the room"), yet he won't pay five measly shakedown dollars to escape the slugging. But he easily gives ten dollars to two nuns eating their breakfast of toast and coffee, because "I hate it if I'm eating bacon and eggs or something and somebody else is only eating toast and coffee." Holden lived and Allie died; life itself is a bacon-and-eggs injustice. Death is the rain beating down on Allie's grave, "on the grass on his stomach." Life smirks its grief, puts its flowers on Allie's stomach and runs for its plush sedans when the rain starts, to "go somewhere nice for dinner." Confused and sickened by human conduct, Holden fears what is new, including the life within. His compulsive wanderings lead him back to New York, to old scenes, to his childhood[149] and to Phoebe. He sees himself as the preserver of innocence, the catcher in the rye.

IV

Especially in its characterization of the hero, *The Catcher in the Rye* is a haunting reminder of *Huckleberry Finn*.

Holden wants to shepherd the young, to be the only big person around; but Huck is the youthful liberator of a grown man, and whether he knows it or not his effort is directed toward making maturity possible. Holden is a conscious idealist who yet says, "I kept wishing I could go home." Huck lives humbly and prudently to get what he wants, but for *his* future home he chooses hell. Mr. Antolini is warning Holden when he says that the immature man wants to die nobly for a cause, while the mature man wants to live humbly for one—but he might have been approving Huck. The hope in Mark Twain's novel is that a ragamuffin pre-adolescent acts maturely for what is good in an open society. The underlying despair of Salinger's book is that a privileged adolescent wants to act immaturely for what he believes is good in a society thickened into vulgarity.

Yet Holden is truly a kind of latter-day, urbanized Huck. He is acutely sensitive to places and times, whether groping through a dark foyer in the early morning hours or relaxing in the cozy auditorium of the Museum of Natural History, where it "always smelled like it was raining outside, even if it wasn't..." He knows the uniqueness of things: the feel of a roller-skate key is unforgettable, everlasting, shimmering with human meaning. With every nerve he feels the moral character of others. He sharply registers the unguarded phrase or facial expression—the prostitute Sunny's childish "Like fun you are," or the beauty of Phoebe's open-mouthed sleep. Although Huck can easily spot "phonies"—witness the Widow Douglas, who approved of taking snuff "because she done it herself"—Holden is violently allergic to them: Carl Luce, a specialist in extracting intimate sex confessions from young boys but a sorehead "if you started asking *him* questions about *himself*"; or the popular entertainer Ernie who, when playing the piano, "*sounds* like the kind of a guy that won't talk to you unless you're a big shot." But the kettle drummer in the Radio City orchestra, whom Holden had observed closely for years, never looked bored even though he might bang the drums only twice during a piece. "Then when he does bang them, he does it so nice and sweet, with this nervous expression on his face." The drummer is what "Jesus *really* would've liked" in all the lavish Radio City Christmas pageant.

Holden has Huck's judicious mind and his respect for fact and knowledge. Huck "studies," Holden "analyzes." Both will generously grant any person his particular points. Harris Macklin, for instance, is the biggest bore[150] Holden knows, but Harris is an inimitable whistler—"So I don't know about bores.... They don't hurt anybody, most of them, and maybe they're secretly all terrific whistlers or something." But Holden is not equally generous with himself. He is the "only really dumb one" in his family, "very yellow" and a "sacrilegious atheist." His relentless self-criticism is alerted by the slightest stirring of "phoniness" within. As with Huck, his humility ironically reveals his goodness and integrity.

This realist Holden is as skeptical of men and as wary of circumstances as is Huck. He cultivates the timely maneuver and the saving lie to get out of tight spots, although he is not the slippery character Huck is. Dr. Thurmer, Headmaster at Pencey, does not admit the inevitability of tight spots. He preaches that Life is a rewarding game if played "according to the rules," and Pencey teaches the rules. "Some game," Holden thinks. "If you get on the side where all the hot-shots are, then it's a game, all right." In this game "people always clap for the wrong things," "people never believe you" and "people are always ruining things for you." It's a game that favors money-grubbers and callous egotists. Holden observes that a sentimental movie-goer weeping over the "putrid" movie characters is "as kindhearted as a goddam wolf" to her child. Here, as in the Grangerford episode, sentimentality reinforces inhumanity. Human kindness sometimes shines forth unexpectedly, but Holden's attitude is that "the sun only comes out when it feels like coming out," and you can't count on it.

In this corrupt world Holden miraculously keeps the uncorrupted heart that most reminds us of Huckleberry Finn. He genuinely loves natural beauty and the socially unspoiled. Freer than Huck from conventional responses, he is an instinctive moralistic democrat whose feelings recall Whitman's "By God! I will accept nothing which all cannot have their counterpart of on the same terms." He sympathizes with the kindhearted, the suffering and the helpless. He lies outrageously to protect a mother from the knowledge that her son's basic character is displayed in his passion for snapping, with his soggy knotted towel, the backsides of boys emerging from the shower. In a touching flashback he comforts unhappy Jane Gallagher, whom he values for her human eccentricities and her real quality—her "muckle-mouthed" way of talking, her curious way of playing checkers and her love of poetry. He best conceives peace and virtue in the imagery of physical and mental cripples—the Bible "lunatic...that lived in the tombs and kept cutting himself with stones," and the "poor deaf-mute bastard" Holden himself would like to be. He is haunted by the peace of two nuns he meets, and in several of his actions he unconsciously imitates the compassion of Jesus.

Holden, in short, like Huck, respects human personality and hates whatever[151] demeans it. He knows that snobbery is aggression, and that subordinating people to ideas and things destroys fruitful human intercourse. A self-styled pacifist, he strives to create relationships with others through discussion, a kind of decent and creative give-and-take.

"That's the way you can always tell a moron. They never want to discuss anything..." He likes books chiefly for the quality that makes "you wish the author that wrote it was a terrific friend of yours and you could call him up on the phone whenever you felt like it." But Ring Lardner and "old Thomas Hardy," two favorites, can't be reached by telephone; something nearly always prevents human intimacy. Possessions, "Goddam money" and creeds get in the way. Holden remembers that his budding friendship with Louis Shaney, a Catholic boy, was tainted because "you could tell he would've enjoyed [our conversation] *more* if I was a Catholic and all." Also Holden defends Richard Kinsella, his very nervous classmate who was academically hazed, by order of the Oral Expression instructor, for digressing in his class speeches. "It's nice when somebody tells you about their... father's farm and then all of a sudden get[s] more interested in their uncle. I mean it's dirty to keep yelling 'Digression!' at him when he's all nice and excited."

Unselfish love and spontaneous joy—Holden values these expressions of the uncontaminated spirit above all. So rarely are they found and so often thwarted in adult life that their slightest appearance saddens him. As he prepares to leave Pencey and packs the brand-new ice skates his mother had just bought him, he can see her "going in Spaulding's and asking the salesman a million dopey questions—and here I was getting the ax again. It made me feel pretty sad." Later on, Sunny, who sells her love at so much a throw, wants Holden to hang up her new dress to prevent wrinkles. Again he feels sad as he thinks of her buying it and "nobody in the store knowing she was a prostitute and all. The salesman probably just thought she was a regular girl when she bought it." But the little boy singing "Comin' Thro' the Rye" is a regular kid, happy, fulfilled, innocently insulated from the disagreeable. "He had a pretty little voice, too.... The cars zoomed by, brakes screeched all over the place, his parents paid no attention to him, and he kept on walking next to the curb and singing 'If a body catch a body coming through the rye.' It made me feel better." Holden is happy in the world of innocence that creates its own conditions. Desperately lonesome, he reveals his need for human intimacy by using the word "catch."

Clearly Holden and Huck, who so often shape their experience in similar patterns, have similar qualities. Holden's acute self-consciousness and his evident neuroticism do not diminish the reality or worth of what he is[152] and feels. Nor do they invalidate the comparison between the two boys. Rather, by appropriately distinguishing a typically modern personality from Huck Finn, still predominantly one of the "Divine Inert" but already, in his extreme and sensitive youth, bearing the scars of harsh experience, they help define the direct descent of Holden from Huck.

V

Huckleberry Finn and *The Catcher in the Rye* are akin also in ethical-social import. Each book is a devastating criticism of American society and voices a morality of love and humanity.

In many important matters, as we have just seen, Huck and Holden —not to speak of others like Jim and Phoebe—affirm goodness, honesty and loyalty. Huck does so almost unconsciously, backhandedly, often against his conventional conscience, and Holden does so with an agonizing self-consciousness and a bitter spirit. In each the perception of innocence is radical: from their mouths come pessimistic judgments damning the social forms that help make men less than fully human. "Human beings *can* be awful cruel to one another," observes Huck after seeing the Duke and Dauphin tarred and feathered. And Huck assumes his share of the guilt. Holden, with searingly honest insight that gets to the root of sadistic practices and class jealousies, remarks: "I can even get to hate somebody, just *looking* at them, if they have cheap suitcases with them....it's really hard to be roommates with people if your suitcases are much better than theirs... You think if they're intelligent...they don't give a damn whose suitcases are better, but they do. They really do." To Aunt Sally's question whether anybody was hurt in the steamboat accident, Huck replies, "No'm. Killed a nigger," and the blindness of a civilization is bared with terrible casualness. The same ironic exposure comes in Holden's apology for having to like a girl before he can get sexy—"I mean *really* sexy" with her. So he remarks, "My sex life stinks." And Carl Luce, the modern expert on love, answers: "Naturally it does, for God's sake."

Such examples might easily be multiplied: the vision is often identical. Yet we must grant that the reliability and quality of Holden's vision are complicated, far beyond Huck's straightforward objectivity, by the loss he has sustained. As Holden recognizes, he is mentally ill. "I don't get hardly anything out of anything. I'm in bad shape. I'm in *lousy* shape." Bad as the modern world is, his view of it adds a distortion not found in Huck's picture. Almost everyone in Holden's world is "phony"—headmasters, students, alumni, bartenders, movie actors, movie goers, people who say "Glad to've met you" or "Good luck!" or "Grand!," virile handshakers,[153] Holy Joe ministers, even partially bald men who hopefully comb their hair over the bald spot. The book reeks with Holden's revulsion and nausea. He experiences things in an aura of disgusting physical details. The park is "lousy" with "dog crap, globs of spit and cigar butts." A chair is "vomity" looking. A cab smells as though someone had "tossed his cookies in it." Moreover, although Holden keeps his innocent heart, his adolescence has riddled the innocence of mind, that naiveté, which Huck in good measure still possesses. What Holden's heart seeks and responds to, his mind sees is violated everywhere by the mere fact of human maturity. Adult activities become expressive masks for adult sexuality. The four-letter word he reads with horror—and erases—on the wall of Phoebe's school, follows him wherever he goes. In the quiet tomb of Pharaoh in the Museum, he feels at peace for the first time—until suddenly he sees the same word in red crayon on the wall. Desparingly, hysterically, he thinks that even in death he will not escape that word which someone surely will write on his tombstone. A great difference between the two boys is measured by Huck's sensitive but reserved opinion of the obscene words on the wall of the abandoned house floating down the June rise: "the ignorantest kind of words..."

Certainly if Huck's vision reveals both the limitations and promises of democracy—the hope and despair—Holden's, in direct descent from Huck's, focuses upon the despair. In the predatory wasteland of the city, Holden can foresee no future refuge or good. (Is it by accident that some lines of weary futility from "The Love Song of J. Alfred Prufrock" are echoed in Holden's words to Sally Hayes: "It wouldn't be the same at all. You don't see what I mean at all"?) If he and Sally were married, Holden knows he would be an office worker "making a a lot of dough, and riding to work in...Madison Avenue buses, and reading newspapers, and playing bridge all the time, and going to the movies and seeing a lot of stupid shorts and coming attractions and newsreels." He accurately describes the commercialized Christmas spirit as something over which "old Jesus probably would've puked if He could see it." He damns the competitive drive for status. Even the cab drivers, primitives of the city, are suspicious, raw-nerved. And nowhere is there peace. Holden's view of modern war concludes: "I'm sort of glad they've got the atomic bomb invented. If there's ever another war, I'm going to sit right the hell on top of it. I'll volunteer for it..." Neurotic or not, Holden's criticism often hits home.

Like Holden, Huck knows the meaning of respectable routine, competition and violence, but the difference is that what is organized nightmare in Holden's world is merely nascent in Huck's. Everyone can remember[154] the brutal and degenerate persons Huck encounters and some of the dozen or more corpses that bloody up his story. Holden's society holds far more possibilities for horror and depravity, and on a massive scale. Feverishly, obsessively on the move, it has more irritants and fewer profound satisfactions than does Huck's. Holden's cherished memory of one little duck pond in Central Park replaces Huck's Jackson's Island and lazy days on the Mississippi. The three or four lights Huck sees, "twinkling where there were sick folks, maybe," are not so much, compared to the health, the beauty, the freedom of the river. The sparkling metropolis Holden sees looming over the forlorn duck pond is inescapable, portentous. The life Huck explores, despite its evil and treachery, is still daring and redemptive, not just sodden, mean and self-destructive.

Given such contrasting conditions, what moral destiny confronts the individual in the worlds Salinger and Mark Twain create? Like the Central Park ducks in winter, Holden is essentially homeless, frozen out. But Huck, although an outcast, is a true home-maker wherever he is. Allie's baseball mitt is all that is left to Holden of Allie's love, and unlike Huck, he seems unable to break through the ring of hostility to find new sources of affection. Deprived of real opportunity for the sort of soul-shaking sacrifice Huck makes for Jim, Holden expresses his love for Phoebe by the gift of a phonograph record—which breaks. Of greater significance, Huck has Jim; but Holden, so desperately in need of love, is one of the loneliest characters in fiction. Obviously Huck is not as critically wounded as Holden. He has far more resilience, a stronger power of renewal. Necessity shows him the wisdom of prudence, and his natural environment provides therapeutic primal sanities. Both boys are rebels—with a difference. Huck can often go naked, but Holden can defy convention only by wearing his "corny" red hunting cap. Capable of making a free choice, Huck outwits his enemies and rises above the compulsions within. He is a practical rebel like Thoreau. He runs away to confront and modify reality, and thereby he proves, for his day, the explosive force of individual ethical action. Holden runs off too, but his actions are usually ineffective, and the path of escape leads him deeper into the mire of his personal difficulties.

Huckleberry Finn, in short, recognizes both necessity and freedom, the restrictions limiting moral accomplishment and its possibility. *The Catcher in the Rye* leaves us doubtful that the individual, even assisted by the analyst's best efforts, can ever truly escape the double trap of society and self. How well the two concluding scenes contrast these moral outlooks! Throughout *The Catcher in the Rye* Holden makes, and is, a telling criticism of our civilization: his "madness" in itself is a damning fact of our times; yet, doubly damning, what the "madman" says is often true,[155] what he feels often unimpeachable. Supremely ironical, then, is our last glimpse of Holden making recovery and adjustment in the sanitarium—a prelude to compromise in the outside world—as Father Peter in Mark Twain's *The Mysterious Stranger* can not do. Holden says: "I sort of *miss* everybody I told about. Even old Stradlater and Ackley, for instance. I think I even miss that goddam Maurice. It's funny. Don't ever tell anybody anything. If you do, you start missing everybody." Modern therapy takes over, Holden will return. For Holden's sake we wouldn't have it otherwise, even though it's a return to the big money and dopey newsreels. But we remember Huck with admiration and with confidence in his personal future as, Jim freed and the Duke and Dauphin in limbo, he says: "I reckon I got to light out for the Territory ahead of the rest, because Aunt Sally she's going to adopt me and sivilize me and I can't stand it. I been there before."

No wonder Holden wants to remain forever the catcher in the rye—*his* free Territory—oblivious to the trap that maturity finally springs. His recessive traits suggest that the logical, perhaps desirable, end for him and his civilization is the pure silence of death, the final release from imperfect life. *Huckleberry Finn,* as Philip Young has recently realized, appeals to rescuing death in the series of escapes—gliding, still and dark—made by Huck and Jim as the raft slips into the flowing, mythic river.[1] Huck, too, has guilt-feelings that, if sufficiently intensified, could conceivably lead to self-destruction. But such suggestions are muted in Huck's story, for Huck is committed to life. In Salinger's book death symbols are more pronounced, and death openly fascinates Holden not only for its horror but for the peaceful refuge it offers from the consciousness of life. Beneath the appealing and often hilarious humor, comparable to some of the best of Mark Twain's, life is felt in this book fundamentally as a ceaseless, pushing round of activity that one would be well rid of. Holden carries with him a dim sense of the eternal and transcendental. He is something like a soul unknowingly striving to rise from the muck of this world to the peace of nirvana. Jane Gallagher is always beyond his reach; he must settle for Sally Hayes, the "queen of the Phonies." Like Teddy McArdle in Salinger's story "Teddy," Holden might have called his contemporaries a "bunch of apple-eaters." Like Jean in Salinger's "De Daumier-Smith's Blue Period," Holden might have felt that in this life he "would always at best be a visitor in a garden of enamel urinals and bedpans, with a sightless, wooden dummy-deity standing by..." But for Jean, "the sun came up." Sudden spiritual insight transforms that garden into a "shimmering field of[156] exquisite, twice-blessed, enamel flowers." Nirvana is here and now. Holden, of course, has hardly begun to find the peace and illumination inherent in a full understanding of the Zen koan inscribed in Salinger's second book, *Nine Stories:*

> We know the sound of two hands clapping.
> But what is the sound of one hand clapping?

but the urge to find them works deeply within him. Salinger's social criticism, it would seem, has a mystical base, a support more profound than mere belief in Holden's Christian virtues, though that belief is present too. It constantly implies a religious feeling, possibly a conviction, that dimly hints a way out of the life-trap. Mark Twain's social criticism in *Huckleberry Finn* is more simply that of the rational democrat and humanitarian who has not lost faith in the practical effectiveness of the good heart on this earth.

---

[1] Philip Young, *Ernest Hemingway* (New York: Rinehart and Company, 1952), p. 181 ff.

We have seen that *Huckleberry Finn* and *The Catcher in the Rye* share certain ethical and social attitudes. Yet Salinger's critical view assumes a cultural determinism that in *Huckleberry Finn,* although always present, permits freedom through self-guidance. Salinger's viewpoint also draws upon a mystical sense merely inchoate in Mark Twain's imagination. We have seen too that Holden's neuroticism is both literary cause and social effect. It is Salinger's means of etching the modern picture the more deeply, and a product of the culture it so sweepingly condemns on moral grounds. But Mark Twain's moral vision is projected through the prevailing normality of Huck's temperament. It is eminently central; fundamentally there is nothing rigged about Huck's experience or eccentric in his responses. So Huck on a raft, as profoundly symbolic today as Thoreau in his cabin, is ever more meaningful as our national experience hurtles us along routes more menacing than the Mississippi. *The Catcher in the Rye,* always cautionary, often horrifying in moral tone, creates an overwhelming sense of that hurtling. The point is not that Salinger's moral vision is therefore defective. Rather, because his vision is lit by the sick lamps of civilization, *The Catcher in the Rye* is as appropriate to our age as *Huckleberry Finn* is to an earlier America. Salinger's novel, in fact, suggests great truths about our times, as Whitman's *Democratic Vistas* did, in polemic form, about an earlier age that was cankered, crude, materialistic, depraved. *The Catcher in the Rye* has the same awesome relevance to our collective civilized fate that more subtly pervades Mark Twain's masterpiece. Nowhere is its literary descent from *Huckleberry Finn* more clearly seen than in its critical modern dramatization of moral and social themes.[157]

VI

To conclude, the two novels are clearly related in narrative pattern and style, characterization of the hero and critical import—the three areas discussed in this paper. The relationship argues the continuing vitality of Huck's archetypal story, absorbed by generations and still creatively at work in contemporary thought and art. *The Catcher in the Rye* takes its place in that literary tradition—spreading beyond Anderson, Lardner, Hemingway, Faulkner—that has one of its great sources in *Huckleberry Finn.*[2] But the literary kinship of these two

---

[2] See, for example: Horace Gregory (ed.), *The Portable Sherwood Anderson* (New York: The Viking Press, 1949), pp. 8–9; Irving Howe, *Sherwood Anderson* (New York: William Sloane Associates, 1951), pp. 94, 124–27; Gilbert Seldes (ed.), *The Portable Ring Lardner* (New York: The Viking Press, 1946), pp. 1–2, 13–15; Carlos Baker, *Hemingway the Writer as Artist* (Princeton, N.J.: Princeton University Press, 1952), pp. 180–81; Philip Young, *Ernest Hemingway* (New York: Rinehart and Company, 1952), pp. 159–61, 181–212;

novels presupposes a type of cultural continuity more basic than the dynamics of literary tradition or than the persistence of Huck's story in the popular imagination. We have seen that each author responds sensitively to the times he depicts, appropriately choosing his facts and shaping his language and meaning to portray the social and moral realities clustered in and about his hero. Yet the resulting differences do not obscure the similarity in the conformations of character and social relationships that emerge. Fundamentally these books are brothers under the skin because they reflect a slowly developing but always recognizable pattern of moral and social meaning that is part of the active experience of young Americans let loose in the world, in this century and the last. Independently and in his own right, each author has probed beneath surface facts—so dramatically contrasted in Huck's and Holden's environments—to the experiential continuity of American life.[158]

ALBERT FOWLER

> "Alien in the Rye," *Modern Age,* I, No. 2 (Fall 1957), 193–197. Reprinted by permission of *Modern Age: A Conservative Review.*

J. D. Salinger's picture of man sickened by society reflects the idea propounded by Rousseau and the disciples of naturalism of the individual born good and corrupted by his institutions. Both in the novel *The Catcher in the Rye* and in the stories like *For Esmé—with Love and Squalor* he shows an adolescent trailing clouds of childhood and very much at odds with the world. The argument that Salinger has inherited from a long tradition of writers is that nature is norm and ideal, civilization the alien and warping form imposed against the grain. Many have been the voices raised in support of this theme, and none more significant for the present century than that of Sigmund Freud who said: "My secret conclusion was: since we can only regard

---

Malcolm Cowley (ed.), *The Portable Faulkner* (New York: The Viking Press, 1946), p. 22; Randall Stewart and Dorothy Bethurum (eds.), *Modern American Narration, Mark Twain, Ernest Hemingway, William Faulkner* (Chicago: Scott Foresman and Company, 1954), "Foreword."

the highest civilization of the present as disfigured by a gigantic hypocrisy it follows that we are organically unfit for it."

The cause of the alienation is placed at the doors of schools,
churches, business houses, government bureaus. They are charged with
thwarting human aspirations,[1931] frustrating conscience, outraging
sensitivity. Salinger's stand for the individual and against the world,
for the heaven of inner desire and opposed to the hell of outward
circumstance, brings up the question posed by the disciples of naturalism how deep the split is between moral man and immoral society.
Is it a superficial alienation, a literary idea caught between the covers
of a book, a figure of speech confined to the imaginative events of
novel and story, or does it have roots in the behavior of real men and
women in everyday life? Is this a romantic notion handed down
through two centuries of naturalism, or a basic flaw in the makeup
of the western body social?

Although Freud was explicit in his belief that man is being con-
strained almost to the breaking point by social code and convention,
his famous disciple and biographer Ernest Jones does not place Salinger's novel in this frame of reference. His review of *The Catcher in
the Rye* distinguishes between actual alienation and the sense of alienation he finds in Holden Caulfield, whose feeling of being cut off from
his fellows, from parents, friends, school and society, Dr. Jones insists
has been common to every sensitive adolescent for the past two hundred years. He considers it only a phase of growing up, only an intimation and intuition of disaffection.

Despite Ernest Jones' and a few other unsympathetic reviews, the
critics generally have dealt kindly with the novel, and Salinger's stories
have enjoyed an impressive vogue in *The New Yorker*. He is praised
as intelligent, poignant, profound; his writing original, serious, and
beautiful. Now the *Western Humanities Review* has presented an
evaluation of the body of his work under the title *J. D. Salinger: Some
Crazy Cliff* by Arthur Heiserman and James E. Miller, Jr. What they
have to say about the alienated individual deserves careful attention.

They place *The Catcher in the Rye* in the epic tradition of the
Quest, which seems to them the most profound in western fiction, and
range Holden Caulfield beside those great outcasts, Stephen Dedalus,
Hans Castorp, Huck Finn and Prince Myshkin. The young man is
pictured full of love and courage, innocent and good, a wise sheep
forced into lone wolf's clothing. He pierces the shams and deceits and
vulgarity of a phony society which botches things so terribly that at
last Holden has no escape except a mental institution.

The final sentences of this perceptive Salinger analysis give an
answer to the question how deep the present split is between the
individual and his society.

> As we leave Holden alone in his room in the psychiatric
> ward, we are aware of the book's last ironic incongruity. It is
> not Holden who should be examined for a sickness of the
> mind, but the world in which he has sojourned and found
> himself an alien. To "cure" Holden, he must be given the
> contagious, almost universal disease of phony adultism; he
> must be pushed over that "crazy cliff."

This position can be buttressed by similar remarks by other writers in
the university quarterlies. Lawrence Lipton, in his *Disaffiliation and
the Art of Poverty* in the *Chicago Review*, says Holden rebels against
the moral cowardice of an age that jails the victims and lets the crimi-
nals rule. Lipton supports Nelson Algren's opinions expressed in *The
Man with the Golden Arm* that society creates the sinner, that the
guilty ones are the judges and the lawyers, and that the writer's duty
is forever with the accused. This idea that society is so meanly organized it forces the individual to perpetrate villainies goes back to
Dostoievski, as Algren points out, and beyond the Russian to Rousseau[194] and to an age which discarded the discipline of the church
for personal freedom, the bondage to manual labor for scientific technology.

The novelist's right to condemn society without fear of criticism
has been defended by Wayne Burns in *The Novelist as Revolutionary*
in the *Arizona Quarterly*. He claims that first and foremost the
novelist is an artist, and as such cannot be judged on the basis of moral
and religious values. If he is not granted complete and unqualified
freedom to write as he pleases, Burns argues, the novelist must somehow contrive to wrest that freedom from society or cease to be an artist.

> This is the price of modern fictional art; and if we are
> to pay that price, we must be prepared to accept and encour-
> age the serious novelist as we do the scientist—as a kind of
> licensed madman and revolutionary.

The pertinent part of the bargain is that while the artist is free to
castigate society for its sins, society is warned to withhold its criticism
of the artist for fear of maiming or killing him. It is on the naturalistic
premise that the good is found in the individual and the evil in society
that such a bargain can be struck.

The argument that the world is sick and that its sickness is forcing
the healthy person to alienate himself from society gains strength
from the widespread and continuing growth of mental disturbance
like that of Holden Caulfield. The neurotic and psychotic constitute
an increasing group that is crowding the capacity of mental institutions and living a separate existence largely cut off from the main
body social. An occasional doctor, psychiatrist, and religious teacher is
convinced it would be dangerous to try to persuade the neurotic to

adjust to his society because that society may be too sick to insure its own survival. They describe him as a fascinating and beautiful rebel, one of the few in a moribund culture who is spiritually alive, a wise seeker from whom a desperately ill world has much to learn. To ask him to accept his environment and his institutions would be to propose that he exchange a precious if precarious health for a mortal affliction.

Further support for the belief that a breach too deep for bridging has been opened between the individual and society may be found in the current fear of subversion and the cry for loyalty oaths and security screens. Even the occasionally hysterical investigations of so-called un-American activities might be cited as evidence of a dread that the body social is split by disaffection. But this aspect of the argument is clouded by the presence of contrary witnesses, and if there are individuals seceding from society there are others like the Negroes who are beginning to leave their ghetto status and join as partners and equals in the business of building a stronger community.

Salinger expresses the alienation in another way by contrasting the child with the adult, early innocence and goodness with later cynicism and corruption, on the naturalistic theory that the farther one goes from the purity of the cradle the more tainted one becomes from contact with society. As a child Holden Caulfield had known truth and "non-phoniness," say the authors of the *Western Humanities Review* evaluation, and he retains the courage and wisdom to refuse to compromise with adulthood and its necessary adulteries. They confess that his heroism, like that of Dostoievski's princely idiot, finally drives him out of his mind, but they insist the hero must either flee his institutions or defy them in the search for what is real. These critics see beyond the romantic aspect of their argument, for they realize how horrified Wordsworth would have been at Freud's discoveries about the child as father of the man and [195] they declare that when Freud made the cult of childhood clinical he made it rampant.

The goal of Holden's quest is what Heiserman and Miller describe as that inner peace found in the midst of nature "when you're naked of civilization and in company with an outcast more untarnished and childlike than yourself..." The figure of the hunter seems to them to personify man stripped to his essence because in this role he has left behind him, like the boy in Faulkner's story *The Bear,* whatever is unnatural or convenient. They feel the wilderness requires an integrity of life from the man who faces it alone, a courage and a fury which lie at the core of human nature unspoiled by contact with society.

Is the flight from civilization prompted by an unusual maturity or by an undisciplined nostalgia for childhood? Is it based on a wise appraisal of a society stricken beyond rescue or on an inherited assumption that society is evil? As one studies Heiserman's and Miller's evaluation of Salinger, his reverence for childhood, his canonization of the child's innocence and inability to do any wrong, make one wonder whether there is about him some bias against manhood, against the choices and conciliations the adult must make in everyday life. And one is moved to wonder further whether some of the disaffected refuse the challenge of their society partly because it necessitates the response of a mature mind and educated emotions.

Much of the persuasive power in Salinger's naturalism stems from the artificial division it makes between the good and the evil. The world of experience is a bewildering combination of good and evil, and neither in society nor in the individual is the good or the bad to be found by itself. If the novelist is free to do what the disciples of naturalism have done with impunity since Rousseau, to separate good from bad, to endow the hero with the good qualities and his society with the bad ones, this falsification will continue to charm the reader as long as it can command belief. The weakness of naturalism becomes apparent whenever it tackles the problem of evil as part of the makeup of the individual without foisting it off on the external world.

It is convenient and comforting to forget that almost as soon as Rousseau proclaimed man was born good, his contemporary the Marquis de Sade proclaimed man was born evil. It is becoming increasingly difficult to dismiss Sade's maleficent individual as a force in history after the series of events that were touched off in 1914 and 1939. Naturalism has been about as busy celebrating maleficent as his beneficent counterpart, and his friends and defenders form a famous line from Sade through Baudelaire to Nietzsche. So little attention has been paid to this side of naturalism, however, that it is hard to name more than a handful of well reasoned books devoted to the subject, notable among which are Mario Praz' *The Romantic Agony* and Albert Camus' *The Rebel*. But enough work has been done to show that as long as Rousseau's idea of man good in essence persists, Sade's idea of man evil in essence will flourish beside it.

If it is true that Salinger follows Rousseau in concentrating the good in his adolescent hero Holden Caulfield and concentrating the evil in the surrounding environment, Heiserman and Miller aid the process by making explicit what they believe he implied. They have set this novel beside the work of the greatest writers, raising it to the high level of a holy quest and teasing from it implications of the tremendous. They find here the search for Virtue and Truth in the face of grave danger. "The phoniness of society forces Holden Caulfield to leave it.... For Holden loves the world more than the world can bear." But for him,[196] they explain, there is no Ithaca that waited for Ulysses after his trials. "Ithaca has not merely been defiled by a horde of suitors; it has sunk beneath waves of phoniness." To be a catcher of men as Holden wanted to be, to save them from the crazy cliff of destruction, is possible only at the price of breaking with the world. "To be good is to be a 'case,' a 'bad boy' who confounds the society of men." According to this searching interpretation, Holden is a truly tragic figure, a wanderer with no place to call his own, a pilgrim kept forever from Jerusalem.

It is as a critique of the contemporary world that Harvey Breit in *The Atlantic Monthly* considered the novel a failure. Its seriousness seemed always overwhelmed by the greater power of the comic element, and he found the book a brilliant *tour de force* capable of making the reader laugh aloud. Again and again the reviews refer to the quality of Salinger's humor, and one is tempted at the beginning of *The Catcher in the Rye to* wonder whether it will turn out to be a side-splitting satire on the modern romantic theme of the good man in a naughty world. Heiserman and Miller understand how common is the writer's flight into the Eden of innocence, how nonexistent was Rousseau's noble savage, and how obsessed western literature has been since his time with the charms of childhood as solutions to social problems. But in spite of their insight these critics insist with Eudora Welty that the distinctive mark of Salinger's humor is its ability to intensify the heartbreak and the horror, to bring out the catch in the throat that accompanies all the laughs. It is important to them not that he has a saving sense of the comical but that he uses it to point up the tragic, to make his hero's plight more poignant.

In the light of their critical analysis Salinger appears to be presenting a tragedy without a catharsis. As they interpret his message it seems to be a counsel of despair. In it one catches an echo of Freud's remark: "We have to abdicate, and the Great Unknown, He or It, lurking behind Fate, will sometime repeat such an experiment with another race." Civilization is pictured here as phony beyond succor, the individual as casting loose from society and taking with him whoever he can rescue at the risk of his life. This dismay at the evil of the external world, this tendency to throw up one's hands in horror and withdraw from the body social in desperation at its depravity, seems to be the result of the Rousseau wedge driven between good and evil, confining the good in the individual and the evil in social institutions.

Rousseau's assumption of man noble and innocent at birth, endowed by nature with all beautiful and loveable qualities only to have them tainted and poisoned by contact with society, has held an enormous appeal ever since the west began to discard the discipline of the church and to depend for its existence on the technology of science. From the seventeenth century on men have been fascinated with the possibility that the church had misled them, that perhaps they were not born both good and evil, perhaps life was not a battleground between the good and the bad but was instead a paradise of virtue waiting to welcome them once they could see through the church's deception. But no matter how hard they have tried to believe in the human soul as essentially good they have never succeeded in ridding it of the essence of evil. The shining figure of Rousseau is forever shadowed by Sade, and the good and evil they argue for continue to struggle together in the individual as well as in society.[197]

FRANK KERMODE

"Fit Audience," *The Spectator,* CC (May 30, 1958), 705–706. Reprinted by permission of *The Spectator,* London.

What meaning, if any, can one attach to the expression 'a key book of the present decade'? It is used as a blurb in a new reprint of Mr. J. D. Salinger's famous novel,[1] which was first published in 1951. Whoever remembers the book will suppose that this is a serious claim, implying perhaps that *The Catcher,* as well as being extremely successful, is a work of art existing in some more or less profound relationship with the 'spirit of the age.' It is, anyway, quite different from saying that *No Orchids for Miss Blandish* is a key book. On the other hand, there is an equally clear distinction between this book and such key novels as *Ulysses* or *A Passage to India.* For it is elementary that, although these books have been read by very large numbers of people, one may reasonably distinguish between a smaller, 'true' audience and bigger audiences which read them quite differently, and were formerly a fortuitous addition to the 'highbrow' public. But although Salinger is certainly a 'highbrow' novelist, it would be unreal to speak of his audience, large though it is, as divided in this way. What we now have is a new reader who is not only common but pretty sharp. This new reader is also a pampered consumer, so that the goods supplied him rapidly grow obsolete; which may explain why I found *The Catcher* somewhat less enchanting on a second reading.

It is, of course, a book of extraordinary accomplishment; I don't know how one reviewer came to call it 'untidy.' Nothing inept, nothing that does not look good and work well as long as it is needed, will

---

[1] *The Catcher in the Rye* (Penguin Books, 2s. 6d.).

satisfy this new public. Structural virtuosity is now taken for granted, particularly in American novels. This one is designed for readers who can see a wood, and paths in a wood, as well as sturdy, primitive trees —a large, roughly calculable audience: fit audience though many.

At the level of its untidy story, the book is about an adolescent crisis. A boy runs away from his expensive school because he is an academic failure and finds intolerable the company of so many phoneys. He passes a lost weekend in New York, mostly in phoney hotels, night clubs and theatres, avoids going to bed with a prostitute and is beaten up by her ponce, meets some phoney friends, talks to taxi-drivers, wonders endearingly where the ducks from Central Park Lake go in winter, secretly visits his kid sister, indulges various fantasies of much charm and finally falls ill with exhaustion. He tells his story in a naive sophisticated dialect, partly in the Homeric Runyon tradition, partly something more modern. Repetitive, indecent, often very funny, it is wonderfully sustained by the author, who achieves all those ancient effects to be got from a hero who is in some ways inferior, and in others superior, to the reader. (His wisdom is natural, ours artificial.) The effect is comfortably compassionate; the boy, ungifted and iso-lated as he thinks himself to be, is getting his last pre-adult look at the adult world, our world, into which he is being irresistibly projected. He can't stand the adolescent world either; clean, good children turn into pimply shavers with dirty minds. For sex is what alters the good-ness of children. Of the girls Holden Caulfield knows, one is nice and lovable—for her he admits no sexual feeling, though her date with a crumby seducer helps to work him up to this crisis; one is a prostitute, operating in a hotel which is a comic emblem of the perverted adult world; and one is an arty phoney. Growing up is moving out of crumby phoneyness into perverted phoneyness. These phoneys, they come in at the goddam window, using words like 'grand' and 'marvellous,' reading and writing stories about 'phoney lean-jawed guys named David...and a lot of phoney girls named Marcia that are always lighting all the goddam Davids' pipes for them.' Successful people, even the Lunts, turn into phoneys because of all the phoneys who adore them. Holden, near enough to Nature to spot this, is himself know-ingly infected by the false attitudes of the movies, the greatest single source of phoneyness. Only children are free of it, especially dead children.

This much you get from listening to the boy, and it sounds untidy. What Mr. Salinger adds is design. Holden is betrayed at the outset by a schoolmaster (phoney-crumby) and at the end by another (phoney-perverted). The only time his parents come into the story, he has to remain motionless in the dark with his sister. The boy's slang is used to suggest patterns he cannot be aware of: whatever pleases him 'kills' him, sends him off to join his dead brother; almost everybody, even the disappointed whore, is 'old so-and-so,' and 'old' suggests the past and stability. More important, the book has its big, focal passages, wonderfully contrived. Holden hears a little neglected boy singing, 'If a body catch a body, etc.' This kills him. Then he helps a little girl in Central Park to fasten her skates. Next he walks to the Museum of Natural History, which he loved as a child; it seemed 'the only nice, dry cosy place in the world.' Nothing changed there among the stuffed Indians and Eskimos; except *you*. You changed every time you went in. The thought that his little sister must also feel that whenever she went in depresses him; so he tries to help some kids on a see-saw, but they don't want him around. When he reaches the museum he won't go in. This is a beautiful little parable, and part of my point is that nobody will miss it. Another is the climactic scene when Holden is waiting for his sister to come out of school. Full of rage at the '—— yous' written on the school walls, he goes into the Egyptian Room of the museum and explains to a couple of scared children why the mummies don't rot. Of course, he likes mummies; though the kids, naturally, don't. But even in there, in the congenial atmosphere of undecaying death, somebody has written '—— you' on the wall. There is nowhere free from crumbiness and sex. He retreats into his catcher fantasy as Phoebe rides the carousel; and then into illness.

This is only a hint of the complexity of Mr. Salinger's 'highbrow' plotting. There is much more; consider the perfectly 'placed' discussion between the boy and his sister in which he tells her about the phoneys at school. She complains that he doesn't like *anything*, and challenges him to mention something he does. After a struggle, he speaks of two casually encountered nuns, a boy who threw himself out of a window, and his dead brother. He daren't grow up, for fear of turning into a phoney; but behind him Eden is shut for ever.

Why, then, with all this to admire, do I find something phoney in the book itself? Not because there is 'faking,' as Mr. Forster calls it. In his sense, 'faking' doesn't lead one directly to some prefabricated attitude, and this does happen in *The Catcher*. The mixed-up kid totters on the brink of a society which is corrupt in a conventional way; its evils are fashionably known to be such, and don't have to be proved, made valid in the book. Similarly, the adult view of adolescence, insinuated by skilful faking, is agreeable to a predictable public taste. Again, we like to look at the book and see the Libido having a bad time while the Death Wish does well, as in the museum scenes; but I don't feel that this situation occurs in the book as it were by natural growth, any more than sub-threshold advertising grows on film. *The Catcher* has a built-in death wish; it is what the consumer needs, just as he might ask that a toothpaste taste good *and* contain a smart prophylactic against pyorrhœa. The predictable consumer-reaction is a double one; how good! and how clever! The boy's attitudes to religion, authority, art, sex and so on are what smart people would like other people to have, but cannot have themselves because of their superior understanding. They hold together in a single thought purity and mess, and feel good. The author's success springs from his having, with perfect understanding, supplied their demand for this kind of satisfaction.

It is this rapport between author and public, or high-class rabblement, that would have astonished Joyce. Its presence in *The Catcher* may be roughly established by comparison with Keith Waterhouse's *There is a Happy Land,* obviously influenced by Salinger. It is in some ways a more genuine book; the growth of a positive evil out of the sordid innocence of a proletarian childhood is worked out in a way that prevents anybody feeling superior about it. But it isn't a 'key' book, because it is not designed for the smart-common reader. These may seem hard sayings, when[705] *The Catcher* has given me so much pleasure. But I speak as a consumer myself, asking why the book, a few years on, seems so much less impressive. The answer seems to be that new needs are readily engendered in us, and readily supplied. Books will not last us any longer than motorcars. Of the rabblement from which we came, we retain one characteristic, its fickleness. What pleases us will not keep, of its very nature. Joyce was right not to seek his readers in the walks of the *bestia trionfante,* Forster to stand by his aristocracy. Mr. Salinger is not like them. Since few men will write for nobody, this fine artist writes for the sharp common reader.[706]

MAXWELL GEISMAR

From *American Moderns: From Rebellion to Conformity* by Maxwell Geismar. New York: Hill & Wang, Inc., 1958. Copyright © 1958 by Maxwell Geismar. Reprinted by permission of Hill & Wang, Inc.

. . .

These are handsome prose passages, and *The Catcher in the Rye* is eminently readable and quotable in its tragicomic narrative of preadolescent revolt. Compact, taut, and colorful, the first half of the novel presents in brief compass all the petty horrors, the banalities, the final mediocrity of the typical American prep school. Very fine—and not sustained or fulfilled, as fiction. For the later sections of the narrative are simply an episodic account of Holden Caulfield's "lost week end" in New York City which manages to sustain our interest but hardly deepens our understanding.

There are very ambiguous elements, moreover, in the portrait of this sad little screwed-up hero. His urban background is curiously shadowy, like the parents who never quite appear in the story, like the one pure adolescent love affair which is now "ruined" in his memory. The locale of the New York sections is obviously that of a comfortable middle-class urban Jewish society where, however, all the leading figures have become beautifully Anglicized. Holden and Phoebe Caulfield: what perfect American social register names which are presented to us in both a[197] social and a psychological void! Just as the hero's interest in the ancient Egyptians extends only to the fact that they created mummies, so Salinger's own view of his hero's environment omits any reference to its real nature and dynamics.

Though the book is dedicated to Salinger's mother, the fictional mother in the narrative appears only as a voice through the wall. The touching note of affection between the brother and sister is partly a substitute for the missing child-parent relationships (which might indeed clarify the nature of the neurotic hero), and perhaps even a sentimental evasion of the true emotions in a sibling love. The only real creation (or half-creation) in this world is Holden Caulfield himself. And that "compassion," so much praised in the story, and always expressed in the key phrase, "You had to feel sorry"—for him, for her, for them—also implies the same sense of superiority. If this hero really represents the nonconformist rebellion of the Fifties, he is a rebel without a past, apparently, and without a cause.

The Catcher in the Rye protests, to be sure, against both the academic and social conformity of its period. But what does it argue *for?* When Holden mopes about the New York museum which is almost the true home of his discredited childhood, he remembers the Indian war-canoes "about as long as three goddam Cadillacs in a row." He refuses any longer to participate in the wealthy private boys' school where "you have to keep making believe you give a damn if the football team loses, and all you do is talk about girls and liquor and sex all day, and everybody sticks together in these dirty little goddam cliques." Fair enough; while he also rejects the notion of a conventional future in which he would work in an office, make a lot of dough, ride in cabs, play bridge, or go to the movies. But in his own private vision of a better life, this little catcher in the rye sees only those "thousands of little children" all playing near the dangerous cliff, "and nobody's around—nobody big, I mean—except me" to rescue them from their morbid fate.

This is surely the differential revolt of the lonesome rich child, the conspicuous display of leisure-class emotions, the wounded affections, never quite faced, of the upper-class orphan. This is the *New Yorker* school of ambiguous finality at its best. But Holden Caulfield's real trouble, as he is told by the equally precocious Phoebe is that he doesn't like *any*thing that is happening.[198] "You don't like any schools. You don't like a million things. You *don't*." This is also the peak of well-to-do and neurotic anarchism—the one world of cultivated negation in which all those thousands of innocent, pure little children are surely as doomed as their would-be and somewhat paranoid savior. "I have a feeling that you're riding for some kind of a terrible, terrible fall," says the last and best teacher in Holden's tormented academic career. But even this prophetic insight is vitiated by the fact that Mr. Antolini, too, is one of those flits and perverty guys from whom the adolescent hero escapes in shame and fear.

He is still, and forever, the innocent child in the evil and hostile universe, the child who can never grow up. And no wonder that he hears, in the final pages of the narrative, only a chorus of obscene sexual epithets which seem to surround the little moment of lyric happiness with his childlike sister. The real achievement of *The Catcher in the Rye* is that it manages so gracefully to evade just those central questions which it raises, and to preserve both its verbal brilliance and the charm of its emotions within the scope of its own dubious literary form. It is still Salinger's best work, if a highly artificial one, and the caesuras, the absences, the ambiguities at the base of this writer's work became more obvious in his subsequent books.[199]

DONALD P. COSTELLO

From "The Language of *The Catcher in the Rye*," *American Speech*, XXXIV (October 1959), 172–181. Reprinted with permission from *American Speech*, Copyright Columbia University Press, 1959.

A study of the language of J. D. Salinger's *The Catcher in the Rye* can be justified not only on the basis of literary interest, but also on the basis of linguistic significance. Today we study *The Adventures of Huckleberry Finn* (with which many critics have compared *The Catcher in the Rye*) not only as a great work of literary art, but as a valuable study in 1884 dialect. In coming decades, *The Catcher in the Rye* will be studied, I feel, not only as a literary work, but also as an example of teenage vernacular in the 1950s. As such, the book will be a significant historical linguistic record of a type of speech rarely made available in permanent form. Its linguistic importance will increase as the American speech it records becomes less current.

Most critics who looked at *The Catcher in the Rye* at the time of its publication thought that its language was a true and authentic rendering of teenage colloquial speech. Reviewers in the Chicago *Sunday Tribune,* the London *Times Literary Supplement,* the *New Republic,* the New York *Herald Tribune Book Review,* the New York *Times,* the *New Yorker,* and the *Saturday Review of Literature* all specifically mentioned the authenticity of the book's language. Various aspects of its language were also discussed in the reviews published in *America,* the *Atlantic,* the *Catholic World,* the *Christian Science Monitor,* the *Library Journal,* the Manchester *Guardian,* the *Nation,* the *New Statesman and Nation,* the New York *Times Book Review, Newsweek,* the *Spectator,* and *Time.*[1] Of these many reviews, only the writers for the *Catholic World* and the *Christian Science Monitor* denied the authenticity of the book's language, but both of these are religious journals which refused to believe that the 'obscenity' was realistic. An examination of the reviews of *The Catcher in the Rye* proves that[172] the language of Holden Caulfield, the book's sixteen-year-old narrator, struck the ear of the contemporary reader as an accurate rendering of the informal speech of an intelligent, educated, Northeastern American adolescent.[2]

---

[1] See reviews in *America,* LXXV (August 11, 1951), 463, 464; *Atlantic,* CLXXXVIII (1951), 82; *Catholic World,* CLXXIV (1951), 154; Chicago *Sunday Tribune,* July 15, 1951, Part 4, p. 3; *Christian Science Monitor,* July 19, 1951, p. 9; *Library Journal,* LXXVI (1951), 1125; *Times* (London) *Literary Supplement,* September 7, 1951, p. 561; Manchester *Guardian,* August 10, 1951, p. 4; *Nation,* CLXXIII (September 1, 1951), 176; *New Republic,* CXXV (July 16, 1951), 20, 21; *New Statesman and Nation,* XLII (August 18, 1951), 185; New York *Herald Tribune Book Review,* July 15, 1951, p. 3; New York *Times Book Review,* July 15, 1951, p. 5; New York *Times,* July 16, 1951, p. 19; *New Yorker,* XXVII (August 11, 1951), 71–76; *Newsweek,* XXXVIII (July 16, 1951), 89, 90; *Saturday Review of Literature,* XXXIV (July 14, 1951), 12, 13; *Spectator,* CLXXXVII (August 17, 1951), 224; *Time,* LVIII (July 16, 1951), 96, 97.

[2] If additional evidence of the authenticity of the book's language is required, one need only look at the phenomenal regard with which *The Catcher in the Rye* is held by today's college students, who were about Holden's age at the

In addition to commenting on its authenticity, critics have often remarked—uneasily—the 'daring,' 'obscene,' 'blasphemous' features of Holden's language. Another commonly noted feature of the book's language has been its comic effect. And yet there has never been an extensive investigation of the language itself. That is what this paper proposes to do.

Even though Holden's language is authentic teenage speech, recording it was certainly not the major intention of Salinger. He was faced with the artistic task of creating an individual character, not with the linguistic task of reproducing the exact speech of teenagers in general. Yet Holden had to speak a recognizable teenage language, and at the same time had to be identifiable as an individual. This difficult task Salinger achieved by giving Holden an extremely trite and typical teenage speech, overlaid with strong personal idiosyncrasies. There are two major speech habits which are Holden's own, which are endlessly repeated throughout the book, and which are, nevertheless, typical enough of teenage speech so that Holden can be both typical and individual in his use of them. It is certainly common for teenagers to end thoughts with a loosely dangling 'and all,' just as it is common for them to add an insistent 'I really did,' 'It really was.' But Holden uses these phrases to such an overpowering degree that they become a clear part of the flavor of the book; they become, more, a part of Holden himself, and actually help to characterize him.

Holden's 'and all' and its twins, 'or something,' 'or anything,' serve no real, consistent linguistic function. They simply give a sense of looseness of expression and looseness of thought. Often they signify that Holden knows there is more that could be said about the issue at hand, but he is not going to bother about going into it. . . .[173] But just as often the use of such expressions is purely arbitrary, with no discernible meaning. . . . Donald Barr, writing in the *Commonweal*, finds this habit indicative of Holden's tendency to generalize, to find the all in the one:

---

time the book was written. In its March 9, 1957, issue, the *Nation* published a symposium which attempted to discover the major influences upon the college students of today. Many teachers pointed out the impact of Salinger. Carlos Baker, of Princeton, stated: 'There is still, as there has been for years, a cult of Thomas Wolfe. They have all read J. D. Salinger, Wolfe's closest competitor.' Stanley Kunitz, of Queens College, wrote: 'The only novelist I have heard praised vociferously is J. D. Salinger.' Harvey Curtis Webster, of the University of Louisville, listed Salinger as one of the 'stimulators.' R. J. Kaufman, of the University of Rochester, called *The Catcher in the Rye* 'a book which has complexly aroused nearly all of them.' See 'The Careful Young Men,' *Nation*, CLXXXIV (March 9, 1957), 199–214. I have never heard any Salinger partisan among college students doubt the authenticity of the language of their compatriot, Holden.

Salinger has an ear not only for idiosyncrasies of diction and syntax, but for mental processes. Holden Caulfield's phrase is 'and all'—'She looked so damn *nice,* the way she kept going around and around in her blue coat and all'—as if each experience wore a halo. His fallacy is *ab uno disce omnes;* he abstracts and generalizes wildly.[3]

Heiserman and Miller, in the *Western Humanities Review,* comment specifically upon Holden's second most obvious idiosyncrasy: 'In a phony world Holden feels compelled to reenforce his sincerity and truthfulness constantly with, "It really is" or "It really did." '[4] S. N. Behrman, in the *New Yorker,* finds a double function of these 'perpetual insistences of Holden's.' Behrman thinks they 'reveal his age, even when he is thinking much older,' and, more important, 'he is so aware of the danger of slipping into phoniness himself that he has to repeat over and over "I really mean it," "It really does." '[5] Holden uses this idiosyncrasy of insistence almost every time that he makes an affirmation.

Allied to Holden's habit of insistence is his 'if you want to know the truth.' Heiserman and Miller are able to find characterization in this habit too:

> The skepticism inherent in that casual phrase, 'if you want to know the truth,' suggesting that as a matter of fact in the world of Holden Caulfield very few people do, characterizes this sixteen-year-old 'crazy mixed up kid' more sharply and vividly than pages of character 'analysis' possibly could.[174][6]

Holden uses this phrase only after affirmations, just as he uses 'It really does,' but usually after the personal ones, where he is consciously being frank. . . .

These personal idiosyncrasies of Holden's speech are in keeping with general teenage language. Yet they are so much a part of Holden and of the flavor of the book that they are much of what makes Holden to be Holden. They are the most memorable feature of the book's language. Although always in character, the rest of Holden's speech is more typical than individual. The special quality of this language comes from its triteness, its lack of distinctive qualities.

Holden's informal, schoolboy vernacular is particularly typical in its 'vulgarity' and 'obscenity.' No one familiar with prep-school speech

---

[3] Donald Barr, 'Saints, Pilgrims, and Artists,' *Commonweal,* LXVII (October 25, 1957), 90.

[4] Arthur Heiserman and James E. Miller, Jr., 'J. D. Salinger: Some Crazy Cliff,' *Western Humanities Review,* X (1956), 136.

[5] S. N. Behrman, 'The Vision of the Innocent,' *New Yorker,* XXVII (August 11, 1951), 72.

[6] Heiserman and Miller, *op. cit.,* p. 135.

could seriously contend that Salinger overplayed his hand in this respect. On the contrary, Holden's restraints help to characterize him as a sensitive youth who avoids the most strongly forbidden terms, and who never uses vulgarity in a self-conscious or phony way to help him be 'one of the boys' . . .[175]

The use of crude language in *The Catcher in the Rye* increases, as we should expect, when Holden is reporting schoolboy dialogue. When he is directly addressing the reader, Holden's use of such language drops off almost entirely. There is also an increase in this language when any of the characters are excited or angry. Thus, when Holden is apprehensive over Stradlater's treatment of Jane, his *goddams* increase suddenly to seven on a single page (p. 39).[7]

Holden's speech is also typical in his use of slang. I have catalogued over a hundred slang terms used by Holden, and every one of these is in widespread use. Although Holden's slang is rich and colorful, it, of course, being slang, often fails at precise communication. Thus, Holden's *crap* is used in seven different ways. It can mean foolishness, as 'all that David Copperfield kind of crap,' or messy matter, as 'I spilled some crap all over my gray flannel,' or merely miscellaneous matter, as 'I was putting on my galoshes and crap.' It can also carry its basic meaning, animal excreta, as 'there didn't look like there was anything in the park except dog crap,' and it can be used as an adjective meaning anything generally unfavorable, as 'The show was on the crappy side.' Holden uses the phrases *to be a lot of crap* and *to shoot the crap* and *to chuck the crap* all to mean 'to be untrue,' but he can also use *to shoot the crap* to mean simply 'to chat,' with no connotation of untruth, as in 'I certainly wouldn't have minded shooting the crap with old Phoebe for a while.'

Similarly Holden's slang use of *crazy* is both trite and imprecise. 'That drives me crazy' means that he violently dislikes something; yet 'to be crazy about' something means just the opposite. In the same way, to be 'killed' by[176] something can mean that he was emotionally affected either favorably ('That story just about killed me.') or unfavorably ('Then she turned her back on me again. It nearly killed me.'). This use of *killed* is one of Holden's favorite slang expressions. Heiserman and Miller are, incidentally, certainly incorrect when they conclude: 'Holden always lets us know when he has insight into the absurdity of the endlessly absurd situations which make up the life of a sixteen-year-old by exclaiming, "It killed me." '[8] Holden often uses this expression with no connection to the absurd; he even uses it for his beloved Phoebe. The expression simply indicates a high degree of emo-

---

[7] A footnote omitted earlier points out that page references to *The Catcher in the Rye* are to the Signet paperback reprint. [Eds.]
[8] Heiserman and Miller, *op. cit.*, p. 136.

tion—any kind. It is hazardous to conclude that any of Holden's slang has a precise and consistent meaning or function. These same critics fall into the same error when they conclude that Holden's use of the adjective *old* serves as 'a term of endearment.'[9] Holden appends this word to almost every character, real or fictional, mentioned in the novel, from the hated 'old Maurice' to 'old Peter Lorre,' to 'old Phoebe,' and even 'old Jesus.' The only pattern that can be discovered in Holden's use of this term is that he usually uses it only after he has previously mentioned the character; he then feels free to append the familiar *old*. All we can conclude from Holden's slang is that it is typical teenage slang: versatile yet narrow, expressive yet unimaginative, imprecise, often crude, and always trite.

Holden has many favorite slang expressions which he overuses. In one place, he admits:

> 'Boy!' I said. I also say 'Boy!' quite a lot. Partly because I have a lousy vocabulary and partly because I act quite young for my age sometimes. (12.)

But if Holden's slang shows the typically 'lousy vocabulary' of even the educated American teenager, this failing becomes even more obvious when we narrow our view to Holden's choice of adjectives and adverbs. The choice is indeed narrow, with a constant repetition of a few favorite words: *lousy, pretty, crumby, terrific, quite, old, stupid*—all used, as is the habit of teenage vernacular, with little regard to specific meaning. Thus, most of the nouns which are called 'stupid' could not in any logical framework be called 'ignorant,' and, as we have seen, *old* before a proper noun has nothing to do with age.

Another respect in which Holden was correct in accusing himself of having a 'lousy vocabulary' is discovered in the ease with which he falls into trite figures of speech. We have already seen that Holden's most common simile is the worn and meaningless 'as hell'; but his often-repeated 'like a madman' and 'like a bastard' are just about as unrelated to a literal meaning and are[177] easily as unimaginative. Even Holden's nonhabitual figures of speech are usually trite: 'sharp as a tack'; 'hot as a firecracker'; 'laughed like a hyena'; 'I know old Jane like a book'; 'drove off like a bat out of hell'; 'I began to feel like a horse's ass'; 'blind as a bat'; 'I know Central Park like the back of my hand.'

Repetitious and trite as Holden's vocabulary may be, it can, nevertheless, become highly effective. For example, when Holden piles one trite adjective upon another, a strong power of invective is often the result. . . . And his limited vocabulary can also be used for good

---

[9] *Ibid.*

comic effect. Holden's constant repetition of identical expressions in countless widely different situations is often hilariously funny.

But all of the humor in Holden's vocabulary does not come from its unimaginative quality. Quite the contrary, some of his figures of speech are entirely original; and these are inspired, dramatically effective, and terribly funny. . . .

Another aspect in which Holden's language is typical is that it shows the general American characteristic of adaptability—apparently strengthened by his teenage lack of restraint. It is very easy for Holden to turn nouns into adjectives, with the simple addition of a -y: 'perverty,' 'Christmasy,' 'vomity-looking,' 'whory-looking,' 'hoodlumy-looking,' 'show-offy,' 'flitty-looking,' 'dumpy-looking,' 'pimpy,' 'snobby,' 'fisty.' Like all of English, Holden's language shows a versatile combining ability: 'They gave Sally this little blue butt-twitcher of a dress to wear' (117) and 'That magazine was some little cheerer upper' (176). Perhaps the most interesting aspect of the adaptability of Holden's language is his ability to use nouns as adverbs: 'She sings it very Dixieland and whorehouse, and it doesn't sound at all mushy' (105).

As we have seen, Holden shares, in general, the trite repetitive vocabulary which is the typical lot of his age group. But as there are exceptions in his figures of speech, so are there exceptions in his vocabulary itself, in his word stock. An intelligent, well-read ('I'm quite illiterate, but I read a lot'), and educated boy, Holden possesses, and can use when he wants to, many words[178] which are many a cut above Basic English, including 'ostracized,' 'exhibitionist,' 'unscrupulous,' 'conversationalist,' 'psychic,' 'bourgeois.' Often Holden seems to choose his words consciously, in an effort to communicate to his adult reader clearly and properly, as in such terms as 'lose my virginity,' 'relieve himself,' 'an alcoholic'; for upon occasion, he also uses the more vulgar terms 'to give someone the time,' 'to take a leak,' 'booze hound.' Much of the humor arises, in fact, from Holden's habit of writing on more than one level at the same time. Thus, we have such phrases as 'They give guys the ax quite frequently at Pency' and 'It has a very good academic rating, Pency' (7). Both sentences show a colloquial idiom with an overlay of consciously selected words.

Such a conscious choice of words seems to indicate that Salinger, in his attempt to create a realistic character in Holden, wanted to make him aware of his speech, as, indeed, a real teenager would be when communicating to the outside world. Another piece of evidence that Holden is conscious of his speech and, more, realizes a difficulty in communication, is found in his habit of direct repetition: 'She likes me a lot. I mean she's quite fond of me.' (141), and 'She can be very snotty sometimes. She can be quite snotty.' (150). Sometimes the repetition is exact: 'He was a very nervous guy—I mean he was a very nervous guy.' (165), and 'I sort of missed them. I mean I sort of missed them.' (169). Sometimes Holden stops specifically to interpret slang terms, as when he wants to communicate the fact that Allie liked Phoebe: 'She killed Allie, too. I mean he liked her, too' (64).

There is still more direct evidence that Holden was conscious of his speech. Many of his comments to the reader are concerned with language. He was aware, for example, of the 'phony' quality of many words and phrases, such as 'grand,' 'prince,' 'traveling incognito,' 'little girls' room,' 'licorice stick,' and 'angels.' Holden is also conscious, of course, of the existence of 'taboo words.' He makes a point of mentioning that the girl from Seattle repeatedly asked him to 'watch your language, if you don't mind' (67), and that his mother told Phoebe not to say 'lousy' (160). When the prostitute says 'Like fun you are,' Holden comments:

> It was a funny thing to say. It sounded like a real kid. You'd think a prostitute and all would say 'Like hell you are' or 'Cut the crap' instead of 'Like fun you are.' (87.)

In grammar, too, as in vocabulary, Holden possesses a certain self-consciousness. (It is, of course, impossible to imagine a student getting through today's schools without a self-consciousness with regard to grammar rules.) Holden is, in fact, not only aware of the existence of 'grammatical errors,' but knows the social taboos that accompany them. He is disturbed by a schoolmate who is ashamed of his parents' grammar, and he reports that his former[179] teacher, Mr. Antolini, warned him about picking up 'just enough education to hate people who say, "It's a secret between he and I"' (168).

Holden is a typical enough teenager to violate the grammar rules, even though he knows of their social importance. His most common rule violation is the misuse of *lie* and *lay*, but he also is careless about relative pronouns ('about a traffic cop that falls in love'), the double negative ('I hardly didn't even know I was doing it'), the perfect tenses ('I'd woke him up'), extra words ('like as if all you ever did at Pency was play polo all the time'), pronoun number ('it's pretty disgusting to watch somebody picking their nose'), and pronoun position ('I and this friend of mine, Mal Brossard'). More remarkable, however, than the instances of grammar rule violations is Holden's relative 'correctness.' Holden is always intelligible, and is even 'correct' in many usually difficult constructions. Grammatically speaking, Holden's language seems to point up the fact that English was the only subject in which he was not failing. It is interesting to note how much more 'correct' Holden's speech is than that of Huck Finn. But then Holden is educated, and since the time of Huck there had been sixty-seven years of authoritarian schoolmarms working on the likes of Holden. . . .

Now that we have examined several aspects of Holden's vocabulary and grammar, it would be well to look at a few examples of how he puts these elements together into sentences. The structure of Holden's sentences indicates that Salinger thinks of the book more in terms of spoken speech than written speech. Holden's faulty structure is quite common and typical in vocal expression; I doubt if a student who is 'good in English' would ever create such sentence structure in writing. A student who showed the self-consciousness of Holden would not *write* so many fragments, such afterthoughts (e.g., 'It has a very good academic rating, Pency' [7]), or such repetitions (e.g., 'Where I lived at Pency, I lived in the Ossenburger Memorial Wing of the new dorms' [18]).

There are other indications that Holden's speech is vocal. In many places Salinger mildly imitates spoken speech. Sentences such as 'You could tell old Spencer'd got a big bang out of buying it' (10) and 'I'd've killed him' (42) are repeated throughout the book. Yet it is impossible to imagine Holden taking pen in hand and actually writing 'Spencer'd' or 'I'd've.' Sometimes, too, emphasized words, or even parts of words, are italicized, as in 'Now[180] *shut up*, Holden. God damn it—I'm *warning ya*' (42). This is often done with good effect, imitating quite perfectly the rhythms of speech, as in the typical:

> I practically sat down on her *lap,* as a matter of fact. Then she *really* started to cry, and the next thing I knew, I was kissing her all over—*any*where—her eyes, her *nose,* her forehead, her eyebrows and all, her *ears*—her whole face except her mouth and all. (73.)

The language of *The Catcher in the Rye* is, as we have seen, an authentic artistic rendering of a type of informal, colloquial, teenage American spoken speech. It is strongly typical and trite, yet often somewhat individual; it is crude and slangy and imprecise, imitative yet occasionally imaginative, and affected toward standardization by the strong efforts of schools. But authentic and interesting as this language may be, it must be remembered that it exists, in *The Catcher in the Rye,* as only one part of an artistic achievement. The language was not written for itself, but as a part of a greater whole. Like the great Twain work with which it is often compared, a study of *The Catcher in the Rye* repays both the linguist and the literary critic; for as one critic has said, 'In them, 1884 and 1951 speak to us in the idiom and accent of two youthful travelers who have earned their passports to literary immortality.'[181] 10

---

10 Charles Kaplan, 'Holden and Huck: the Odysseys of Youth,' *College English,* XVIII (1956), 80.

EDWARD P. J. CORBETT

"Raise High the Barriers, Censors," *America,* CIV (January 7, 1961), 441–443. Reprinted from *America,* National Catholic Weekly Review, 920 Broadway, New York 10, New York.

About six years ago, at a Modern Language Association convention, a group of professors were discussing job openings, as is their wont at such gatherings. One of the teachers mentioned an offer he had had from a West Coast college. A pipe-smoker in the group blurted out: "For heaven's sake, stay away from *that* place. They recently fired a man for requiring his freshman students to read *The Catcher in the Rye.*"

That firing may have been the earliest instance of a teacher getting into serious trouble over J. D. Salinger's book. Since that time, reports of irate protests from school boards, principals, librarians and parents have multiplied. The most publicized recent stir about the book was the reprimand that Mrs. Beatrice Levin received from her principal for introducing *The Catcher in the Rye* to her 16-year-old students at Edison High School in Tulsa, Okla. Scores of subsequent letters to the editor revealed other bans on the book in schools and libraries. Curiously enough, the same kind of censure was once visited upon the book to which *The Catcher in the Rye* has most often been compared— Mark Twain's *Huckleberry Finn.*

Adult attempts to keep *The Catcher in the Rye* out of the hands of young people will undoubtedly increase, for it is the one novel that young people of the postwar generation have been reading and discussing avidly. I had firsthand evidence of students' reactions when *The Catcher in the Rye* was one of the three novels (the other two were Huxley's *Brave New World* and Conrad's *Under Western Eyes*) eligible for review two years ago in the Jesuit English Contest, an annual event among ten Midwestern Jesuit colleges and universities. At least 90 per cent of our students elected to write on Salinger's book. In fact, I have never witnessed on our campus as much eager discussion about a book as there was about *The Catcher in the Rye.* There were a few repercussions from adults outside the university, but these subsided when the question was raised: "Would the Jesuit Educational Association assign a book that was going to corrupt young people?"

To the many people who have come to love the book and its hero, Holden Caulfield, all this controversy is puzzling and disturbing. They regard even the suggestion that the book needs defending as sacrilegious—almost as though they were being asked to vindicate the Con-

54

stitution. Although their feelings of outrage are understandable, I feel that in view of the vast and continuing popularity of the book the objections should be confronted and appraised. My arguments in defense of *The Catcher in the Rye* are the common ones, quite familiar to those acquainted with other controversies about "forbidden" books.

The language of the book is crude, profane, obscene. This is the objection most frequently cited when the book has been banned. From one point of view, this objection is the easiest to answer; from another point of view, it is the hardest to answer.

Considered in isolation, the language *is* crude and profane. It would be difficult to argue, however, that such language is unfamiliar to our young people or that it is rougher than the language they are accustomed to hear in the streets among their acquaintances. But there is no question about it, a vulgar expression seen in print is much more shocking than one that is spoken. Lewd scribblings on sidewalks or on the walls of rest-rooms catch our attention and unsettle our sensibilities; and they become most shocking when they are seen in the sanctity of the printed page. Traditionally, novelists have been keenly aware of the shock value of printed profanities. Stephen Leacock has a delightful essay in which he reviews the many circumlocutions and typographical devices that novelists since the 18th century have employed to avoid the use of shocking expressions.

Granting the shock potential of such language, especially to youngsters, must we also grant it a corrupting influence? To deny that words can shape our attitudes and influence our actions would be to deny the rhetorical power of language. But to maintain that four-letter words of themselves are obscene and can corrupt is another matter. Interestingly enough, most reports about the banning of this novel have told that some principal or librarian or parent hastily paged through the book and spotted several four-letter words. That was evidence enough; the book must go. It is natural, although not always prudent, for adults to want to protect the young from shock. And this concern may be sufficient justification for adults wanting to keep the book out of the hands of grade-school children or the more immature high school students. But one of the unfortunate results of banning the book for this reason is that the very action of banning creates the impression that the book is nasty and highly corrosive of morals.

As has happened in many censorship actions in the[441] past, parts are judged in isolation from the whole. The soundest defense that can be advanced for the language of this novel is a defense based on the art of the novel. Such a defense could be stated like this: Given the point of view from which the novel is told, and given the kind of character that figures as the hero, no other language was possible. The integrity of the novel demanded such language.

But even when readers have been willing to concede that the bold language is a necessary part of the novel, they have expressed doubts about the authenticity of Holden's language. Teen-age girls, I find, are especially skeptical about the authenticity of the language. "Prep-school boys just don't talk like that," they say. It is a tribute, perhaps, to the gentlemanliness of adolescent boys that when they are in the company of girls they temper their language. But, whatever the girls may think, prep-school boys do on occasion talk as Holden talks. As a matter of fact, Holden's patois is remarkably restrained in comparison with the blue-streak vernacular of his real-life counterparts. Holden's profanity becomes most pronounced in moments of emotional tension; at other times his language is notably tempered—slangy, ungrammatical, rambling, yes, but almost boyishly pure. Donald P. Costello, who made a study of the language of *The Catcher in the Rye* for the journal *American Speech* (October, 1959), concluded that Salinger had given "an accurate rendering of the informal speech of an intelligent, educated, Northeastern American adolescent." "No one familiar with prep school speech," Costello goes on to say, "could seriously contend that Salinger overplayed his hand in this respect."

Holden's swearing is so habitual, so unintentional, so ritualistic that it takes on a quality of innocence. Holden is characterized by a desperate bravado; he is constantly seeking to appear older than he really is. Despite that trait, however, Holden's profanity does not stem from the same motivation that prompts other adolescents to swear— the urge to seem "one of the boys." His profanity is so much ingrained by habit into the fabric of his speech that he is wholly unaware of how rough his language is. Twice his little sister Phoebe reminds him to stop swearing so much. Holden doesn't even pause to apologize for his language; he doesn't even advert to the fact that his sister has reprimanded him. And it is not because he has become callous, for this is the same boy who flew into a rage when he saw the obscenity scribbled on a wall where it might be seen by little children.

Some of the episodes in the book are scandalous. The episode commonly cited as being unfit for adolescents to read is the one about the prostitute in the hotel room. A case could be made out for the view that young people should not be exposed to such descriptions. It would be much the same case that one makes out in support of the view that children of a certain age should not be allowed to play with matches. But a convincing case cannot be, and never has been, made out for the view that vice should never be portrayed in a novel.

One shouldn't have to remind readers of what Cardinal Newman once said, that we cannot have a sinless literature about a sinful people. That reminder, however, has to be made whenever a censorship controversy comes up. The proper distinction in this matter is that no novel is immoral merely because vice is represented in it. Immorality creeps in as a result of the author's attitude toward the vice he is portraying and his manner of rendering the scene.

Let us consider the scene in question according to this norm in order to test the validity of the charge that it is scandalous. First of all, neither the novelist nor his character regards the assignation with the prostitute as proper or even as morally indifferent. The word *sin* is not part of Holden's vocabulary, but throughout the episode Holden is acutely aware that the situation in which he finds himself is producing an uncomfortable tension, a tormenting conflict, within him. And that vague awareness of disturbance, of something being "wrong," even if the character doesn't assign the label "sin" to it, is enough to preserve the moral tone of the scene in question.

Some readers seem to forget, too, that Holden didn't seek this encounter with the prostitute. He was trapped into it; he was a victim, again, of his own bravado. "It was against my principles and all," he says, "but I was feeling so depressed I didn't even *think*." Nor does he go through with the act. Embarrassment, nervousness, inexperience— all play a part in his rejection of the girl. But what influences his decision most, without his being aware of it, is his pity for the girl. That emotion is triggered by the sight of her green dress. It is that pity which introduces a moral note into Holden's choice. Nor does Salinger render this scene with the kind of explicit, erotic detail that satisfies the pruriency of readers who take a lickerish delight in pornography. All of the scenes about sexual matters are tastefully, even beautifully, treated. Is it any wonder that devotees of the novel are shocked by the suggestion that some of the scenes are scandalous?[442]

Holden, constantly protesting against phoniness, is a phony himself. With this objection we move close to a charge against the novel that is damaging because it is based on sounder premises than the other two objections. No doubt about it, Salinger likes this boy, and he wants his readers to like the boy, too. If it could be shown that Salinger, despite his intentions, failed to create a sympathetic character, all the current fuss about the novel would be rendered superfluous, because the novel would eventually fall of its own dead weight.

Holden uses the word *phony* or some derivative of it at least 44 times. *Phoniness* is the generic term that Holden uses to cover all manifestations of cant, hypocrisy and speciosity. He is genuinely disturbed by such manifestations, so much so that, to use his own forthright term, he wants to "puke." The reason why he finds the nuns, his sister Phoebe and children in general so refreshing is that they are free of this phoniness.

But, as a number of people charge, Holden is himself a phony. He is an inveterate liar; he frequently masquerades as someone he is not;

he fulminates against foibles of which he himself is guilty; he frequently vents his spleen about his friends, despite the fact that he seems to be advocating the need for charity. Maxwell Geismar puts this objection most pointedly when he says: *"The Catcher in the Rye* protests, to be sure, against both the academic and social conformity of its period. But what does it argue *for?"* Because of this inconsistency between what Holden wants other people to be and what he is himself, many readers find the boy a far from sympathetic character and declare that he is no model for our young people to emulate.

These readers have accurately described what Holden *does,* but they miss the point about what he *is.* Holden is the classic portrait of "the crazy, mixed-up kid," but with this significant difference: there is about him a solid substratum of goodness, genuineness and sensitivity. It is just this conflict between the surface and the substratum that makes the reading of the novel such a fascinating, pathetic and intensely moral experience. Because Holden is more intelligent and more sensitive than his confreres, he has arrived prematurely at the agonizing transition between adolescence and adulthood. He is precocious but badly seasoned. An affectionate boy, yearning for love and moorings, he has been cut off during most of his teen-age years from the haven of his family. Whatever religious training he has been exposed to has failed to touch him or served to confuse him. Accordingly, he is a young man adrift in an adult world that buffets and bewilders him.

The most salient mark of Holden's immaturity is his inability to discriminate. His values are sound enough, but he views everything out of proportion. Most of the manners and mores that Holden observes and scorns are not as monstrous as Holden makes them out to be. His very style of speech, with its extraordinary propensity for hyperbole, is evidence of this lack of a sense of proportion. Because he will not discriminate, he is moving dangerously close to that most tragic of all states, negation. His sister Phoebe tells him: "You don't like *any*thing that's happening." Holden's reaction to this charge gives the first glimmer of hope that he may seek the self-knowledge which can save him.

Holden must get to know himself. As Mr. Antolini, his former teacher, tells him: "You're going to have to find out where you want to go." But Holden needs most of all to develop a sense of humor. One of the most startling paradoxes about this book is that although it is immensely funny, there is not an ounce of humor in Holden himself. With the development of a sense of humor will come the maturity that can straighten him out. He will begin to see himself as others see him.

The lovely little scene near the end of the book in which Phoebe is going around and around on the carousel can be regarded as an objective correlative of Holden's condition at the end of his ordeal by disillusionment. Up to this point, Holden has pursued his odyssey in a more or less straight line; but in the end, in his confusion and heart-sickness, he is swirling around in a dizzying maelstrom. In the final chapter, however, it would appear that Holden has had his salutary epiphany. "I sort of *miss* everybody I told about," he says. Here is the beginning of wisdom. The reader is left with the feeling that Holden, because his values are fundamentally sound, will turn out all right.

I suspect that adults who object to Holden on the grounds of his apparent phoniness are betraying their own uneasiness. Holden is not like the adolescents in the magazine ads—the smiling, crew-cut, loafer-shod teen-agers wrapped up in the cocoon of suburban togetherness. He makes the adults of my generation uncomfortable because he exposes so much of what is meretricious in our way of life.

In defending *The Catcher in the Rye,* one is liable to the danger of exaggerating J. D. Salinger's achievement and potential. As George Steiner has warned in the *Nation* (Nov. 14, 1959), there is a vigorous "Salinger industry" under way now, which could put Salinger's work badly out of focus. Judged in the company of other postwar fiction, *The Catcher in the Rye* is an extraordinary novel. His earlier short stories, especially "For Esmé—with Love and Squalor," are truly distinguished. But the last two long, diffuse stories to appear in the *New Yorker,* "Zooey" and "Seymour," have been something of a disappointment. They are fascinating as experiments with the short-story form, but they strike me as being an accumulation of finger exercises rather than the finished symphony. If we admirers of Salinger can keep our heads about us, maybe we can make it possible for Salinger to build on the promise of his earlier work.

In the meantime, some concession must be made, I suppose, to the vigilantes who want to keep *The Catcher in the Rye* out of the hands of the very young. Future controversy will probably center on just what age an adolescent must be before he is ready for this book. That may prove to be a futile dispute. But I would hope that any decisions about the book would be influenced by the consideration, not that this is an immoral, corrupting book—for it is certainly not—but that it is a subtle, sophisticated novel that requires an experienced, mature reader. Above all, let the self-appointed censors *read* the novel before they raise the barriers.[443]

PETER J. SENG

"The Fallen Idol: The Immature World of Holden Caulfield," *College English,* XXIII (December 1961), 203–209. Reprinted with the permission of the National Council of Teachers of English and Peter J. Seng.

A recent article in the New York *Times Book Review*[1] pointed out that J. D. Salinger's *The Catcher in the Rye,* first published in 1951, was still selling about 250,000 copies a year in its paperback edition. A report like this is news about any novel ten years after its first appearance. While *Majorie Morningstar, The Adventures of Augie March,* and *By Love Possessed* have almost faded from sight, Salinger's novel seems to go on and on and on. In fact it regularly attracts attention to itself on the *front* pages of newspapers, usually when an irate school superintendent, parent, or local PTA discovers what the children have been reading in the classrooms and decides that something must be done to keep English courses moral.

The prominence of Salinger's novel in book supplements and news columns is significant evidence that *The Catcher in the Rye* is no longer merely a trade book but has become a college and high school text as well. Further evidence is provided by the articles that the "little magazines" and scholarly journals have been printing for the past six years: essays written by instructors who have apparently been teaching the novel to their classes. If it is possible to guess a pedagogical viewpoint from a critical article, then it seems likely that the school superintendents, parents, and[203] PTAs who want to censor the book may sometimes be doing the right thing for the wrong reason. Perhaps the teacher ought to be banned and not the book. The extant academic criticism on *The Catcher in the Rye* for the most part deposes, openly or covertly, an assessment of the book which reflects a romantic view of life. I think such an interpretation represents a wholly unfair view of a novel which is in fact realistic, sensible, moral, and very hard-headed.

To talk about morality in connection with a modern novel is a distinctly unfashionable enterprise, just as unfashionable as William Dean Howells' efforts to talk about realism in the novel in the 80's and 90's. The parallel is, I think, a valid one. At the end of the last century Howells was deeply concerned with the effects of "novel-reading" on young people, especially on the protected young ladies of his era. From

---

[1] January 15, 1961, p. 38.

the romantic novels of his time Howells felt that a young lady might come to believe

> that Love, or the passion or fancy she mistook for it, was the chief interest of a life, which is really concerned with a great many other things; that it was lasting in the way she knew it; that it was worthy of every sacrifice, and was altogether a finer thing than prudence, obedience, reason; that love alone was glorious and beautiful.... More lately she has begun to idolize and illustrate Duty, and she is hardly less mischievous in this new role....[2]

It is melancholy to reflect now, seventy years after Howells' warnings, that perhaps our concern ought to be directed to the effects of a romantic misreading of a contemporary novel on the moral attitudes of young men.

Howells defined realism in the novel as "nothing more and nothing less than the truthful treatment of material," and he defined morality in the same terms. What he asked of a novel was:

> Is it true?—true to the motives, the impulses, the principles that shape the life of actual men and women? This truth, which necessarily includes the highest morality and the highest artistry—this truth given, the book cannot be wicked and cannot be weak.[3]

Judged by this criterion *The Catcher in the Rye* is certainly not an immoral book. On the contrary the great appeal this book has for young people is due, I think, to the fact that it is a valid, "realistic" representation of the adolescent world. Some parents and teachers may object to Holden's thoughts, language, and activities as "immoral"; but I doubt that modern adolescents are as innocent of these things as those parents and teachers suppose. The adults would do better to mount their moral attack not against the novel but against the interpretation that it may be given (or allowed) in the classroom. If that interpretation is not a "truthful treatment of material"—that is, a truthful treatment of the realities of life—then adults ought to be exercised far more than they are. If Holden Caulfield is being held up to students as the ideal youth, as a Galahad who carries his pure white banner undefiled through a world of sordid adults, only to fall at the novel's end as a pathetic victim of their machinations against him, then *The Catcher in the Rye* becomes an immoral novel—precisely in Howells' terms. Howells' objection to romantic novels in the nineteenth century was not an objection to wicked passages in them; rather his objections were grounded on the fact that those novels were

---

[2] *Criticism and Fiction and Other Essays*, ed. Clara Marburg Kirk and Rudolf Kirk (1959), pp. 47–48.

[3] The same, p. 49.

idle lies about human nature and the social fabric, which it behooves us to know and to understand, that we may[204] deal justly with ourselves and with one another.[4]

The moral issue here is not negligible. If, as the *Times* reports, a million and a half copies of Salinger's book have been distributed in the past ten years, most of them in paperback, then *The Catcher in the Rye* is more solidly entrenched in a number of schools than the classics are. I have no objection to the entrenchment; it could be a good thing; but I think there is some reason for fear about what goes on in the trenches. Therefore I would like to suggest an interpretation of the novel which is, I think, realistic in Howells' terms.

The plot of *The Catcher in the Rye* concerns the three-day odyssey of Holden Caulfield after he has been expelled from Pencey Prep for bad grades and general irresponsibility. At the beginning of the story Holden is in a sanitarium in California recovering from a mental breakdown. He says that he is not going to tell his life-story but just the story of "this madman stuff that happened to me around last Christmas just before I got pretty run-down and had to come out here and take it easy" (p. 5).[5] In the final chapter he speculates about what he is going to do when he is released and reflects on "all this stuff I just finished telling you about.... If you want to know the truth, I don't *know* what I think about it" (p. 192). Between these important framing limits the story proper is contained. It reads like an edited psychoanalysis, an illusion which is sustained by the rambling first-person narrative.

Sensitive and perceptive as Holden is, he is still an adolescent and so an immature judge of adult life. His viewpoint is as limited as that of Hazlitt's young man who thinks that he will never die. Like many young people Holden is intolerant of sickness and the debility of old age. Recalling his visit to "Old Spencer" he says,

> there were pills and medicine all over the place, and everything smelled like Vicks Nose Drops. It was pretty depressing. I'm not too crazy about sick people, anyway. What made it even more depressing, old Spencer had on this very sad, ratty old bathrobe that he was probably born in or something. I don't much like to see old guys in their pajamas and bathrobes anyway. (p. 10)

Nor can he bear the old history teacher's garrulity and physical habits. While Holden is quick to pass severe judgments on others he is not so quick to see the faults in himself. A number of the picayune traits he

---

[4] The same, pp. 46–47.
[5] All quotations are from the paperback Signet Edition, New American Library, 1960. The page number is cited in parentheses following the quotation.

hates Ackley for in Chapter 3 are traits he reveals in himself in Chapter 4 when he talks to Stradlater. A comparison of these two chapters reveals interesting things both about Holden's character and about Salinger's narrative technique. It might be said that Holden's chief fault is his failure "to connect" (to use Forster's phrase); he hates lies, phoniness, pretense, yet these are often his own sins.

He is enraged at the thought that Stradlater may have "made time" with Jane Gallagher. His rage springs partly from the fact that he regards Jane as his own property, partly from his suspicion that Stradlater is a heel; yet there are further implications in this episode that he most deeply resents Stradlater's apparent self-possession in an area where he himself is ill-at-ease. Stradlater may have "made time" with Jane (though the reader of the novel tends to see his testimony as an adolescent's boast); but the moment Holden arrives in New York he attempts to "make time" first with a burlesque stripper and then with a hotel call-girl. There is, to be sure, a difference in the objects of each boy's affections, but the difference is not so great as[205] Holden, not "connecting," might think. His failure in both attempts is probably adequately explained by his confession:

> Sex is something I really don't understand too hot. You never know *where* the hell you are. I keep making up these sex rules for myself, and then I break them right away. Last year I made a rule that I was going to quit horsing around with girls that, deep down, gave me a pain in the ass. I broke it, though, the same week I made it.... Sex is something I just don't understand. (p. 59)

While Holden responds to the common chord to which all fleshly creatures vibrate, he is nonetheless contemptuous of its varied—and sometimes perverse—manifestations in others.

In a similar fashion he passes harsh verdicts on people who do not measure up to his standards of taste and urban sophistication. When the tourists from Seattle—Bernice, Marty, and Laverne (the very names spell out a whole aesthetic)—plan to see the first show at Radio City Music Hall their taste depresses him; yet the following day he goes there himself. Buying drinks for the girls from Seattle he puts on a pretense of New Yorkish world-weary sophistication. On the other hand he cannot bear that sort of pretense in others, and has only contempt for the kind of people who say that something is "grand," or affect a fashionable critical attitude about Lunt and Fontanne, or who make polite social noises at each other (social noises that have to be made if society is going to endure).

What disturbs Holden about the world in which he finds himself is adults and adult values. He sees that the world belongs to adults, and it seems to him that they have filled it with phoniness, pretense, social compromise. He would prefer a world that is honest, sincere, simple. He is looking, as one critic notes, for the "simple truth."[6] Such a quest is doomed from the start: *there are no simple truths*. In a complex modern society truth, too, is complex, and a certain amount of social compromise is necessary.

This kind of civilizing compromise Holden is unwilling to make. The world he wants is a world of children or children-surrogates like the nuns. He would people it with little girls whose skates need tightening, little girls like his adored sister Phoebe; with little boys like the ones at the Museum of Natural History, filled with exquisite terror at the prospect of seeing the mummies. It would include small boys with poems on their baseball gloves like his brother Allie who died some years ago from leukemia and so has been arrested in permanent youth by death. The chief citizens of Holden's world would be the little boys who walk along the curbstone and sing,

> If a body catch a body
> Coming through the rye.

Holden's chief fantasy is built on this memory: he sees himself as the "catcher in the rye," the only adult in a world of children:

> I keep picturing all these little kids playing some game in this big field of rye and all. Thousands of little kids, and nobody's around—nobody big, I mean—except me. And I'm standing on the edge of some crazy cliff. What I have to do, I have to catch everybody if they start to go over the cliff—I mean if they're running and they don't look where they're going I have to come out from somewhere and *catch* them. That's all I'd do all day. I'd just be the catcher in the rye and all. (p. 156)

Holden has other fantasies as well, and these are less healthy. He imagines himself living all alone in a cabin in the far west pretending to be a deaf-mute. If anyone wanted to communicate with[206] him, he says, that person would have to write him a note (a prescription that would also include his wife who would be deaf and dumb, too). "They'd get bored as hell doing that after a while, and then I'd be through with having conversations for the rest of my life" (p. 179). Both the "catcher" and the "deaf-mute" fantasies are rooted in a single desire: a wish to escape from an adult world with which Holden feels that he cannot cope.

His mental breakdown is a direct result of his inability to come to terms with adult reality. Consequently he invents other fantasies, tinged with paranoia, in which he sees himself as a martyr-victim. In front of Ackley he play-acts at going blind: " 'Mother darling, give me

---

[6] Ihab H. Hassan, "Rare Quixotic Gesture," *The Western Review*, XXI (1956), 271.

your *hand*. Why won't you give me your hand?' " (p. 23). Roughed up
by a pimp-bellhop he imagines that he has been shot, and fancies himself walking down the stairs of the hotel bleeding to death. In a third
fantasy he imagines his own death and funeral in great detail. Finally,
in his recollections of previous events he seems to identify with a
schoolmate, James Castle, who jumped from a high window rather
than submit to the brutality of prep school bullies.

The crucial chapter in *The Catcher in the Rye* seems to me to be
the one in which Holden calls on his former English teacher Mr.
Antolini. For all his own weaknesses Antolini sees to the heart of the
matter and gives saving advice to Holden; the advice is rejected because Holden measures it against impossibly absolute standards. If this
view of the novel is correct then Holden's interview with Antolini is
also the high point of irony in *The Catcher in the Rye*: the proffered
offer of salvation comes from a teacher whom Holden enormously admires, but the counsel is nullified when Holden discovers that Antolini,
like all adults, has feet of clay. From the moment the boy leaves Antolini's apartment his mental breakdown commences. This sequence of
events seems to be Salinger's intention.

If the Antolini episode is crucial, as I think it is, it deserves examination in some detail. The relationship between Mr. and Mrs. Antolini is immediately clear to the reader, if not to Holden. Mrs. Antolini
is older than her husband and rich. They have an elegant apartment
on Sutton Place, belong to the West Side Tennis Club in Forest Hills,
and are ostentatiously affectionate in public. Yet in Holden's un-
comprehending phrase, they are "never in the same room at the same
time" (p. 164).

Holden's attachment to this teacher is in sharp contrast to his antip-
athy for "old Spencer" at the beginning of the novel. There is ease
and *rapport* between the older man and the younger one. As Mrs.
Antolini retires for the night to leave "the boys" alone, her husband
has a stiff highball, obviously not his first. As he drinks he gives advice
to Holden, all of it very much to the point:

> "I have a feeling that you're riding for some kind of a ter-
> rible, terrible fall. But I don't honestly know what kind.
> ... It may be the kind where, at the age of thirty, you sit in
> some bar hating everybody who comes in looking as if he
> might have played football in college. Then again, you may
> pick up just enough education to hate people who say, 'It's
> a secret between he and I.' Or you may end up in some busi-
> ness office, throwing paper clips at the nearest stenogra-
> pher." (p. 168)

It is instructive to re-examine the previous episodes of the novel in the
light of this assessment of Holden's character. What Antolini predicts

for the future already, in part, exists in the present. After another drink he goes on:

> This fall I think you're riding for—it's a special kind of fall, a horrible kind. The man falling isn't permitted to feel or hear himself hit bottom. He just keeps falling and falling. The whole arrangement's[207] designed for men who, at some time or other in their lives, were looking for something their own environment couldn't supply them with. ... So they gave up looking. They gave it up before they ever really even got started." (p. 169)

Antolini writes out for Holden an epigram from the works of the psychoanalyst Wilhelm Stekel: " 'The mark of the immature man is that he wants to die nobly for a cause, while the mark of the mature man is that he wants to live humbly for one' " (p. 170). This epigram is a penetrating insight into the personality of an adolescent who continually views himself as a martyr or savior, but never sees himself as modestly attempting to cope with a humdrum and very imperfect world. In effect what Antolini is saying is, "You are not alone; we have all been through this." You are not the first one, he tells Holden,

> "who was ever confused and frightened and even sickened by human behavior. You're by no means alone on that score, you'll be excited and *stimulated* to know. Many, many men have been just as troubled morally and spiritually as you are right now. Happily, some of them kept records of their troubles. You'll learn from them—if you want to." (pp. 170–171)

He makes up a bed for the boy on the couch and then retires to the kitchen, presumably for another drink. Holden lies awake for a few seconds

> thinking about all that stuff Mr. Antolini'd told me.... He was really a pretty smart guy. But I couldn't keep my goddam eyes open, and I fell asleep. (p. 173)

That sleep is symbolic as well as literal. Suddenly waking during the night Holden finds Antolini sitting on the floor next to his couch-bed patting him on the head. Panicked by what he regards as something "perverty" he flees from the apartment.

The irony built into this denouement is clear: the saving advice that Antolini has given Holden has been rendered useless because the idol who gave it has fallen. Antolini is a shabby adult like all the others. In his reactions Holden is like the man in the Stephen Crane poem who climbed to the top of the mountain only to cry out:

> "Woe to my knowledge!
> I intended to see good white lands

And bad black lands,
But the scene is grey."

It is worth noting that Salinger takes pains to keep the end of the Antolini episode ambiguous: that is to say, while there can be little doubt in a reader's mind about Antolini's propensities, his gesture toward Holden is considerably short of explicit. In fact Salinger raises this very doubt in Holden's mind:

> I wondered if just maybe I was wrong about thinking he was making a flitty pass at me. I wondered if maybe he just liked to pat guys on the head when they're asleep. I mean how can you tell about that stuff for sure? You can't. (p. 175)

Whatever doubts he may have about Antolini's motives, there can be no doubts about the meaning of his own feelings as he walks up Fifth Avenue the next day:

> Then all of a sudden, something very spooky started happening.... Every time I came to the end of a block and stepped off the goddam curb, I had this feeling that I'd never get to the other side of the street. I thought I'd just go down, down, down, and nobody'd ever see me again. (p. 178)

This, of course, is the beginning of the fall which Antolini had predicted.

So much for the edited psychoanalysis of Holden Caulfield. It seems to me that if *The Catcher in the Rye* is viewed along the lines suggested above it is a moral novel in the fullest sense of that word. According to this interpretation[208] Holden is not a mere victim of modern society, but is in some sense a tragic figure. His temporary mental defeat is brought about by a flaw in his own character: a naive refusal to come to terms with the world in which he lives. To regard him, on the other hand, as a pure young man who is martyred in his unavailing struggle against a sordid world of adult phoniness, is to strip him of any real dignity. Such an interpretation makes the novel guilty of idle romanticism. Howells would have called it immoral romanticism because he would have seen it as filled with "idle lies about human nature and the social fabric," areas where we must know the truth if we are to deal "justly with ourselves and with one another."

Salinger himself is reported to have said that he regretted that his novel might be kept out of the reach of children.[7] It is hard to guess at the motives behind his remark, but one of them may have been that he was trying to tell young people how difficult it was to move from

---

7 *Twentieth Century Authors*, First Supplement, ed. Stanley J. Kunitz, New York, 1955, p. 859.

their world into the world of adults. He may have been trying to warn them against the pitfalls of the transition.

To my mind one of the most penetrating reviews of *The Catcher in the Rye* was the one which appeared in *The Nation* in 1951 when the novel first came out:

> It reflects something not at all rich and strange but what every sensitive sixteen-year-old since Rousseau has felt, and of course what each one of us is certain he has felt.... *The Catcher in the Rye* [is] a case history of all of us.[8]

The reviewer was Dr. Ernest Jones, and for the sickness he diagnosed he also prescribed a remedy. His prescription was a line from Auden: "We must love one another or die."

Holden will survive; but first he must learn to love other human beings as well as he loves children. He must acquire a sense of proportion, a sense of humor.[9] He must learn compassion for the human, the pompous, the phoney, the perverse; such people are the fellow inhabitants of his world, and behind their pitiful masks are the faces of the children in the rye. In Stekel's phrase, he must learn to live humbly for a cause.[209]

BERNARD S. OLDSEY

"The Movies in the Rye," *College English*, XXIII (December 1961), 209–215. Reprinted with the permission of the National Council of Teachers of English and Bernard S. Oldsey.

Several good novels—including F. Scott Fitzgerald's *The Last Tycoon*, Nathanael West's *The Day of the Locust*, and Budd Schulberg's *The Disenchanted*—have registered the effect of the movies, Hollywood style, on the American imagination. J. D. Salinger's *Catcher in the Rye* should be added to this list, since, in addition to its literary merit,

---

[8] September 1, 1951, p. 176.
[9] This observation is E. P. J. Corbett's, "Raise High the Barriers, Censors," *America*, January 7, 1961, p. 442.

it is as much a Hollywood product (that is to say, anti-Hollywood product) as we have had.

The unrecognized fact is that the[209] movies constitute a major influence on Salinger's novel and play a peculiarly functional part in it. This is particularly true in respect to thematic development and character revelation rather than form.[1] Thematically, the novel is intent on exposing the phoniness of life in these United States, the tawdriness of a Barnum-and-Bailey world remade by Metro-Goldwyn-Mayer. This anti-phoniness theme is developed through a series of related character reactions and revelations—all filtered through the censuring lens of Holden Caulfield, who is himself not left unmarred in the process. The way individuals react to phoniness—of a dramatic and literary sort too,[2] but especially cinematic—becomes the infallible metric aid by which he assesses character.

Actually, the novel opens and closes on a note of character assessment, with Holden the reluctant and, at the end, unwitting re-assessor. In the very first paragraph, as he begins his story from inside a mental hospital, he exhibits great concern over what is happening to his older brother, D. B., in Hollywood (which is "not too far from this crumby place"). As the author of a "terrific book of short stories," D. B. has been Holden's idol; but the idol is crumbling, may even have crumbled, for D. B. has become a movie writer, or as Holden bluntly puts it: "Now he's out in Hollywood, D. B., being a prostitute."

In the last paragraph of the novel, this concern lingers wonderingly on. And it is easy to understand why: Holden has already lost one brother to death and is extremely reluctant to admit having lost the other to Hollywood. Nevertheless, he must report that on his last visit to the mental hospital, D. B., already equipped with one of those little Jaguars "That can do around two hundred miles an hour," has brought with him a familiar Hollywood opiate: "He drove over last Saturday with this English babe that's in this new picture that he's writing. She was pretty affected, but very good-looking." This may be but a final, weaker echo of the lines with which Holden leads into his

---

[1] In form, the book is an extended flashback framed by an introductory paragraph and three short concluding paragraphs, and to some extent it does resemble a movie adaptation script, with built-in camera angles, bare character suggestions, and fast scenic shifts. But of course the long interior ramble by which Holden tells his story not only subtly reveals his character and controls the thematic tone of the book, but also helps distinguish the novel from a movie script.

[2] For comments on phoniness in drama and literature see *The Catcher in the Rye* (Boston, 1951), pp. 152–53, 164–65, 182. All references in parentheses are to this edition. [In the Signet paperback edition these comments are on pp. 89–90, 96–97, 107. References in the text of this article have been changed to conform to the Signet edition. (Eds.)]

story proper: "If there's one thing I hate, it's the movies. Don't even mention them to me" (p. 7).

Yet it is Holden himself who mentions the movies afterward, and keeps on mentioning them. As a child of his times he is automatically a child of the movies; even his name, one suspects, is an ironic amalgam of the last names of movie stars William Holden and Joan Caulfield.[3] His imagination—à la Mitty's—battens on the movies; his reveries revolve around them; and his narrative depends heavily upon them.

Holden has a habit, for instance, whenever in trouble or "just horsing around," of slipping into a convenient movie role. One of the first times he does this is in watching his roommate shave; he gets bored just sitting there on a washbowl; so, urged on by the acoustics of the "stone" floor, he taps his way into a screen role:

> I started imitating one of those guys in the movies. In one of those *musicals*. I hate the movies like poison, but I get a[210] bang imitating them. Old Stradlater watched me in the mirror.... "I'm the goddam Governor's son," I said. I was knocking myself out.... "He doesn't want me to be a tap dancer. He wants me to go to Oxford. But it's in my goddam blood, tap-dancing." Old Stradlater laughed. He didn't have too bad a sense of humor.... (p. 27)

Holden's favorite role, however, is not musical, but the kind made famous by James Cagney and Humphrey Bogart. He uses it several times, the first for Ackley's benefit: "What I did," Holden explains, "I pulled the old peak of my hunting hat around to the front, then pulled it way down over my eyes.... 'I think I'm going blind,' I said in this very hoarse voice. 'Mother darling, everything's getting so *dark* in here'" (p. 18). He uses it again when slugged by Maurice, the elevator-operating pimp. Though not knocked unconscious (earlier he has informed us, when hit by Stradlater, that "It's pretty hard to knock a guy out, except in the goddam movies"), Holden is rather stunned by the blow to the stomach; his mind slips and he begins to imagine things:

> But I'm crazy. I swear to God I am. About halfway to the bathroom, I sort of started pretending I had a bullet in my guts. Old Maurice had plugged me.... I pictured myself coming out of the goddam bathroom, dressed and all, with my automatic in my pocket.... Then I'd walk down a few floors— holding onto my guts, blood leaking all over the place— and then I'd ring the elevator bell. As soon as old Maurice

---

[3] The plausibility of this conjecture is increased by the fact that these two actors costarred in the well-known 1947 movie version of *Dear Ruth*, the story of a juvenile girl who, in writing to a soldier overseas, tries to appear more mature than she actually is.

opened the doors, he'd see me with the automatic in my
hand and he'd start screaming.... But I'd plug him anyway.... Then I'd crawl back to my room and call up Jane and
have her come over and bandage up my guts. I pictured her
holding a cigarette for me to smoke while I was bleeding
and all.

The goddam movies. They can ruin you. I'm not kidding.
(pp. 80–81)

Once again Holden resorts to this role—after a dispiriting chat with
an acquaintance named Carl Luce, who advises him to see a psychoanalyst and have "the patterns" of his mind clarified. Luce leaves him
alone at the bar, and Holden goes on drinking: "When I was *really*
drunk, I started that stupid business with the bullets in my guts again."
The business includes the same ingredients as before—the supporting
hand inside the jacket, the dripping blood, the hurried phone call to
Jane (p. 113). Certainly by this time one of the patterns of Holden's
mind has been clarified. It is a one-reeler starring Holden the wounded.

On numerous other occasions and in various ways Holden sees himself and others in relationship to the movies. For example, one Saturday
night he considers going to Agerstown with Ackley and Mal Brossard
to see a comedy starring Cary Grant. Eventually they eschew it for
hamburgers; and Holden is just as glad, because he has been to the
movies before with Ackley and Brossard, who laugh "like hyenas at
stuff that wasn't even funny" (p. 32). Another evening, the night he
meets Carl Luce, Holden has some time to kill and goes to the movies
at Radio City. "It was probably the worst thing I could've done," he
explains apologetically, "but it was near, and I couldn't think of anything else" (p. 104). On this occasion he sees the film version of James
Hilton's *Random Harvest*.[4] Taking two and a quarter pages to outline
its implausible, tear-jerking plot, he finishes with a short analysis of the
maudlin woman who sits next to him during the performance. She
cries throughout the show, but will not allow her suffering child to go
to the toilet. "You take somebody that cries their goddam eyes out over
phony stuff in the movies,"[211] Holden concludes, "and nine times out
of ten they're mean bastards at heart."

His apologetic explanation for going to Radio City becomes clear
when we consider what Holden has said about others on this score
earlier. The three girls he dances with in the Lavender Room are all
movie struck; their fondest hope, after coming all the way from Seattle,
is to see some movie celebrities in New York. Until Holden meets them
they have had little success, having caught sight only of Peter Lorre (so
at least they claim). To revenge himself on one of them, the heavy-
dancing Marty, Holden pretends to have spotted Gary Cooper on the

---

4 See Frederick L. Gwynn and Joseph L. Blotner, *The Fiction of J. D. Salinger*
(Pittsburgh, 1958), p. 29.

opposite side of the dance floor and makes him disappear before the hopeful Marty can turn in that direction. Later, though, Holden feels sorry for the lot of them, when they announce they have to get up early next day to fulfill their intentions: "If somebody...comes all the way to New York—from Seattle, *Washington*, for God's sake—and ends up getting up early in the morning to see the goddam first show at Radio City Music Hall, it makes me so depressed I can't stand it. I'd've bought the whole three of them a *hundred* drinks if only they hadn't told me that" (p. 60).

Lillian Simmons and Sunny, the youthful whore, also fall victim to Hollywood's attraction. Lillian, an old girl-friend of D. B.'s, simply gushes when Holden informs her D. B. is in Hollywood writing for the movies (p. 68). Holden thinks her one of the biggest—in all respects but one—phonies he has ever met. Sunny is a more complicated case: She claims to be from Hollywood; she thinks Holden resembles this movie actor, Whosis (appeared in "that pitcher with Mel-vine Douglas"); and she confesses to having no other activities (besides those demanded by her profession) except sleeping and going to the movies. She depresses Holden even more than the Lavender Room girls: "*She* was depressing. Her green dress in the closet and all. And besides, I don't think I could ever do it with somebody that sits in a stupid movie all day long" (p. 75).

Holden considers two other girls—much more important to the novel than either Lillian or Sunny—in terms of the movies; namely, his sister, Phoebe, and the girl he really cares for, Jane Gallagher. Phoebe passes every test. Her innocence is proof against the phoniness of Hollywood. She tends toward foreign films and those with serious themes. She liked seeing *The Baker's Wife,* with Raimu; and her favorite is *The 39 Steps,* with Robert Donat. Holden has taken her to the latter at least ten times; she knows it so well that she can put in bits of dialogue and the missing-finger business at just the right places (p. 54). When Holden first sees Phoebe after he has been dropped from Pencey, one of the first things she must tell him about is a problem movie, *The Doctor:* " 'It's a special movie they had at the Lister Foundation. Just this one day they had it....' " He tries several times to discuss more immediate problems, but Phoebe rushes on with her rapt summary: " 'It was all about this doctor in Kentucky and everything that sticks a blanket over this child's face that's a cripple and can't walk. Then they send him to jail and everything. It was excellent' " (pp. 122–123).

This summary of *The Doctor,* with its central problem of euthanasia, underscores Holden's own problem. Like the doctor in the movie, he, too (though by different means), wishes to protect the young from the cruelties and indignities of the world. For their pains, the doctor goes to prison, Holden to a mental hospital.

The movie with the doctor in it also moves us closer to Jane Gallagher's problem. Jane is a strange, intelligent, attractive girl, whose muckle-mouth seems to go "in about fifty different[212] directions" when she talks. The most peculiar thing about her, however, is that in playing checkers she never takes her kings out of the back row—a fact so significant as to be mentioned at least four times. In spite of these peculiarities, or probably because of them, Holden is very fond of Jane. He feels as protective toward her as toward Phoebe and the kids in the museum and the ducks on the pond. When his roommate, Stradlater, takes her lightly and hints of intimate relations with her, Holden flies into a quixotic rage and absorbs a physical beating in her honor.

Actually, Jane is product of a movie and book. The stage is set for the main treatment of her in chapter eleven, where Holden declares, "I know old Jane like a book," and again—"I still couldn't get her off my brain. I knew her like a book" (p. 60). The movie and book in question, which concerns not one but three doctors, is Henry Bellaman's Kings Row (1940), a well-known novel that was made into a very popular and, in risking censorship, courageous movie in 1942. Kings Row shares with The Catcher in the Rye three notable elements: youthful innocence in a world of adult cruelty, possible confinement in a mental institution, and a muted theme of incest.[5]

Jane Gallagher, like Cassandra Tower and Louise Gordon of Kings Row, fills the role of the fearful daughter; only in her case incest possibilities are heightened by the fact that she is a stepdaughter. Keeping her kings in the back row has already been interpreted as a fear manifestation by Gwynn and Blotner.[6] But it is necessary to go an inferential step further and fill out the syndrome with incestuous qualification. If evidence for such a step seems at first highly circumstantial, there is additional support in Holden's account of a certain afternoon when he and Jane come closest to "necking." As he describes the situation— "It was a Saturday and it was raining like a bastard out, and I was over at her house, on the porch.... We were playing checkers. I used to kid her once in a while because she wouldn't take her kings out of the back row" (p. 61). There follows an explanation about how he dislikes kidding Jane too much because he senses something perhaps over-sensitized in her. "Anyway," he continues, "I was telling you about that afternoon.... It was raining like hell and we were out on her porch, and all of a sudden this booze hound her mother was married to came

5 The incest motif of Kings Row was a much discussed topic of the day; for critical commentaries on the handling of the problem in the movie version, see Russell Maloney, "A Good Movie," The New Yorker (February 7, 1942), p. 56; and Otis Ferguson, "More Sound than Fury," The New Republic (February 16, 1942), pp. 237–38.
6 The Fiction of J. D. Salinger, p. 30.

out on the porch and asked Jane if there were any cigarettes in the house" (p. 62). Holden here provides another analysis of Jane's step-father, Cudahy, whom he has already described for Stradlater as an alcoholic playwright who runs "around the goddam house, naked" (p. 29). Then he goes on—"Anyway, old Jane wouldn't answer him when he asked her if she knew where there was any cigarettes.... Finally the guy went inside the house. When he did, I asked Jane what the hell was going on. She wouldn't even answer *me*, then" (p. 62).

Jane begins to cry, and one of her tears, a big one, plops right onto the checkerboard. Suddenly Holden finds himself comforting her, kissing her all over, except on the lips: "She sort of wouldn't let me get to her mouth." And finally, miraculous to say, they go to "a goddam movie," with Holden still in the dark as to what has happened between Jane and her stepfather: "I asked her,[213] on the way, if Mr. Cudahy had ever tried to get wise with her. She was pretty young, but she had this terrific figure, and I wouldn't've put it past that Cudahy bastard. She said no, though. I never did find out what the hell was the matter. Some girls you practically never find out what's the matter" (p. 62).

So the incestuous matter with Jane is left about as ambiguous as the homosexual matter with Mr. Antolini; but both contribute to the education of young Caulfield. It is an education which by now includes the matters of the transvestite and the water-squirting perverts at the Edmont Hotel, and the matter of Sunny and her finger-flicking friend, Maurice, as well as the matter of a single word, scrawled everywhere, reducing human relationships to the level of travesty. It is an education, moreover, that makes Holden more determined than ever to be a pro-tector of innocence.

The movies are connected with Holden's protective desire to be-come a catcher in the rye. The idea comes to him while he watches a small boy walking perilously toward, or on, Broadway. The boy, oblivi-ous to the traffic and crowds around him, sweetly sings what Holden takes to be "If a body catch a body coming through the rye" (p. 88). In contrast to the boy, who cheers him up, there are the mobs of people, who depress him, because "Everybody was on their way to the movies —the Paramount or the Astor or the Strand or the Capitol...." It is by now a familiar form of depression; another pattern of Holden's mind is clarified: "I can understand somebody going to the movies because there's nothing else to do, but when somebody really *wants* to go...then it depresses hell out of me. Especially if I see millions of people stand-ing in one of those long, terrible lines, all the way down the block...." (p. 89).

It is an unpleasant vista of mass man in pursuit of phoniness. Holden—whose favorite phrase is "if you *really* want to know"—is in revolt against this phoniness. As a Wordsworthian or Rousseauistic version of the little boy lost, Holden represents Romantic innocence in search of continuing truth. He seeks a truth as durable as that figuring with beauty on Keats's Grecian urn ("For ever warm and still to be enjoyed,/For ever panting, and for ever young...."). In fact, speaking of the displays at the Museum of Natural History, he produces a modern version of Keats's "Ode," with truth and beauty held in kinetic bond: "The best thing, though, in that museum was that everything stayed right where it was.... You could go there a hundred times, and that Eskimo would still be just finished catching those two fish, the birds would still be on their way south, the deers would still be drinking out of that water hole..., and that squaw with the naked bosom would still be weaving that same basket. The only thing different would be you" (p. 93).

Thus Holden is as anxious to hold onto beauty and truth as he is those children who might fall off a cliff into some abyss of death, or untruth. He explains most of his occupational desire to be a Protector to Phoebe, and he also explains what he does not want to be: he will not be a corporation lawyer, like his father; nor will he even chance being a lawyer who goes around saving "innocent guys' lives" (p. 129). For this too might turn out to be phony, as it often does "in the dirty movies"; and Holden must be sure: "How would you know you weren't being a phony? The trouble is you wouldn't." He really suffers from a form of "phoniphobia" and must keep checking himself. Once he almost succumbs when, as a very good golfer, he is asked to appear in a golfing short—"but I changed my mind at the last minute. I figured[214] that anybody that hates the movies as much as I do, I'd be a phony if I let them stick me in a movie short" (p. 61).

He must be pure to be the catcher in the rye, saving little children who might be rushing to their doom, and living in his own peaceful cabin. There, one of his few visitors would be Phoebe. As for his brother D. B., a proviso is necessary: "...I'd let D. B. come out and visit me for a while if he wanted a nice, quiet place for his writing, but he couldn't write any movies in my cabin, only stories and books. I'd have this rule that nobody could do anything phony when they visited me. If anybody tried to do anything phony, they couldn't stay" (p. 153).

So the boy of sanity, of peace and truth and beauty, lights out for his own rye-covered territory and finds his own retreat, which ironically is "not too far" from Hollywood, as things turn out. There is a certain amount of literary ambiguity implicit in the geographical juxtaposition. Hollywood is not too far from insanity; but, on the other hand, Holden's "insanity," or neurosis, or whatever it is that troubles him is not far removed from Hollywood. If someone were to ask him (as Captain Delano does Benito Cereno), "What has cast such a shadow upon you?" Holden might very well answer, "The movies." In fact, he has already given the equivalent answer with "If there's one thing I hate, it's the movies" and "The goddam movies. They can ruin you."[215]

"Kings in the Back Row: Meaning Through Structure, A Reading of Salinger's *The Catcher in the Rye.*" This article is reprinted from *Wisconsin Studies in Contemporary Literature,* II (Winter 1961), 5–30, with the permission of the editors.

I

The impressive accumulation of critical views on Salinger's *The Catcher in the Rye* is a tribute not only to the exciting qualities of the book but also to the awareness and resourcefulness of academic commentators. It has been compared to other fictional treatments of the crushing moral problems of sensitive American adolescents confronted by a hostile society. Critics, for the most part, have lavished an affectionate understanding upon a Holden Caulfield who regards his fellows with religious compassion and at the same time, out of his own durable honesty, reacts against the phony in both institutions and people. On this score there has been, so far as I know, only one conservative protest, wholly unconvincing, against Salinger's alleged Rousseauistic philosophy.[1] In another quarter *The Catcher* has been regarded as itself a conservative protest, along with *The Great Gatsby, H. M. Pulham, Esq.,* and the work of William Faulkner, against the anarchic drift of society and the shortcomings of the "natural man"; but in this view *The Catcher* is dismissed as providing a merely negative answer to the question of social chaos, and the conclusion of the novel can hardly serve "as a creed to live by."[2] If such an undiscerning approach amounts to a begging of the question, several rewarding insights, on the other hand, have emerged from detailed analysis of parallels in narrative pattern and characterization in *Huck Finn* and *The Catcher;* and one judges that such expansive comparisons between Huck and Holden require correction only in several premature unfavorable impressions of Holden.[3] A profitable view has arisen from the exploration of the epic motifs of alienation and quest; and from this vantage point Holden is observed to keep company not only with Huck Finn but also with Ulysses, Aeneas, Ishmael, Alyosha, Stephen

---

[1] Albert Fowler, "Alien in the Rye," *Modern Age,* I (Fall, 1957), 193–197.

[2] Hugh Maclean, "Conservatism in Modern American Fiction," *College English,* XV (March, 1954), 315–325. See pp. 321–322 especially.

[3] Edgar Branch, "Mark Twain and J. D. Salinger: A Study in Literary Continuity," *American Quarterly,* IX (Summer, 1957), 144–158.

Dedalus, and[5] Hans Castorp.[4] Still another view discloses Holden as an American Don Quixote, indulging with rare gestures of the spirit in "behavior that sings" and thus, in spite of his adolescent disaffiliation, affirming values of truth and imagination.[5]

There is, nevertheless, some critical unhappiness with a Holden who refuses to mature and with a distinctly unsatisfactory conclusion to the novel; and on both counts *The Catcher* suffers in comparison with *Huck Finn*. If Holden displays a superiority over Huck in certain traits of character, his neurotic psychology, intensified by sexual conflicts from which Huck was free and aggravated by a vulgar, dehumanized society, leads the boy to the psychoanalytical couch in a thoroughly pessimistic novel, whereas *Huck Finn* ends on a resolute note of courage in Huck's rejection of his society with his escape into the farther West.[6]

Thus we may summarize a commentary at once elaborate, precise, and generally correct as far as it goes; and yet all these approaches, however sophisticated the insight, remain discursively short of the critical goal because they fail to acknowledge the terms for understanding that the novel itself, as a work of art, has furnished. Except in scattered and fragmentary flashes, it has thus far escaped attention that Salinger sharply accentuates the portrayal of Holden with a symbolic structure of language, motif, episode, and character; and when the complex patterns are discovered, the effect is to concentrate our scrutiny on a masterpiece that moves effortlessly on the colloquial surface and at the same time uncovers, with hypnotic compulsion, a psychological drama of unrelenting terror and final beauty.

If Holden's suffering is the measure as well as the product, in part, of the outrageous assault on private innocence by social depravity, it does not follow that Salinger's philosophy is Rousseauistic. If we ac-

---

4 Arthur Heiserman and James E. Miller, Jr., "J. D. Salinger: Some Crazy Cliff," *Western Humanities Review,* X (Spring, 1956), 129–137.

5 Ihab H. Hassan, "Rare Quixotic Gesture: The Fiction of J. D. Salinger," *The Western Review,* XXI (Summer, 1957), 261–280.

6 See especially Branch, pp. 147 *et passim.* For Branch Holden is "the sex-conscious boy who yearns for the uncomplicated state of Huck" (p. 147); the carrousel scene represents "a dynamic moment of happy, static immaturity" (p. 149); "the underlying despair of Salinger's book is that a privileged adolescent wants to act immaturely" (p. 150). For Heiserman and Miller, Holden "seeks the role of a child" (p. 131). This is substantially the view in Leslie A. Fiedler's *Love and Death in the American Novel* (New York, 1960). But see Charles H. Kegel's brief reply to Heiserman and Miller: "Incommunicability in Salinger's *The Catcher in the Rye,*" *Western Humanities Review,* XI (Winter, 1957), 188–190. This excellent note fails, unfortunately, to present the full complexity of the problem; but Kegel does see that Holden matures.

knowledge that a personality has been split to the very core, such a discovery does not support the view that Holden, unlike the resourceful Huck, wishes to remain immature. Nor, as we shall learn, does the conclusion of *The Catcher* present a "creed" of any kind in the sense demanded by one critic; and the conclusion, furthermore, is neither pessimistic nor, for that matter, ironical in any sense perceived thus far. An immature Holden is not being delivered up to the unmerciful process of adjustment to a society he detests. The irony is profounder than that because the meaning is profounder: a Holden who has accepted both the mood and the act of responsibility with Phoebe does[6] not require psychoanalytical therapy, for he has miraculously wrought his own cure and has thus spiritually escaped the social rigidities that would be imposed upon him. The conclusion is, therefore, optimistic and affirmative, not in any credal sense but in terms of the unconquerable resources of personality.

Now, the thesis of the present study is that all or most of this psychological and philosophical insight can be gained only through a recognition of the interlocking metaphorical structure of *The Catcher*. We may thus perceive that Salinger has employed neurotic deterioration, symbolical death, spiritual awakening, and psychological self-cure as the inspiration and burden of an elaborate pattern—verbal, thematic, and episodic, that yields the meaning as the discursive examination of Holden's character and problem out of metaphoric context can never do. Structure *is* meaning.

As a start, the readiest way of understanding *The Catcher* lies in an awareness of the dualism or ambivalence of language, for Holden employs both the slob and the literate idiom. He mingles them so nicely, however, and with such colloquial ease that the alternating modes have heretofore escaped attention; and however we look at the two languages, each is, in effect, employed both realistically and metaphorically. Holden's slob speech is obviously justified as a realistic narrative device, since it is the idiom of the American male; yet from the psychological point of view, it becomes the boy's self-protective, verbalized acceptance of the slob values of his prep school contemporaries. He thus may justify himself in his overt being and may hope to secure immunity from attack and rationalize his "belonging"; slob language, therefore, hits off two important social themes—security and status. But the psychological intent becomes symbolical portent when we see that the mass idiom emphasizes a significant distinction between two worlds—the phony world of corrupt materialism and Holden's private world of innocence, which, in its corporate love, embraces a secret goldfish, Holden's dead brother Allie, his sister Phoebe (all children, in fact), Jane Gallagher, nuns, and animals (ducks and zoo animals, the Doberman that belonged to Jane's family, and the dog that Olivier-Hamlet patted on the head). For his private world Holden uses a literate and expressive English, and so the profounder psychological and symbolical purposes of slob language may be detected only as that idiom functions in polarized relationship with the other. We need not[7] labor the point that the full range of Salinger's portrayal would never be disclosed without an awareness of the ambivalence of language.

The literary Salinger has, of course, created a literate and even literary and artistic Holden, capable of acute aesthetic as well as moral judgments. Thus, Ernie, the piano player in Greenwich Village, was phony in his mingled real snobbery and false humility, and the Lunts overdid their acting and were *too* good. It is such a perceptive Holden that opens the narrative on a confessional note—"all that David Copperfield kind of crap"; and it may be observed in passing, as a literary parallel, that if Dickens portrays a young Victorian immoralist, Steerforth, Salinger gives us Stradlater, a "secret slob" and "sexy bastard." Holden's literary taste provides depth of background for a boy who said of himself, "I'm quite illiterate, but I read a lot." Favorite authors are his own brother D. B., Ring Lardner, and Thomas Hardy. Holden dismisses Hemingway as phony but approves of Fitzgerald's *The Great Gatsby*, from which, amusingly, he has borrowed Gatsby's nonchalant and phony habit of address—"old sport"; thus Holden refers to "old Spencer," "old Mrs. Morrow," "old Ernie," "old Phoebe." If this literary borrowing represents merely Holden's linguistic "horsing around," there is, on the other hand, real bite to his reporting Allie's verdict that Emily Dickinson was a better war poet than Rupert Brooke, the idea being that imagination imparts meaning to experience; and the discerning reader will keep this in mind as a gloss for Holden's concluding observation on his traumatic adventures.

Presumably, Holden's literary judgments are as perceptive as Allie's. Holden "wouldn't mind calling...up" Isak Dinesen, the author of *Out of Africa*; and his reason, open to readers of the Danish noblewoman, springs from his own suffering, for a writer so warmly understanding of children and animals would make an appropriate *confidante*. The slob Holden is more prominent, but the literate Holden is more intrinsic, for like Isak Dinesen he can use language to express sensitive insights and humane joys. As we proceed we shall note that although some of the literary sophistication is solely for background, a few works enter into and reenforce the moral, psychological, and symbolic range of *The Catcher*.

The literary precision with which Holden employs slob language for a public world that is varyingly indifferent and cruel and usually phony and literate speech for his private world emerges beautifully[8] when he explains how he met Jane Gallagher: "The way I met her, this Doberman pinscher she had used to come over and *relieve* himself on our lawn, and my mother got very irritated about it. She called up

Jane's mother and made a big *stink* about it. My mother can make a very big *stink* about that kind of stuff" (italics mine).

Once we have recognized the ambivalence of language we are prepared to discover Salinger's elaborate use of several kinds of pattern that support and help to develop the narrative. The first verbal pattern to be examined stands in an ironic and mutually illuminating relationship with the image of the secret goldfish at the head of the narrative symbolizing Holden and his secret world. In D. B.'s short story "The Secret Goldfish" the boy would not let others see the goldfish "because he'd bought it with his own money." Holden likewise was to pay in far more than money for his secret world; and as a further parallel, nobody ever saw (or cared to see) this secret world, although Holden invites inspection in the confessional mode, "if you really want to hear about it." This mode is maintained throughout with frequent interpolations of "if you want to know the truth" or "if you really want to know." As the story uncovers more and more of Holden's dilemma, these phrasings, although employed in the most casual manner, transcend their merely conversational usage and become psychologically portentous. The inference is that society, including his own parents, has no desire to recognize the truth about Holden or its own obsessions. In the middle of the tale Holden learns from the psychoanalytical snob, Carl Luce, that his father had helped him to "adjust"; and the blunted resolution of the narrative on the Freudian couch represents society's final humiliating indifference to truth. Recognition of the truth would embrace the love and compassion that it has no time for but that Holden himself not only lavishes on his secret world but extends to the public world in episodes and reflections rounded off with a minor verbal pattern, "You felt sort of sorry for her" or "I felt sorry as hell for him." The confessional mode embraces still another verbal pattern put variously, "People never notice anything," "He wasn't even listening," "People never believe you," and morons "never want to discuss anything." The failure in communication could not be more bleakly confirmed; and there is an immense irony in the contrast between Holden's telling the truth and the indifference surrounding him. Note, then, that the confessional mode, developed by several verbal patterns, provides[9] a beautifully formulated enclosing structure for the tale—with the symbolic image of the secret goldfish at the start and at the end the equally symbolic talking couch.

Two other patterns ironically reenforce the confessional mode. At Pencey Dr. Thurmer had talked to Holden "about Life being a game," and Mr. Spencer added for the truant's benefit, "Life *is* a game that one plays according to the rules." Toward the end Mr. Antolini sustained the cliché in his overblown rhetoric. Considering Holden's own honesty and the indifference of his seniors, "playing the game" becomes a grisly farce; and there is further irony in the fact that Holden is him-

ance for public show (he was handsome in a Year Book way), but filthy in his private habits. His razor "was always rusty as hell and full of lather and hairs and crap." He was "madly in love with himself" and spent half his life in front of a mirror, and he could never whistle in tune. Since it is the despoiling and humiliation of Holden Caulfield, the cynically indifferent invasion and stripping bare of his person, property, and secret imaginative world that is the burden of this episode, we note with fascinated attention how Stradlater possesses himself of all things that are Holden's, one after another. He uses Holden's Vitalis on his "gorgeous locks," he borrows Holden's hounds-tooth jacket for his date, and yawning all the while, he expects Holden to write his theme for him. A sovereign indifference to all about him is Stradlater's salient characteristic. He could not be bothered to get Jane Gallagher's first name right; he called her Jean. When Holden, with his studious[12] care for the other person, asked whether Jane had enjoyed the game, Stradlater didn't know. A bitter humiliation for Holden is that he must ask this gorgeous phony, who has made a theme-slave of him, not to tell Jane that he is being expelled from Pencey; most galling for the reader is Holden's admission that Stradlater probably won't tell "mostly...because he wasn't too interested."

It is, however, the imminently dangerous quality of sex that is frightening. In chapter four when Holden heard that Stradlater was to have a date with Jane Gallagher, he "nearly dropped *dead*" and "nearly went crazy," and in chapter six, through all the mounting ordeal, he "went right on smoking like a madman." The psychological significance of these verbalisms is unmistakable, for Stradlater has invaded Holden's secret world and violated a symbol of innocence and respect. Indeed, in the elaborate pattern of this episode, Stradlater, the "secret slob," matched Holden's secret world with his own, for when Holden was driven to ask the crude but important question, he announced with all the taunting impudence of his kind, "That's a professional secret, buddy."

When Holden recalls for this "sexy bastard" how he had met Jane and goes on to say that he used to play checkers with her, Stradlater's contemptuous comment is, *"Checkers,* for Chrissake!" This girl, who had had a "lousy childhood" with a booze hound for stepfather running "around the goddam house naked," always kept her kings in the back row. As Holden put it, "She just liked the way they looked when they were all in the back row." Half earnestly, half facetiously, he requests Stradlater to ask Jane whether she still keeps her kings in the back row; the symbolism of this imagery, portraying defense against sexual attack, is the central motif of the episode. Stradlater cannot, of course, know what a shocking and menacing figure he has become, for on the simple realistic level the request is merely casual reminiscence; but in the psychological context danger signals have begun fluttering in Holden's mind. If the request may be construed as Holden's desire to send Jane a secret warning against the slob who would himself be the bearer of the message, this defensive gesture, nevertheless, cannot issue in decisive action, and it remains no less symbolical than Holden's wearing his red hunting hat "with the peak around to the back and all." But these gestures indicate, so early in the narrative, that Holden is unconsciously preparing for his subsequent role as a catcher in the[13] rye. In chapter six the futile best that he can do is to invite a beating at Stradlater's hands, and after the struggle he cannot, for a while, find the hat. All the protective gestures have dissolved in impotence, and with his nose "bleeding all over the place" Holden has had a thorough lesson in the game of life.

This lesson is all the more pathetic because in chapter five we have the first full glimpse of Holden's secret world and hence some indication of how, given a chance, Holden would play the game. The subject of his theme is his dead brother Allie's outfielder's mitt that has "poems written all over the fingers and pocket and everywhere." The mitt symbolically indicates that Holden would like to play the game with sensitivity and imagination, and Stradlater's crude rejection of the theme is itself a symbolic gesture, and a final one, shutting off all hope of communication. Holden tears the theme into pieces. But it should be added that, like Jane's kings in the back row, Holden's private world is impotent, and the effort at self-revelation in the theme is of a piece with this futility. His rapidly worsening neurotic condition has frozen him in this posture of feebleness, and indeed Holden must take Antolini's "special kind of fall" and disappear into the museum room where the mummies are and thus symbolically encounter death before he may be reborn to an active defense of his world. But this is to anticipate; meanwhile, on the night of his humiliation, several hours later and many hours before the precious Antolini disgorged his wisdom, Holden reflected, "It just drove me stark staring mad when I thought about her and Stradlater parked somewhere in that fat-assed Ed Banky's car [Stradlater is the conscienceless, universal borrower]. Every time I thought about it, I felt like jumping out the window." Holden's fantasying about suicide (and young Castle *did* jump) provides final evidence of frozen impotence, and action is not outwardly directed but inwardly as an impulse toward self-destruction.

The "crazy" pattern continues throughout the middle portion of the book and reaches a climax in the Sally Hayes episode; thereafter, since Holden's neurosis has by then been established, it occurs less frequently, and other patterns come into prominence. Meanwhile in the lobby of the New York hotel Holden's obsessive imagination presents a picture to him of Stradlater with Jane that "almost drove [him] crazy." After the incident with the prostitute and Maurice, Holden's violent fantasying (of which, more later) compels him to say, "But I'm crazy. I swear to God I am." The literary talk with the nuns provides some[14] relief before the scene with Sally Hayes, but even here Holden's reflections are violent, though interestingly varied from the obsession with Jane. The talk is about *Romeo and Juliet*; his favorite character, Mercutio, leads him to the private comment, "The thing is, it drives me crazy if somebody gets killed—especially somebody very smart and entertaining and all...." It is part of Salinger's intricately patterned structure that Holden's favorite character in the play should have been killed in a duel and that Holden himself was the manager of the Pencey fencing team and had "left all the foils and equipment and stuff on the goddam subway." Of greater import is the recollection of Allie in Holden's words about Mercutio, "somebody very smart and entertaining and all." Furthermore, this brief literary interlude brings together the "crazy" and "kill" patterns; and in a moment we shall pursue the latter.

The episode with Sally Hayes provides an explosive self-revelation, in which Holden (we have previously noted his apologizing "like a madman") admits that he is crazy and swears to God that he is a madman. What is a madman? Earlier in the fight with Stradlater Holden was "practically yelling"; and here Sally must ask him twice to stop shouting. Certainly, in his neurotic condition, Holden is scarcely master of himself, and yet, for the reader's sake if not for Sally's, he expresses his urge to withdraw from society with some semblance of rational discourse. His proposal that Sally and he escape to New England on his small bank account is, of course, fatuous; but what lies behind the proposal is not fatuous, and Salinger, indeed, permits us to penetrate the moral quality of Holden's secret world. Earlier that world was presented largely in terms of pathetic sentiment and instinctive honesty, but now our view of it is compellingly moral. Whereas Holden is nervously protective in the Stradlater episode, he is now aggressive and attacks modern urban life and mores. He protests that he doesn't like automobiles, even *"old"* cars." "I'd rather have a goddam horse. A horse is at least *human,* for God's sake." As Holden sees matters, life has become so inhumanly mechanized that in his secret world animals move up a notch to assume the status of humans. Swift would approve such misanthropy.

III

We observe, then, that the "madman" and "crazy" patterns are employed most effectively in episodes, chiefly in the first two thirds of[15] the book, that reveal Holden's neurotic condition and, as above, his sense of alienation. The psychological substratum is the frightening ambivalence of fantasy, with all the highly charged emotional responses flashing back and forth between the negative and positive poles; and we must now explore this dominant pattern.

Holden's fantasy begins at the obvious and apparently extroverted level of "horsing around." With Ackley Holden pretends to be a "blind guy," saying, "Mother darling, give me your *hand*. Why won't you give me your *hand?*" Considering the view we get later of parental care *in absentia* or by remote control, and considering, furthermore, what has already been disclosed of the highly wrought design of *The Catcher,* we should not fail to note, so early in the novel, the motif of mutilation and the implied charge that a mother has not provided guidance and owes her son the hand that he has broken; with Holden the extroverted simply does not exist. Ackley's response is, "You're nuts, I swear to God." Ackley calls Holden's hat a "deer shooting hat," and Holden facetiously retorts, "I shoot people in this hat"; and once again, in the sequel, the facetious may be seen to envelop aggressive tendencies. The hat, indeed, is the central symbol of Holden's fantasy and so of the book—not only, as here, for aggression, but later for his humanitarian role, faintly foreshadowed, as we have already noted, in the Stradlater episode; and a third symbolic function of the hat is to hit off Holden's quest, which is in a large measure hysterical flight, as he rushes about New York before he comes home to Phoebe. Aggression and withdrawal follow each other rapidly in the opening scenes, the first with Stradlater when Holden leaps on him "like a goddam panther," and the second when he wakes up Ackley and asks about joining a monastery.

In his hotel room, after "old Sunny," the prostitute, has gone, he talks "sort of out loud" to Allie and expresses guilt feelings about his having refused to take Allie with him and a friend on a luncheon bike-trip because Allie was just a child. Since Allie's death, whenever Holden becomes depressed, he tries to make up for this past cruelty by saying that he may go along. Here, then, in his guilt feelings we have an explanation of why Holden broke his hand against the garage windows, and we may trace all the elements of his fantasying to this psychological cause. Mutilation is itself the physical symbol of a psychological state of self-accusation and self-laceration. Hence, when[16] Holden, after discovering that he cannot pray, reflects that next to Jesus the character in the Bible that he likes best is the lunatic that lived in the tombs and cut himself with stones, we observe a consistent psychological development of the motif of mutilation and, linked to it, the death-wish; and recalling the verbal patterns of "madman" and "crazy" we note further that Holden identifies himself with a madman. In *Mark* V:1–20, we are told of the lunatic that broke all chains and fetters, for no man could tame him. Jesus drove the spirits that possessed him into the swine and told him to go home to his friends. If we are to comprehend what really happens in *The Catcher* we must attribute prime importance to this little scene of about two pages at the head of chapter fourteen; for Holden will subsequently break his morbid psychological fetters, he will go home to Phoebe, and, in a manner of speaking, he will be able to pray.

Before all this may occur, however, society in the form of Maurice, the "elevator guy," intrudes for his shake-down and sadistic treatment of Holden, who, in consequence, is plunged into his most elaborate fantasy of mutilation, death-wish, and aggression. He pretends that in a gun fight with Maurice he receives a bullet in his abdomen, and Jane Gallagher bandages him and holds a cigarette for him to smoke as he bleeds. "The goddam movies. They can ruin you. I'm not kidding." The function of Hollywood is to glamorize and distort and, in consequence, to disparage private suffering for an entranced national audience. This view is scarcely fresh-minted in *The Catcher,* but it is substantially Holden's criticism in the comment above when he realizes that he has given his own genuine difficulty the *ersatz* Hollywood form.

As the supreme national incarnation of the phony, Hollywood (and by extension, California) figures prominently in the tale from first to last, for it provides another enclosing pattern. We learn quite early that D. B. has prostituted himself by going to Hollywood to write scenarios; and at the end we see Holden in the clutches of a California psychoanalyst, who is interested not in the cause of suffering, not even in the person suffering, but rather in the "desirable" social result of adjustment. The suffering, in any case, would not have arisen or assumed such neurotic proportions had there been parental care instead of a nomadic existence at expensive prep schools. As Phoebe tells Holden, "Daddy can't come. He has to fly to California."[17]

When Holden visits Radio City he is confronted by a phony image of withdrawal and escape matching his own genuine urge. Indeed, the fantasy projected upon the screen also matches his own most persistent fantasy of mutilation, for the hero, "this English guy," who is a Duke, suffers from the mutilation of amnesia. Furthermore, the adult audience is sentimentally phony, for sitting next to Holden is a woman who, weeping copiously, refuses to take her boy to the lavatory but keeps him squirming in his seat. "She was about as kindhearted as a goddam wolf." If Holden is sick and escapes into fantasy, so too the nation; and although it may be going too far to suggest that a movie touched off Holden's recovery, it is nonetheless true that in the last third of the narrative the emphasis is on maturity and an affirmative, curative psychology.

Following the movie, Holden meets Carl Luce in the Wicker Bar of the Seton Hotel, where Holden, at his most amusingly raffish, "horses around" conversationally to the boredom and vexation of his older prep school friend, who has taken up with Eastern philosophy and a Chinese mistress rather older than himself. Three separate times Luce is driven to comment on Holden's immaturity: "Same old Caulfield. When are you going to grow up?" After Luce has gone Holden starts "that stupid business with the bullets in [his] guts again," but quite likely the phony movie and Luce's rather exalted talk have helped to take some of the steam out of "that stupid business." Certainly, the reader is being prepared for a turning point. Before Holden leaves the hotel he is told five times to go home; the psychological direction of the novel, under the narrative surface, is by now unmistakable. Although Luce "couldn't care less, frankly" about Holden's growing up, Holden will mature, and in the terms supplied subsequently by Antolini out of Stekel: "The mark of the immature man is that he wants to die nobly for a cause, while the mark of the mature man is that he wants to live humbly for one."[7]

IV

The visit to Central Park and then home to Phoebe must be regarded as the two halves of a single, unfolding psychological experience; they provide the hinge on which *The Catcher* moves. Holden had started thinking about the ducks during his talk with "old" Spencer; and in New York he asked two cab drivers about what the ducks did[18] in such wintry weather. Holden knew the park "like the back of [his] hand," for as a child he had roller-skated and ridden his bike there. But now, searching for the lagoon, he is lost, and, as he says, "it kept getting darker and darker and spookier and spookier." The park has become *terra incognita*. When at last he finds the lagoon there are no ducks. Meanwhile he has dropped and broken the *Shirley Bean* record that he had bought for Phoebe, but he carefully gathers up the pieces into his pocket. He sits down on a park bench and shivers "like a bastard" because back at the hotel he had sloshed water over his head, and "little hunks of ice" had formed on his back hair. He

---

[7] Wilhelm Stekel (1868–1940), the colleague of Freud and Jung, was the author of numerous works, based on his own practice, in which infantilism and maturity are a frequent subject of interpretation and comment. Worthy of special mention here is the English translation by James S. Van Teslaar of his *Peculiarities of Behavior: Wandering Mania, Dipsomania, Pyromania and Allied Impulsive Acts* (New York, 2 vols., 1924 and 1943). I do not find Antolini's quotation in this or other works by Stekel, though there are passages in several volumes, in particular the *Autobiography* (New York, 1950), that hit off the same idea. Interestingly, Stekel is mentioned in Dashiell Hammett's *The Thin Man* (1934), in which two adolescents, Dorothy and Gilbert Wynant, exhibit psychological problems arising out of the social chaos around them similar to those of Jane Gallagher and Holden Caulfield. Among other parallels are the "lousy childhood" of Dorothy and Jane (involving a stepfather) and the wandering mania of Dorothy and Holden. Considering the critical emphasis on comparisons between Huck Finn and Holden, it may be plausibly urged that *The Thin Man* is just as acceptable a prototype for *The Catcher* as is *Huck Finn*.

thinks of himself as dying of pneumonia and by easy stages gets on to Allie, whom, significantly, he seems to regard as alive, out there in the cemetery surrounded by "dead guys and tombstones." It nearly drives him crazy to think that visitors could run to their cars when it rained, but Allie could not. To relieve his distress Holden skips what little change he has over the lagoon "where it wasn't frozen." Finally, the thought of Phoebe gives him courage to live. "So I got the hell out of the park, and went home."

The psychological and thematic components of this little scene are profoundly rich and yet beautifully simple. Central Park represents Holden's Dark Tower, Dark Night of the Soul, and Wasteland; the paradise of his childhood is bleak, and the ducks that, in his fantasy, he has substituted for the human, have vanished. In effect, Holden is finished with childhood and is prepared for the burdens of maturity. But all the same he gathers up the pieces to be treasured, and in a final act of childhood profligacy—skipping coins over the lagoon—he symbolically rejects the materialism of the adult world that he is about to enter.

The apartment episode with Phoebe is so brilliant and so densely packed that we must examine it in two stages, here largely from Holden's point of view and later from Phoebe's. The meeting between brother and sister is presented as a conspiracy, for Holden enters the building under false pretenses and slips into his own apartment "quiet as hell." "I really should've been a crook." The anti-social bond is confirmed when Phoebe tells Holden that she has the part of Benedict Arnold in a Christmas play and when he gives her his symbolical hunting hat. They are rebels and seekers both.

Almost the first thing that Holden notices in D. B.'s room where Phoebe usually sleeps when D. B. is away is her fantasying with her[19] middle name, which she changes frequently, the present one being "Weatherfield." The various kinds of fantasy have an important role in *The Catcher* and, in alliance with other motifs, hint at the philosophical question of the narrative: "What is the nature of reality?" From this point onward the novel converges upon the answer. Meanwhile, Phoebe's fantasying "killed" Holden; and in this and later scenes with children his mood is good humored, indulgent, and parental. The word "kill" is used throughout the novel in colloquial fashion, as here; but presently it reflects a rising hysteria when Phoebe exclaims again and again about Holden's leaving school, "Daddy'll *kill* you." Paradoxically, the terror exists not for Holden but for Phoebe, and the boy who had been fleeing from one physical and psychological terror after another now finds himself in the role of the elder who must reassure his young sister that nobody is going to kill him.

The spotlight is, furthermore, powerfully focused upon Holden's problem when Phoebe acts out a killing. She had seen a movie about a mercy killing; a doctor compassionately put a crippled child (on his way up to the apartment Holden, continuing his mutilation fantasy, had been "limping like a bastard") out of its misery by smothering it with a blanket. In symbolic mimicry Phoebe places her pillow over her head and resists Holden's plea to come out from under. Here, indeed, is killing—"mercy" killing, and assuredly one way of dealing with children. But it would be a "mercy" also to save children, to catch them as they are about to fall off "some crazy cliff," and this is the humanitarian solution that Holden expresses to Phoebe. The antisocial conspiracy has blossomed into a benevolent and protective order. Antolini's thesis, coming belatedly as it does, merely renders conceptually the courage and maturity that Holden, with his imaginative heart, had discovered in the stolen moments of domestic affection and security with Phoebe. Salinger is intimating that for the imaginatively endowed the living experience may become the source of precept and rule. The point is that Holden is way ahead of his elders.

Holden's image of salvation is a compound of his own anecdote to Phoebe of how James Castle plunged to his death and of the snatch of song Holden had heard, "If a body catch a body coming through the rye." From this point onward, however, there is a bifurcation in his development, for he is paradoxically headed for both physical capture and psychological escape. Holden's verbal slip with the song (and[20] Phoebe corrects him) is a *leitmotif* for his mood of utter weariness as he leaves the apartment; he had entered as a "crook," and now he "didn't give much of a damn any more if they caught [him]." The weariness is evident, furthermore, in his being unable to concentrate both with Phoebe and with Antolini as a sense of the rigidity of life overwhelms him. With a last immense and frightened effort he rushes from Antolini's apartment, escaping what in his fevered imagination he takes to be Antolini's perverted advances on the living room couch, before society finally flings him upon the Procrustes bed of adjustment. Such a development being clearly established, we may follow Holden's escape into freedom.

Now Holden's fantasying will not be neurotically defensive, but rationally motivated and ethically directed; and the death-wish will disappear. On his walk up to Phoebe's school Holden fantasies about going west; he would pretend to be a deaf-mute, and if anybody wanted to talk to him the person would have to write the conversation on a piece of paper. Whereas earlier in his effort to communicate with society, as in the theme he wrote for Stradlater, society rejected him, he now rejects society. If there is to be no communication it is of his own free, rational choice and not a piece of neurotic withdrawal. At Phoebe's school he sees the obscene word twice inscribed on corridor walls; but now, if he says that it drives him almost crazy, it does so not with a neurotic and inwardly directed thrust, but in an outward direction in defense of Phoebe and other children, for he says that he could kill whoever did it.

On the way up Fifth Avenue Holden has a recurrence of a feeling expressed at the beginning: "I felt like I was sort of disappearing," he had said after crossing a road. Once again he feels that he will never get to the other side of the street; he breaks out into a sweat, and he talks to Allie, begging him not to let him disappear. When he has successfully negotiated a crossing he thanks Allie, who thus assumes his function as a guide, like Virgil for Dante, into the lower regions of the dead, as we are about to see. Hence, in the tremendous culmination of the narrative, the "yellow" pattern has a significance that is effectively all-embracing, and it advances our perceptions beyond the threshold of awareness permitted by the other verbal patterns.

From the start Holden is convinced that by either standard—society's or his own, he is a coward. On returning to his hotel from the[21] Village through the cold night he thinks of his stolen gloves. He calls himself "one of these very yellow guys" and by way of proof explains his likely elaborate and cowardly handling of the affair had he known who the thief was. He would not offer fight, and he would therefore be "partly yellow" since, as he admits, "If you're supposed to sock somebody in the jaw" you should. But his trouble is that he "can't stand looking at the other guy's face"; and this, he concludes, as a veiled revelation to the perceptive reader, is a "funny kind of yellowness." Later when the prostitute and the "elevator guy" knock on his door Holden confesses that he is "pretty scared" and "very yellow about those things." These first two instances show the coercive social standard, but the third, in the apartment with Phoebe, gives us Holden's self-condemnation when he admits that he "was too yellow not to join" a secret fraternity. The final instance, unmistakably illuminating the climax of the book, shows that he is not a coward and that, in effect, he essentially has business to transact only with himself, and he must therefore stop running. In the museum of art when Holden walks down "this very narrow sort of hall" leading to the room containing the mummies, one of the two boys with him bolts and runs, the other says, "He's got a yella streak a mile wide," and then he also flees. Not Holden but society is yellow.

Since Holden's neurosis includes feelings of insecurity stemming from Allie's death and from Jane Gallagher's "lousy childhood" (like his own) and since both Allie and Jane have become inextricably bound together in his mind, Holden conquers the two-fold hysteria at one and the same moment. There is sexual imagery in "this very narrow sort of hall" and the room containing the mummies, especially since the obscene word is written "with a red crayon...right under the glass part of the wall." Once again as in Phoebe's school he reacts with weariness over the corruption of this world and solemnly reflects that if he ever dies and is buried, his tombstone will bear the ugly legend. Here, at last, the identity of the fear of death and the fear of sex is made clear, and these fears are to be seen, actually, as a pervasive fear of violence to body or spirit and the ensuing mutilation. If in the Stradlater episode and throughout the rest of the novel Holden is an innocent, he is so, not so much in terms of our popular literary tradition, but rather in a classical, Christian, or psychoanalytical schema. His very fears yield proof that his innocence represents a harmony of attributes[22] and drives—intellectual, emotional, and physical, so that in the proper regulation of them harm will result neither for the person nor for others.[8] Holden's obsession about faces indicates this fastidious care; the Egyptians tried to conquer the final violence of death by mummification so that, as Holden says, the face "would not rot." In Holden's encounter it is important that the spirit should not rot.

For insight into the psychologically symbolic meaning of the museum episode we turn once again to the structure of the novel. Allie's death has been such a traumatic experience that all Holden knows is death, for when "old" Spencer, who makes him "sound dead," confronts him with the unsatisfactory results of the history examination, it is clear that his historical knowledge is limited to the subject of mummification. It is to this knowledge, at the close of the book, that he returns with a sense of how "nice and peaceful" it all is. The psychological journey from the fear of death to a calm acceptance of it is further highlighted at the beginning when we learn that Mr. Ossenburger, the mortician, has donated the dormitory wing named for him in which Holden has his room.

Holden's victorious encounter with death reveals psychological maturity, spiritual mastery, and the animal faith and resiliency of youth. The charmingly offhand and rather awesome conditional statement, "If I ever die" reminds the reader that in the last quarter of the book it is so difficult for Holden to think of Allie as dead that Phoebe must underscore the fact, "Allie's *dead*." Yet although Holden masters his neurosis he also falls victim to society, for in alternating stress the novel continuously presents two mingled actions—his own inner dealings with himself and society's brutal effect upon him. After his visit to the mummies Holden goes to the lavatory and proceeds to faint, i.e., symbolically dies; and his comment is that he was lucky in falling as he did because he "could've killed" himself. The parallelism with the earlier Stradlater episode leaps instantly to the mind, for then, as we recall, Holden "nearly dropped *dead*"; and that scene also took place

---

[8] By a "psychoanalytical schema" I mean, of course, psychotherapy with the sole purpose of exploring the psychological disturbance and restoring the invalid to his original health; I exclude the sociological motivation of "adjustment" to supposedly "desirable" social ends.

in a lavatory—a fit symbol, in both instances, for a scatalogical society. Significantly, he feels better immediately after; and he is reborn into a new world of secure feelings and emotions, with himself fulfilling the office of catcher in his mature view of Phoebe. Thereafter the psychoanalytical couch can mean little to him, far less than Antolini's couch, to which it is thematically related.[23]

V

The dense contrapuntal effect of the verbal patterns is, finally, enhanced by one that keeps a persistent drum beat in the background until the full thematic range of *The Catcher* is disclosed. If Holden symbolically and psychologically dies only to be reborn into the world of Phoebe's innocence and love, he has all through the novel been announcing the theme of regeneration in the "wake up" pattern. After the Stradlater episode Holden wakes up Ackley, then another schoolmate Woodruff (to sell him a typewriter), and as a derisive parting shot, "every bastard on the whole floor" with his yell, *"Sleep tight, ya morons!"* In New York he wakes up or provides the occasion for having wakened up Faith Cavendish (striptease), Sunny (prostitute: "I was *sleepin'* when that crazy Maurice woke me up"), Sally, Phoebe, and the Antolinis. To round out the pattern, Holden's father "won't wake up even if hit over the head with a chair." Obviously, the thematic implication of the pattern transcends both the episodes and the characters involved; in moral as well as psychological terms Salinger is suggesting that a brutalized society requires regeneration and must arouse itself from its mechanistic sloth.

In a development that parallels the "wake up" pattern Salinger shows that Holden, of course, must wake up in his own way; and it has been the thesis of this reading of *The Catcher* that he does effect his own psychological regeneration. Jane Gallagher's kings in the back row symbolize, as we have already noted, the impotence of Holden's secret world, for kings should range freely over the checkerboard. Similarly Holden has interpreted the Museum of Natural History in terms compatible with his own rigid posture. "The best thing, though, in that museum was that everything always stayed right where it was." But the exhibit in the Indian Room, of which Holden is especially fond, with its portrayal of a vanished life, simply mirrors his own death-wish and the death-like quality of his secret world. Actually, Holden's secret world fails the boy not only outwardly in the encounter with society, but also inwardly in his retreat from circumstance, for it is effectively sealed off, so that, as with the outside world, there is here likewise no communication. The pattern that discloses this aspect of Holden's isolation is "giving old Jane a buzz." Early in the novel Holden thinks of phoning Jane's mother; twice thereafter he thinks of phoning Jane, but instead phones Sally. On two separate occasions phoning Jane[24] is part of his fantasy. Toward the close of the novel he thinks of phoning her before going out west, but this bit of fantasy does not reveal a need for her, since, as we have observed, Holden's mood has become rational and volitional. But in the violent Hollywood fantasy earlier in the middle of the book, Holden does phone Jane, and she does come to succor him; any comfort, however, that the boy might derive from Jane, who is one of the two nodal images in his private world (the other being Allie), is immediately destroyed by the *ersatz* sentimental form of the fantasy. Equally significant for Salinger's purpose in underscoring the psychological remoteness of the image of Jane is the one time when Holden does actually phone her: there is no answer. His own world fails to respond. Thereafter come the visit to Central Park, the return home to Phoebe, and a concomitant spiritual recovery.

We now approach the second and, possibly, profounder level of interpretation for the apartment scene. Phoebe wakes up easily; and after this moment of incitation the currents of life may flow, and the rigid, frozen posture yield to the genial warmth of the natural and simple. We become aware of the benevolent and protective order of rebels and seekers, symbolized by the hunting hat and underscored by Holden's parental view of Phoebe, through all the devices of language, gesture, image, and symbol; but to comprehend the deeper level of significance (where we are enabled, perhaps, to answer the question, "What is the nature of reality?") we must rely, in this scene, almost entirely on image and gesture, with little help from speech; and in the final, cryptic chapter this submerged level is brought to the surface of conscious thought in the manner of a riddle. As it is, the profoundest language of the moment we are reexamining lies in the occult and dramatic postures of a charmingly expressive girl.

Neurotic fixations give clues to healthy, natural emotional needs; and Holden, in his trance-like satisfaction with everything in its place in the Indian Room, is instinctively reacting against the chaos outside and inside himself. Things must be in their place; but the constellation must be living and dynamic, not dead, and life must have a magnetic center around which the affairs of life will arrange themselves. For Holden Phoebe provides that center.

From Alice Holmberg Phoebe had learned how to cross her legs in the Yogi manner, hold her breath, and by concentrating exert the influence of mind over matter. In this position, "smack in the middle of[25] the bed," Phoebe represents the still, contemplative center of life; at the same time she is listening to dance music, and with the impulsiveness of the child she offers to dance with Holden. In this manner Salinger indicates the viable relationship between the contemplative and the active participation in the dance of life—a spiritual perception that is as ancient as the *Bhagavad-Gita*. Although the humanitarian role of saviour that Holden assigns himself stands in the foreground, we must nevertheless not fail to see that Phoebe is the essential source; and if Holden, on the path up out of spiritual dilemma and crisis, must find the verbal and conceptual means of expressing his innermost needs, Phoebe, as easily as she wakes up, expresses an even more fundamental insight through symbolic gesture. The charm of the scene, when fully comprehended from this point of view, lies in the mingling of the naive and childlike with the spiritually occult, in the immense discrepancy between means (a child) and ends (spiritual insight); for adults it is a rather puzzling and even terrifying charm, when they acknowledge it, discoverable in fairy tales and some of the teachings of Jesus.

The source of this dualism or polarity of contemplation and activity lies in the intuitive wisdom of the unfettered personality freely acknowledging that the best satisfaction of human nature lies in what Emerson called the law of undulation. Part of this larger spontaneity is the recognition that much of the mastery of life comes through indirection, and hence the preference for the expressive act over precept. Holden, for example, comments that although he had taught Phoebe how to dance when she was "a tiny little kid," "you can't teach somebody how to *really* dance." A far more dramatic defense of personality against restrictions comes in the following scene at Antolini's apartment when, out of a heightened awareness of his approaching crisis, Holden argues his schoolboy point that digressions should be allowed in Oral Expression; "what I mean is, lots of time you don't *know* what interests you most till you start talking about something that *doesn't* interest you most." Holden liked it when somebody got excited about something.

In Holden's maturing there is no repudiation of childhood or even of the secret world. In the organic processes of life the continuity between childhood and maturity, need not, must not be severed. If the child is father of the man, as Wordsworth said, assuredly society[26] at large and parents in particular have scarcely encouraged this teenaged boy, well over six feet, with a crippled right hand and the right side of his head full of "millions of gray hairs," to think of his days in Wordsworthian fashion as "bound each to each by natural piety." For that reason his secret world, when released from the death-like enchantment of neurosis, may well have been, ultimately, the real source of his salvation. Certainly in the daylight return to Central Park with Phoebe Holden experienced the natural piety that Wordsworth celebrated, being at once child and parent with her, both in the zoo (he need no longer search for the ducks) and at the carrousel, watching Phoebe go round and round, another symbol for the circular activity of life. Here the sense of continuity that Holden demands in his surroundings, as we have noted in his feeling for the exhibit in the Indian

Room—the harmonious relation between the private person and the public world, receives a living affirmation when he comments with so much satisfaction that the carrousel "played that same song about fifty years ago when *I* was a little kid." When, to the adult reader's further amusement, Holden, like any apprehensive parent, says that Phoebe will have to take her chances with falling off the horse when reaching for the ring, the boy has added a cubit to his psychological stature.

The short concluding chapter, far from being the lame and defective appendage to a charming book that some think it, is like so much else in *The Catcher,* a triumph of technical virtuosity. In this reading of the novel the conclusion is blunted, and interestingly so, only because we cannot say what society will do to impose adjustment upon a boy who has effected his own secret cure; and we therefore close the narrative not with psychoanalytical questions, but ethical. In rejecting the formalism of psychonalytical technique for the spontaneous personality Salinger follows D. H. Lawrence; and in boldly proposing that the resources of personality are sufficient for self-recovery and discovery, his book will stand comparison with Herman Hesse's *Steppenwolf,* whose protagonist, Harry Haller, rises above his own neurosis in a discovery, based on Buddhistic thought, that the potentialities of the soul are limitless. Altogether, in this reading the answer to the question, "What is the nature of reality?" is both complex and simple, residing in the living, organic relation between childhood and maturity, continuity and change, the contemplative and the active, the external world and the inner spirit. This reality is not a philosophical[27] abstraction, but an existentialist datum of physical and emotional experience. Since the action of *The Catcher* takes place against the background of the approaching Christmas holidays, the answer is again suggested in the implied contrast between the birth of Jesus and the Egyptian art of mummification.

In the chapter under consideration, as well as in a number of short stories, Salinger has found his rationale in Buddhistic thought. The blunted conclusion is to be understood not only as a realistic narrative device but also as the paradoxical product of a tremendous leap in thought. In Zen Buddhism the koan or riddle lifts one above the level of the conceptualizing intelligence to that of immediate insight, as in the famous koan that Salinger affixed to his *Nine Stories*: "We know the sound of two hands clapping. But what is the sound of one hand clapping?" The Zen riddle presents an intellectual impasse "beyond assertion and denial"; and if the master's answer to the disciple's question often seems impertinent and even frivolous the purpose is to turn the question back upon the disciple to sharpen his awareness of "life's elusiveness and indefinability." As one authority puts it, "Thus when the disciple comes to the final point where the Koan absolutely refuses to be grasped, he comes also to the realization that life can never be grasped, never possessed or made to stay still. Whereupon he 'lets go,' and this letting go is the acceptance of life *as* life, as that which cannot be made another's property, which is always free and spontaneous and unlimited."[9]

Once again there is an immense discrepancy between means (a child) and ends (spiritual insight). When the psychoanalyst (in the role of disciple) asks Holden (the master) whether he intends to apply himself at school, and Holden replies that he doesn't know because you don't know "what you're going to do till you do it," the surface impression is that of a typically unsatisfactory answer from a teen-ager. When D. B. asks him what he thinks about "all this stuff [he] just finished telling...about" and Holden replies that he does not know what to think, the surface impression is the same. Finally, Holden proposes a riddle. He says that he misses everybody, even Stradlater, Ackley, and "that goddam Maurice." "Don't ever tell anybody anything. If you do, you start missing everybody." Here is a shock to the conceptualizing, precept-laden intelligence, a puzzle or paradox that will not yield to logical analysis but that, on the contrary, sends[28] the mind back over the experience recorded, even into the depths of the unconscious where both the malady and the cure lay. In the large, Whitmanesque acceptance of evil there is affirmation of the life-process as the personality "lets go"; and such Zen riddling is easily translatable into existentialist understanding.

In its emphasis on the conflict between the organic and the mechanistic, the secret and the public, reality and appearance, awakening and death, *The Catcher* hits off the strongest Romantic affirmations from Goethe and Wordsworth down to Lawrence, Joyce, and Hesse. Whether at Walden Pond, at Weissnichtwo, or in New York hot spots, the problem of personality remains; one surmises that, after a century and more, as *A Portrait of the Artist* and *Steppenwolf* likewise indicate, the struggle has become intensified. At the close of *The Catcher* the gap between society and the individual has widened perceptibly; and far from repudiating Holden's secret world, Salinger has added a secret of psychological depth. A mechanistic society, represented just as much by Antolini as by the psychoanalyst, may with the glib teacher continue to ignore the boy and talk of "what kind of thoughts your particular size mind should be wearing"; we may all comfort ourselves with the reflection that, after all, Holden is another bothersome case of arrested development, albeit rather charming in a pathetic and oafish manner.

No doubt Salinger has overdrawn the portrayal, but a work of lit-

---

[9] Alan W. Watts, *The Way of Zen* (New York, 1957), pp. 70, 75. See also Christmas Humphreys, *Zen Buddhism* (London, 1958), pp. 124–131.

erature is not a statistic, it is a special vision. In its pathetic and senti-mental tone *The Catcher* faithfully reflects the surface of American life, and insofar, therefore, as it lacks intellectual substance and a valid universality based on a cultural heritage, it falls far below the Roman-tic masterpieces to which I have made passing reference. But as I have tried to make clear, *The Catcher* is strongest where these are strongest. Whatever the dreadful odds, the human spirit, though slain, refuses to stay dead; it is forever hearing the cock crow, forever re-sponding to the Everlasting Yea. So in *The Catcher*; and the blunted, ambiguous ending mingles with this affirmation the doubt whether now at last, in the long travail of the spirit, the odds have not become too dreadful. If, as this reading interprets the book, the scales tip in favor of the affirmation, it is so because the history of youth is almost always hopeful.[29]

GEORGE R. CREEGER

> *"Treacherous Desertion": Salinger's "The Catcher in the Rye."* Middletown, Connecticut: Wesleyan University, 1961. The Graduate Summer School for Teachers, Wesleyan University, Middletown, Connecticut, Copyright 1961 by Wesleyan Uni-versity, used by permission.

. . .

Now it is an important fact that we see the world of the book ex-clusively through Holden's eyes. Like Twain before him, Salinger chose a limited, and in some senses limiting, point of view, quite dif-ferent, for example, from that common in Jane Austen, Melville, or James. The decision has its dangers, chief of which is that to look through the eyes of even an intelligent sixteen-year-old is to narrow one's range of vision. The reader, in exasperation, is likely to attribute this narrowness not only to the author but also to the whole book. One hears rather frequent complaints that Holden in fact knows very little—about the world at large (despite his sophistication), about other human beings, and even about himself. He is condemned as guilty of a whole sequence of false judgments and is hauled into court for being a self-righteous snob. . . .

But to take adolescence as one's subject matter is not proof of adolescence and certainly not of technical ineptitude. Surely Salinger made his decision, having weighed the disadvantages against certain very clear advantages, equally inherent in the limitations of the point of view and of the narrator. Holden's own failures, like those of Hamlet, confirm our corporate weaknesses. (If such a one may be corrupted, what of us?) And the very narrowness of the vision produces a kind of concentration and intensity. Furthermore, when all is said and done, what remarkable eyes we look through! Holden is obviously highly intelligent. We perceive this fact at once and are not fooled by the knowledge of his having flunked out of two prep schools and of his imminent departure in disgrace from a third. Furthermore, he is honest, and the fact that he is also a superb inventive liar does not in the least diminish the quality of his honesty. He is sensitive, particularly in the area of beauty and of morality. And he possesses a real sense of style, a kind of inventive flair, a flamboyance of speech and action that give him[5] the vitality one expects of characters in fiction (probably because we so seldom find it in life). For these reasons I, for one, am content (partly in the Gallic sense) to look through Holden's eyes, and I am perfectly willing to listen to him tell his story.

The telling of a story involves more than point of view, however; it also involves style. The two in this case are closely linked: Holden is both the witness of and participant in the book's action; he is also its narrator. Thus the style of the book is his style—the way in which he talks. Once again very clear limitations present themselves: forever gone are the possibilities inherent in standard literary English. Salinger shut himself off from the effects that can be achieved only through the use and cultivation of that style in all its multiple variations. He made it impossible to present a setting as Scott or Melville might or to create characters like those in Fielding or James. He ran the risk, furthermore, in limiting himself to the vernacular of a prep school adolescent, of simple monotony; and even a friendly and admiring critic must admit that the book is a tour de force (although, for that matter, so is *Huckleberry Finn*). Salinger succeeded, as Twain succeeded before him, but I would entertain arguments that it is a near thing in both cases, as I would arguments that the style can expect a short life at best; already prep school boys speak another jargon, and perhaps in fifty years we shall need a scholarly edition of *The Catcher in the Rye*. There are worse fates: I'll wager that we shall have no annotated editions of *The Late George Apley*!

In any event the style has such genuine counterbalancing virtues—spontaneity, freshness, immediacy, and vitality. One need only read with an attentive inner ear such a famous passage as the one that describes the interchange between Holden and Horwitz, the cabdriver, on the ultimate fate of the ducks in Central Park, to become a believer.

Yet if this passage proves my point, it should not be permitted so to charm us that we fail to see how functional it also is. *The Catcher in the Rye* is one of those rare books in which there are no[6] irrelevant details: however trivial Holden's concern for the ducks may appear on the surface, it is yet another statement (and not the least brilliant) of the book's theme. In the face of the threat posed to the ducks by winter, Holden wants to know what forces operate on their behalf. Horwitz cannot, of course, tell him; his very exasperation at Holden for asking such a damn-fool question is human enough. But the question remains important: if the ducks are unprovided for, then some kind of treacherous desertion has, in Holden's terms, taken place. Once again something of beauty and value faces inexorable destruction.

Since the threatening forces in the book are preponderant, we had better turn to an analysis of them, before considering what arms Holden takes against them.

Physicality and sexuality, which are inextricably linked for Holden, bear a menacing aspect. Holden has an unusually, perhaps abnormally, strong revulsion from all physical ugliness—whether the bare legs of his aging history instructor or the pimply face of Ackley. And it is difficult for him to separate this revulsion from the world of adult sexuality. Almost everywhere he turns he sees sex under the guise of obscenity and perversity, whether in a peep-show display from a hotel window, or in his encounters with the pimp and prostitute, the ambivalent older friend, and the equally ambivalent former teacher. Even in the hallways of his sister's school he finds the familiar mocking obscenity scratched indelibly on the walls. In desperation he concludes that if he ever dies and is buried, the same obscenity will be graven upon his tombstone. What should thus be part of man's power to express love becomes instead the ultimate means of giving vent to hatred and derision.

Nowhere is this situation dramatized more widely than in the episode early in the book where Holden discovers that his aggressively virile and unprincipled roommate, Stradlater, has a date with Jane. Holden had known Jane during the previous summer, had alternately necked and played checkers with her, and remembers her primarily as one who always kept her kings in the back row. Now[7] he must spend an agonizing evening waiting for Stradlater to return, wondering what has happened; but he cannot find out, for Stradlater only taunts him ambiguously. Wild with rage and despair, Holden attempts to fight him but of course loses the physical contest to the older and stronger boy. The whole episode is an expression of Holden's love of the innocent and virginal, his fear for its safety, his helpless rage at the possibility of its corruption.

Holden does not, however, live quite so exclusively in the world of perverse or brutal sexuality as some critics of the book have suggested. There are other forces almost equally powerful in the threat they pose to whatever is lovely, fair, and innocent. Among these are ignorance, stupidity (Holden's favorite epithet of abuse is the word "moron"), and hypocrisy. Wherever he turns, he sees the dull-witted and the phonies congregating. His older brother, who once had shown promise of being a good writer, has gone to Hollywood and prostituted himself there by writing for the movies. A second girl friend, Sally, embodies both a kind of dull bourgeois egotism and a complete devotion to the world of fraud and sham. She *adores* the Lunts. Other examples abound (Old Ossenburger, Old Luce, *et al.*), but I wish to turn, for a moment, to Holden himself. It is bad enough that the world—that which is exterior to self—should apparently be dominated by the perverse, stupid, and hypocritical; it is much worse that the world should have the power to impose its perversity, stupidity, and hypocrisy upon the very individual who loathes them. Like Hamlet, Holden faces the possibility, even the probability, that he too will be forced to brutality, cruelty, hypocrisy, failure of nerve. For what other reason is Holden so distressed when his history teacher reads back to him the cheating inanities he had written on an examination? And why does he remember with such despair the time he had denied his brother Allie ("Get thee to a nunnery, go!")?

In trying to define Holden, it is therefore not enough simply to say that he is an innocent standing aghast before a corrupt world; we must add that he is also an innocent standing aghast before the[8] potentiality of his own interior corruption. And he is afraid. Such fear, as Hamlet discovered, is incapacitating: it reduces one to stasis, for to act is to become involved with corruption, to touch the pitch that defiles; hence one dare not act. In these terms Holden is clearly a neurotic. But there are other terms as well; corruption, whether of the world or the self, is not the only enemy. There is also death.

Holden's experience with death is not very wide, but its impact upon him has been profound: he has seen the suicide of a classmate brought about by the deliberate if unthinking cruelty of companions; more importantly he has seen the death of his beloved brother, Allie, brought about almost solely by chance—inexplicably as it were. Death proves to be the most treacherous of deserters, and the least accessible for purposes of revenge. When Allie died, there was nothing Holden could do to vent his rage and despair except to go out and systematically break the windows of the garage with his bare fist and try, futilely and impotently, to smash those of the stationwagon as well. Yet there was another turn of the screw: not only did death deprive Holden of what he loved most in the world, it also deprived him forever of the chance to make amends to Allie for the moment of desertion of which Holden was guilty; he must perforce live without Allie, as he must live with the burden of guilt. Given this knowledge we should scarcely be surprised that Holden is the victim of acedia, or that he tries desperately throughout the book to find defenses against that which corrupts and that which breaks in and steals. He fights for purity and for those objects and people who embody it for him. What and who are these objects and people? What are his weapons?

To answer the first question: they are not invariably human beings; they may be ducks, for example, or the snow lying pristine upon the grounds of Pencey Prep, or kings lined up in the back row. But usually value is expressed by Holden in people: Jane, for example, or a little boy singing or needing to go to the john, two nuns conversing in a Nedicks about *Romeo and Juliet,* his sister Phoebe. In each of these people he sees innocence, purity, happiness, and[9] intelligence—qualities that constitute a constellation of value for him. For each in turn he is desperately concerned that nothing threaten or destroy this value.

What weapons does Holden use in his fight? Significantly those of daydream and phantasy: he senses from the beginning (and this also is a cause of his despair) that there is in fact nothing whatever he can do to prevent corruption and death (those treacherous deserters) from getting at the things he loves. But repeatedly in daydreams he creates a world of phantasy in which he emerges victorious. Some of these daydreams revolve around the possibility of flight. If one cannot stand up to the treacherous world, perhaps then one can flee and find some place where the world is not. It is this solution that Holden has in mind when he proposes to the incredulous Sally that she run off with him to some small house in New Hampshire. The proposal sounds a bit like that of Lear to Cordelia: "Come, let's away to prison. / We two alone will sing like birds i' th' cage." An alternative solution occurs to Holden that he might take upon himself the role of a deaf-mute and work for the rest of his life in some filling station: at least then he would not have to have any more futile conversations with other people.

Still other daydreams are concerned with the possibility of bringing time to a halt and thereby making impossible that involvement with transience which is also an involvement with change, corruption, and death. In the Museum of Natural History Holden had discovered as a boy a world in which time did, in fact, stop. There, in the tableau of a primitive Eskimo society, he saw a world proof against the "wrackful siege of batt'ring days," somewhat akin to that on Keats's Grecian urn. No matter how many times he returned to the museum, no matter what had happened to him in the meanwhile, he found that everything remained just as it was. The image of a purposeful and protective society in which nourishment and love were provided, of a world in which even small birds were certain of a destination in their flight south—this image remained forever fixed and changeless.[10]

Yet another daydream, comparable in its emphasis upon the stopping of time but also invoking the significant image of falling, is the one in which Holden projects himself as the "catcher in the rye." As he explains the dream to his sister Phoebe, he sees himself as the only big person in a field of rye where little kids are playing. Holden's role is to prevent children from falling off the cliff. This is what he would like to do, but the dream is, as he himself admits, a "crazy" one, however laudable and touching. It is as crazy as his proposal to Sally, his desire to be a deaf-mute working in a filling station, his hope of turning the world into a museum. It is mad for him to wish to keep small children from falling off the cliff into the abyss of adulthood. However much all these dreams seem like ways out of man's involvement with time and change, they will not work; for either they are illusory ("cold pastorals," as Keats says) or, paradoxically, they are themselves forms of death. Furthermore, they shut man off from the possibility of love, which is, as the book suggests, the only answer to the human dilemma.

Phoebe, Holden's ten-year-old, roller-skate-skinny sister, is the one who tells Holden what is wrong with him: he does not like anything. And when Holden insists that he does, that he likes Allie, for example, she points out bluntly that Allie is dead. How profound an observation she has made she does not, of course, know; neither, for that matter, does Holden. But we do; we can see in her judgment the assertion that Holden's loathing of corruption, change, and death is in fact a perverse form of devotion—that of servitude to them, if nothing else; and that as long as he persists in his desperate and hopeless battle, he is perpetually the loser; for the effect of such a battle, as Ahab discovered, is so to isolate oneself within the self that the possibility for love cannot exist. Love can occur only when the self acknowledges other selves, is willing to give up its own absolute sovereignty.

It is therefore a home-truth that Phoebe tells Holden. Furthermore, she is the very embodiment of the power of human love. When her brother decides at the end of the book that the only[11] answer is flight, she insists that she will go with him. She is the negation of treacherous desertion. Even so, like Ahab rounding on Pip, Holden denies her, but she persists, and the force of her persistence holds her brother; he does not flee. Instead, he goes to the carrousel in Central Park, followed by Phoebe, who relents and, no longer mad, climbs up on an old beat-up-looking horse. What follows is one of the most moving passages in modern literature.

As the music plays "Smoke Gets in Your Eyes," and the rain begins to fall, Holden watches Phoebe go round and round, involved in that motion that brings us back to our beginnings, and reaching, like the other children, for the golden ring. In so doing, she runs the risk of falling, but as Holden at last perceives, it is the risk we all must run;

for otherwise we miss the golden ring, symbol at once of the tie that binds, the circle that encloses. It is no wonder, then, that watching her go round and round, Holden should suddenly sense the happiness that is the promise of Advent; or that this happiness should make him want, as he says, to bawl. And even though he admits, with characteristic honesty, that he does not know why the sight of Phoebe brings him close to tears—save that she looks so "damn nice"—he nevertheless perceives the value of the experience and wishes that it could be shared.

His wish is, of course, granted: through the power of Salinger's wonderful fiction we too are present; we share both the knowledge and the human emotions that accompany it. Great art can do no more.[12]

PART TWO

THE ... AND ... ...

PAUL LEVINE

"J. D. Salinger: The Development of the Misfit Hero," *Twentieth Century Literature*, IV (October 1958), 92–99. Reprinted by permission of the author.

No writer of recent years has captured the *New Yorker* market of Connecticut emigres the way J. D. Salinger has. From the defiant Holden Caulfield to the stoic Mrs. Glass all of his characters are strictly the contented-tormented people who inhabit New York City and its suburbs. But Salinger's importance in the school of younger writers comes from a moral awareness as well as a social perception. The hero in every Salinger story becomes a reflection of a moral code arising out of a cult of innocence, love, alienation, and finally redemption. These heroes form a particularly adolescent troupe of spiritual non-conformists, tough-minded and fragile, humorous and heartbreaking.

The basic predicament in Salinger's stories is that of a moral hero forced to compromise his integrity with a pragmatic society. What disaffiliates the hero is his peculiar off-center vision which sensitizes and distorts his sense of truth in a false world. As Salinger's talent develops, his hero's vision becomes his trademark, flowering in the extraordinary Glass family of Salinger's latest *New Yorker* stories. Moreover, the hero's misfitness in the modern world resolves as a moral problem rather than as the bitter fruit of a social injustice. If the significance of Salinger's emphasis on the moral right is kept in mind, then his recent embracing of Christian principles becomes less than surprising; if we are aware of them, there are indications all along the way.

In his second published story Salinger constructs the predicament that all his heroes will subsequently face: a young soldier marches out of step with the rest of his battalion in "Hang of It" (*Collier's*, July 12, 1941). Similarly, in "Varioni Brothers" (*Saturday Evening Post,* July 17, 1943), "Soft-Boiled Sergeant" (*Saturday Evening Post,* April 15, 1944), "This Sandwich Has No Mayonnaise" (*Esquire,* October 1945), and "Stranger" (*Collier's,* December 1, 1945) the hero is a misfit who "can't get the hang of" living in society on its own terms. But in the earliest stories one gets the sense that the hero is justifiably an object of ridicule: in "Heart of a Broken Story" (*Esquire,* September 1941) he is an ineffectual fool named Justin Horgenschlag. In "Varioni Brothers" Salinger, for the first time, portrays his hero as an artist. The story stands as a transition between the hero who is a misfit and the misfit who is a hero. In the character of Joe Varioni, the writer-artist, Salinger crystallizes the character who will dominate his later fiction— the misfit hero. Unlike his predecessors, Joe is talented, kind, and

107

sensitive;[92] yet he stands apart from his society because he is docile as well as brilliant. Unequipped for the tough world around him, Joe's submissiveness leads to his downfall. And what had been funny in "Heart of a Broken Story" became no laughing matter in "Varioni Brothers."

Just as "Varioni Brothers" created the image of the misfit hero, so every succeeding story developed the hero's alienation from, and defeat by, society. All of Salinger's wartime stories accentuated the hero's isolation from the good past and the corrupt world. In "This Sandwich Has No Mayonnaise" the hero, Vincent Caulfield, is separated from his family and removed from his brother, Holden, who is "missing in action." Cut off from love, alienated from the other soldiers by his thoughts, Vincent is "drenched to the bone, the bone of loneliness, the bone of silence." The soldier's initiation into the terrors of war parallels the child's initiation into the sordidness of the adult world. What is so horrifying is neither war's physical brutality nor society's overt prejudices but rather the subtle dehumanization, the insidious loneliness, and the paralyzing lovelessness. Thus each character becomes a war casualty just as the earlier characters were casualties of society. For the G.I. "the thing that was so terrible was the way your mind wanted to tell civilians these things [about war] that was much more terrible than what your voice said." Salinger's world becomes post-war but not peacetime. There always lurks the threat of the next war, "The War with the Eskimos" (*New Yorker*, June 5, 1948).

Salinger's early vision—the vision of something so terrible that it cannot be communicated or forgotten which plagued the young soldier —is culminated in the post-war world of "The Inverted Forest" (*Cosmopolitan*, December 1947) in which an innocent and talented poet destroys himself. Raymond Ford, the talented poet, is Salinger's misfit hero, built from Joe Varioni's image, later to be developed into Seymour Glass. Ford's ascetic childhood left him unequipped to cope with the hard, insensitive world in which he must live. Until he meets Corinne, his wife, he does not smoke or drink because he is afraid of dulling his sense of taste: "a perfect, unimpaired sense of taste" is vital to his character and talent. (Holden and Seymour also exist through and for this sense of taste.) What makes him a misfit in society —the fact that "his equipment differed from that of other men"— cannot be compromised.

The fate of Raymond's vision symbolizes the outcome of his life: real sight and metaphorical sight are one. In his adolescence he read poetry twenty hours a day, badly damaging his eyes. Finally, his impaired vision required him to wear two pair of glasses—one for reading and one for everyday use. In an attempt to reconcile these two worlds —the aesthetic and the real one—Ford ruined himself. He ends as a pathetic figure, taking eye exercises from a quack doctor who forbids him ever to wear any glasses. The vain attempt to adjust his vision costs Ford both worlds. He returns to the miserable state of his childhood when he saw neither poetry nor the real world. Salinger's insight into his hero's dilemma is now clear. The point for Raymond—as for Holden and Seymour—is that he *is* a misfit and can never be[93] accepted by, or accept, society. His vision—like his unimpaired sense of taste—renders his problem insoluble. With it he cannot live in society; without it he cannot live with himself.

In contrast to the selfless hero, Salinger has created a selfish heroine, a pathetic figure who lacks his hero's moral vision. Yet the heroine also stands as an outsider looking in on the unrecoverable private world and outward toward the social world they could never quite make. Like Lois in the earlier story, "The Long Debut of Lois Taggett" (*Story*, September–October 1942), and Eloise in "Uncle Wiggily in Connecticut" (*New Yorker*, March 20, 1948), Ford's wife, Corinne, is suspended between two worlds, removed by some tragedy from one, while unconsciously recognizing the banality of the other. Alienated in her childhood because of her German parentage, Corinne's life is a perpetual attempt to identify with an estranged society. Unhappy, she takes periodic trips back into her childhood and the one thing from it that she loves—Raymond Ford. Corinne needs Ford because he, too, has always been an outcast; yet she needs society because she knows that Ford's private world is closed to her. An orphan, vainly trying to pull her two worlds together, she loses her only chance for happiness when Ford leaves her. The difference between them differentiates their tragedies. Corinne was doomed from the very beginning because she could never belong to either world. Ford destroyed himself through his vision when he sacrificed his personal world to try to bridge the chasm between himself and society.

Ford leaves Corinne for Bunny, Salinger's "other woman." As insensitive and neurotic as the mother-in-law in "Raise High the Roofbeam, Carpenters" (*New Yorker*, November 19, 1955), as immoral as the bed-hopping heroine of "Pretty Mouth and Green My Eyes" (*New Yorker*, July 14, 1951), Bunny symbolizes Salinger's society: the corrupt, materialistic, loveless world of the grown-up where adult and adultery are synonymous. Against this world of false values, false gods, and "phonies" the misfit hero finds that his sense of taste is not enough.

The off-center vision of "The Inverted Forest" is further developed in the first Salinger story to gain any attention, "A Perfect Day for Bananafish" (*New Yorker*, January 31, 1948). In it, the Glass family is born when Seymour Glass, the eldest son in the family, commits suicide at the age of twenty-five. Developing from the mold of Joe Varioni, Vincent Caulfield, and Raymond Ford, Seymour becomes the prototype for the whole Glass family: sensitive, intelligent, imaginative, loving, combining a whimsical sense of humor and an overbearing sense of his own misfitness in the modern world. Like Holden Caulfield, he is too full of love, with no worthy object on which to bestow it. Salinger juxtaposes the delightful conversation Seymour has with the little girl on the beach with his complete inability to communicate with any of the adults around him. Seymour's tragic obsession with his own inability to communicate with the outside world and live with it on its own terms is what kills him and plagues the rest of the Glass family.

In "Uncle Wiggily in Connecticut" Walt Glass is the heroine's—[94] Eloise's—dead lover. Reminiscent of the earlier Lois Taggett, Eloise finds herself caught in a loveless marriage amidst a tawdry suburban environment. Like Holden and Seymour, she can find no object, she thinks, worthy of her love. Thus she loves nothing—neither husband, home, nor child—but the memory of Walt, who was killed in a senseless freak explosion in the war. The story, typical of Salinger's view of society, concerns not only the loss of love and communication but, most of all, the loss of innocence. Eloise's language is constantly impoverished by the mundane: by movies and clothes. Not only is the means of communication lacking but also the object of it. The irony lies in the discrepancy between Eloise's need to get outside of herself and the means and object left open to her: the insensitive, stupid girl friend, Mary Jane. Eloise's myopic daughter, Ramona, confronts her mother with her loss of innocence. Cut off from love, Ramona lives in an imaginary world colored by her thick glasses—her off-center vision. Her imaginary private symbols, Micky Mickareeno and Jimmy Jimmareeno, mirror not only her own loneliness but her mother's marital predicament. Eloise's attack on Ramona, the living reincarnation of Walt's innocence, results in the final insight—that innocence is unrecoverable. Her self-pity is externalized into a compassion that enfolds both innocents—Walt and Ramona. The only thing that remains for Eloise is to reaffirm the possession of innocence in the past: "I was a nice girl, wasn't I?"

If the children in "Down at the Dinghy" (Harper's, April 1949) and "For Esmé—with Love and Squalor" (New Yorker, April 8, 1950)— two of Salinger's finest stories—reaffirm Salinger's cult of innocence, then in "Teddy" (New Yorker, January 31, 1953) and "De Daumier-Smith's Blue Period" (Nine Stories) he offers a chance to recover lost innocence through mysticism. But "Teddy" is marred by an uncharacteristic slickness and "De Daumier-Smith..." suffers from a diffuseness of focus that blurs the effect of the mystical experience. The vagueness of the Experience—the revelation that "everybody is a nun"—is more sharply etched in "Franny," which by no coincidence returns to the firmer footing of the Glass family. On a college party weekend, Franny Glass goes through a crisis in which she repudiates the "phoniness," conformity, and meaninglessness of her collegiate friends. Alienated from her Ivy League boy friend and everything he represents, she turns inward, with the help of a mystical book about a Russian peasant who found God intuned with his heart beat when he repeated the "Christ prayer" over and over. Suffering from psychosomatic cramps induced by an environment she can no longer stomach, Franny rejects the comfort of a public restaurant for the awkward privacy of a lavatory, where, in a curiously fetal position, she can pray. The story resolves itself with a riddle: will Franny choose the way of the pilgrim or the way of the college student?

"Raise High the Roofbeam, Carpenters" (New Yorker, November 19, 1955) delves into the pre-suicidal days of Seymour Glass. That Salinger should resurrect Seymour is important not only because it sheds light on the earlier story, "A[95] Perfect Day for Bananafish," but because it holds the key to further evolution of the misfit hero. The problem becomes no longer one of merely co-existing with society but rather of living the good life. Indeed, this sprawling story—formless in contrast to earlier works like "A Perfect Day for Bananafish" or "Down at the Dinghy"—contains the element found in all of Salinger's stories. Present are the distraught misfit hero, unable to reconcile his Zen Buddhism with his society's Pragmatism; the mundane, misguided girl who cannot share her fiance's extraordinary world; the vulgar antagonist, insensitive and sophisticated enough to be harmful, insinuating that there is something homosexual about Seymour because he is too happy to show up for his own wedding; the narrator who tries to appear detached but obviously has a personal stake in Seymour's life; and the stifling environment in which love, communication and decent values have been lost.

Seymour says: "The human voice conspires to desecrate everything on earth." Indeed, all through Salinger's writing there is distrust of the spoken word: the conversation in "Uncle Wiggily in Connecticut" and the telephone calls in "A Perfect Day for Bananafish" and "Pretty Mouth and Green My Eyes" illustrate the hopelessness of trying to communicate by means of speech. At the same time, Salinger has made the written word the mode of communication for his hero. Joe Varioni is a writer; Raymond Ford a poet; and Teddy and Seymour keep diaries. A letter is the gift of communication in "Boy in France" (Saturday Evening Post, March 31, 1945), "A Girl I Knew" (Good Housekeeping, February 1948), "This Sandwich Has No Mayonnaise," and "For Esmé—With Love and Squalor." For Franny the important thing is her book. More lasting than speech, writing symbolizes both the honesty and the creativity of the artist. Like Stephen Dedalus and Tonio Kruger, but perhaps more like Kafka's Hunger Artist, Salinger's misfit hero is the artist, trying to reconcile his art to his soul.

If the artist communicates by writing, then the religious man communicates by silence: this is the paradox of Zen. Zen Buddhism places

its prime burden on the relationship between man and nature, between the "I" of Martin Buber and any object outside the "I"—the
"Thou." Without this essential relationship there can be no communication. Thus the "sound of two hands clapping" is the sound of the
relationship. Without either partner—call them subject and object if
you like—there can be no sound. The search for "the sound of one
hand clapping" comes to an end in the spiritual life. Thus art is the
way of the imagination and Zen is the way of the soul. Salinger is
primarily interested in the souls of his characters.

However, it is one thing to espouse the way of the soul and quite
another thing actually to follow it. In choosing the private world over
the public the hero has compromised the basic Western principle of
social responsibility. Salinger's heroes attempt not to compromise between the pure spiritual world and the corrupted mundane world
but rather to disaffiliate themselves from the public world and flee to
the private because they have confused the private world with the[96]
soul. Thus Holden would reject his home for a chance to act as a
catcher in the rye, a protector of children's innocence. But Holden
is really unqualified for life in the private world; he loves the outside
world too much and is too weak to really leave it. He remains as he
began: a remarkable adolescent going through a sensitive version of
growing pains. Seymour, likewise, is not strong enough for the way
of Zen. For all his excellent qualities he is unequipped to resolve the
idea of Zen with the fact of the public world in which he must live
daily. The way of the holy man is, truly, a difficult way, too difficult
for either Holden or Seymour. In this sense, Salinger's misfit who is a
hero is really a hero who is a misfit: a misfit in society because he refuses to adjust and a misfit in the private world because he cannot pass
through its "dark night of the soul." Too much a product of his
Western culture to follow Zen, the misfit hero makes the grave error
of assuming that there are only these two alternatives and that one of
them is unthinkable.

Salinger's choice for his hero is essentially a religious problem, that
is, the problem of finding moral integrity, love, and redemption in an
immoral world. We can illuminate the meaningfulness of this interpretation by comparing Salinger's last story, "Zooey" (New Yorker,
May 4, 1957), to T. S. Eliot's The Cocktail Party for the two works
are much closer than one would suspect. In setting up their respective
situations both Salinger and Eliot have used essentially the same pattern and relationships between their characters. In the play, Celia, a
sensitive young woman concerned with the futility of the meaningless
relationships she has established, is faced with the possibilities of her
salvation. Similarly, in "Zooey," we pick up Franny where we last left
her, still sick of her college environment, now at home, trying to decide whether to return to school or become a nun. When Celia says:

"I want to be cured / Of a craving for something I cannot find / And of the shame of never finding it," she also speaks for Franny, who is likewise caught between the necessity of getting out of the tawdry academic atmosphere and the sensed impossibility of ever leaving its environment. Similarly, when Celia says: "It no longer seems worthwhile to *speak* to anyone," it could very well be Franny talking.

Both Franny and Celia suffer from the same symptoms: frustration in love, loneliness and alienation, emptiness and failure. Celia says she feels she must "atone" for her failure while Franny actively does this by murmuring her prayer over and over in an attempt to regain what she feels she has lost. The two women are also presented with the same alternatives. The psychiatrist, Reilly, tells Celia that she must make a choice—"the form of treatment" he calls it—and that choice is between "reconciliation" with the world or rejection of it for the spiritual frontier. Similarly, Zooey tells Franny that she must choose between, in essence, becoming an actress or becoming a nun. It is significant that the terms are not social—the choice is not between being inner-directed or other-directed or between being an intellectual or an organization man—but rather spiritual: between one form of redemption and another.

When Celia asks what her duty[97] is, Reilly answers that whichever way she chooses will prescribe its own duty; when she asks which way is better, he answers that "Neither way is better. / Both ways are necessary. It is also necessary / To make a choice between them." When Zooey explains the terms to Franny he makes it clear that there is no right way but that the way for each person is determined by his desire or desirelessness. "You can't just *walk out* on the results of your own hankerings. Cause and effect, buddy, cause and effect. The only thing you can do now is *act*. Act for God, if you want to—be *God's* actress, if you want to."

Like Eliot, Salinger finds that the path through the world reaches salvation as quickly as the way to the frontier. However, whereas Celia chooses the frontier, Franny chooses the world. In the respective choices lies the difference between the Anglican and American tempers. While William Wiegand points out in the *Chicago Review* (Winter 1958) that Franny's embracing of "Christian love" is a reconciliation of the misfit hero, alias bananafish, to the world, it seems more likely that Franny's defection from the trail to the nunnery indicates a repudiation of the image of the misfit hero. Zooey tells her: "We're freaks, that's all. Those two bastards [Seymour and his twin brother, Buddy, the story's narrator] got us nice and early and made us into freaks with freakish standards, that's all. We're the Tattooed Lady, and we're never going to have a minute's peace, the rest of our lives, till everybody else is tattooed, too." The thing that counts in the religious life is "detachment" but the misfit hero has made the mistake of using his ego as the yardstick of holiness, replacing it with a holier-than-thouness. He has forgotten that "this is *God's* universe, buddy, not yours, and He has the final say about what's ego and what isn't." Like Job, the misfit hero is guilty of the deepest sin, spiritual pride: he has missed the distinction between being religious and being pious, between God's world and his personal world. Thus Franny is so busy searching her spiritual navel that she cannot recognize that her mother's bowl of chicken broth is "consecrated."

But a world of difference separates Franny from the earlier misfit heroes. Whereas Holden Caulfield runs away when he is in trouble, Franny goes home. The misfit hero, who had never been able to reconcile his unique vision with reality, could not find a level on which to communicate with his society. Whereas the riddle of how the moral person lives in an amoral society could only previously be solved in despair, suicide, "the quixotic gesture," or mystical revelation, for Salinger the family now holds the key. In a vast world full of misunderstanding and estrangement, the sensitive innocent must turn in towards the family to find the intimate love and communication that is so lacking in the outside world. It is through the family that he retains his equilibrium, balancing his moral integrity against the social pressures of the outside world. Thus the family becomes the place where self and society meet, where the moral and ethical realms are reconciled. The Glass family is a striking affirmation in an era dominated by the disintegrating families of O'Neill and Wolfe. The affirmation of the family and of the concept of social[98] responsibility is traditionally moral in the sense that it is traditionally Judeo-Christian.

Not only are *The Cocktail Party* and "Zooey" essentially Christian, they are both concerned with the family unit. Arthur Miller has pointed out that the basic weakness of *The Cocktail Party* is that its poetic diction is unsuited to its familial subject matter. Likewise, the form of Salinger's latest stories may weaken their effectiveness. For while the stories retain the semblance of the realism of "Uncle Wiggily..." and "A Perfect Day for Bananafish," they blur the distance between the author and his subject matter. This lack of aesthetic distance creates a personal interplay between author and character rather than between character and character. The stories hold the reader's attention not through the revelation of character but through revelation of author, reducing Salinger's audience to his afficianados and troubled adolescents in general. His audience becomes cultish, his predicament personal, his characters begin "to give off a little stink of piousness," and the meaningfulness of the problem and solution appears both too pat and even ludicrous in its juxtaposition to the facts that he gives. Can Zooey's aesthetic integrity be so brutalized because his mother won't leave the bathroom while he is taking a shower?

Although Salinger's recent experimentation with the short story form may seem strange and strained, we cannot afford to mark it off as merely an interesting but vain attempt at something different. Salinger is too much the conscious and conscientious craftsman to allow stylistic cuteness to dominate over serious content. But whatever the style, his stories continue to contain that off-center moral vision which allows the reader to discover the immensely significant in the apparently trivial and seemingly meaningless. Without bowing to the public opiates of sex, violence, and depravity, without assuming the popular poses of the "beat" or the blasé, he has quietly managed to present with humor and compassion the most significant and complex moral problems we face today.[99]

IHAB HASSAN

From *Radical Innocence: Studies in the Contemporary American Novel*. Princeton: Princeton University Press, 1961. Reprinted by permission of the publisher.

. . .

The dramatic conflict which so many of Salinger's stories present obviously does not lend itself to sociological classification. It is more loving and particular, and it partakes of situations that have been traditionally available to literature. The conflict, however, suggests a certain polarity between what might be called, with all due exaggeration, the Assertive Vulgarian and the Responsive Outsider. Both types recur with sufficient frequency to warrant the distinction, and their interplay defines much that is most central to Salinger's fiction. The[261] Vulgarian, who carries the burden of squalor, stands for all that is crude, venal, self-absorbed, and sequacious in our culture. He has no access to knowledge or feeling or beauty, which makes him all the more invulnerable, and his relationship to the world is largely predicated by Buber's I-It dyad. He or she can be rich or poor: Evelyn Cooney in "Elaine," Mrs. Ford and the Croftses in "The Inverted Forest," Sandra and Mrs. Snell in "Down at the Dinghy," Joanie in "Pretty Mouth and Green My Eyes," The Matron of Honor in "Raise High the Roofbeam, Carpenters," Maurice, Stradlater, or any number of others in *The Catcher in the Rye*. These, in a sense, are Spiritual Tramps, as Seymour called his wife in "A Perfect Day for Bananafish," though he might have better said it of her mother. The Outsider, on the other hand, carries the burden of love. The burden makes of him sometimes a victim, and sometimes a scapegoat saint. His life is like "a great inverted forest/with all foliage underground."[1] It is a quick, generous, and responsive life, somehow preserved against hardness and corruption, and always attempting to reach out from its isolation in accordance with Buber's I-Thou dyad. Often there is something in the situation of the Outsider to isolate him, to set him off, however slightly, from the rest of mankind. He might be a child or an adolescent, might wear glasses or appear disfigured, might be Jewish, though seldom is he as crippled or exotic as the characters of Capote and McCullers often are. His ultimate defense, as Rilke, to whom Salinger refers, put it, is defenselessness. Raymond Ford, Boo Boo Tannenbaum (Glass) and her son, Lionel, Seymour and other members of the Glass family, Holden and Phoebe, in the previous stories, are examples of that type.

The response of these outsiders and victims to the dull or angry world about them is not simply one of withdrawal: it often takes the form of a strange, quixotic gesture. The gesture, one feels sure, is the bright metaphor of Salinger's sensibility,[262] the center from which meaning drives, and ultimately the reach of his commitment to past innocence and current guilt. It is a gesture at once of pure expression and of expectation, of protest and prayer, of aesthetic form and spiritual content—as Blackmur would say, it is behavior that sings. There is often something prodigal and spontaneous about it, something humorous or whimsical, something that disrupts our habits of gray acquiescence and revives our faith in the willingness of the human spirit. But above all, it gives of itself as only a *religious* gesture can. In another age, Cervantes endowed Don Quixote with the capacity to perform it, and so did Twain and Fitzgerald endow their best creations. For the gesture, after all, has an unmistakably American flourish. The quest of American adolescents, as we saw, has always been for an idea of truth. It is this very idea of truth that the quixotic gesture is constantly seeking to embody. The embodiment is style in action: the twist and tang, the stammering and improvisations, the glint and humor of Salinger's language. Hence the examples of the deserted husband who memorizes his wife's farewell note backwards, the woman who, out of pity, starts smacking her husband at the sight of any dead animal, the man about to commit suicide who

---

[1] See J. D. Salinger, "The Inverted Forest," *Cosmopolitan*, December 1947, pp. 73–109.

makes up a story about bananafish for a little girl, the lover who calls the sprained ankle of his sweetheart Uncle Wiggily, the young man who insists on giving half a chicken sandwich to a stranger, the college girl who trains herself to pray incessantly and does so in the toilet of a restaurant, and the bridegroom who is too happy to appear at his wedding. Out of context these may well sound trite or crazy; in their proper place they are nodes of dramatic significance.

But gesture is language too. The quixotic gesture, the central dramatic metaphor, to which Salinger has committed himself defines the limits of his language and the forms his fiction takes. When the gesture aspires to pure religious expression—this is one pole—language reaches into silence. To a writer of[263] fiction, this is a holy dead end, much as the experiments of Mallarmé, say, impose a profane—that is, aesthetic—limit on the language of poetry. (One of "The Four Statements" of Zen, we recall, is: "No dependence upon words and letters.") When, on the other hand, the gesture reveals its purely satiric content—this is the other pole—language begins to lapse into sentimentality. This is the most persistent charge leveled against Salinger. Salinger's "sentimentality," however, is not obedient to the *New Yorker* doctrine of sardonic tenderness, which is really a way of grudging life emotions that the writer feigns to indulge. But if sentimentality means a response more generous than the situation seems objectively to warrant, then Salinger may choose to plead guilty. And he would be right to do so, for the spiritual facts of our situation invite us to reconceive our notions of dramatic objectivity, and the right kind of emotional excess, nowadays, can be as effective as the sharpest irony.

Between the poles of silence and sentiment, language reels and totters. Salinger's cumbersome experiments with character, tense, and point of view in his most recent stories betray his efforts to discover a language which can reconcile the wordless impulse of love to the discursive irony of squalor. In the past, while the quixotic gesture could still convey the force of his vision, reconciliation took the shape of the short story, that genre so richly exploited by the single lyric impulse seeking embodiment in dramatic form. But the quixotic motif seems no longer commensurate with the complex spiritual states by which Salinger has lately been possessed. Language must be refracted into its components—speech, letters, diaries, etc.—and the form of the short story itself must be broken and expanded into something that is neither a short story proper nor yet a novelette. In this development, the risks Salinger has taken with his art are contained in the risks he must take with his religious view of things.[264]

. . .

The Catcher in the Rye inevitably stands out as Salinger's only novel to date. As a "neo-picaresque," the book shows itself to be concerned far less with the education or initiation of an adolescent than with a dramatic exposure of the manner in which ideals are denied access to our lives and of the modes which mendacity assumes in our urban culture. The moving, even stabbing, qualities of the novel derive, to some extent, from Salinger's refusal to adopt a satirical stance. The work, instead, confirms the saving grace of vulnerability; its protest, debunking, and indictments presuppose a willing responsiveness on the part of its hero.

On the surface, Holden Caulfield is Salinger's typical quixotic hero in search, once again, of the simple truth. Actually, Holden is in flight from mendacity rather than in search of truth, and his sensitivity to the failures of the world is compounded with his self-disgust. In comparison with his dear, dead brother, Allie, a kind of redheaded saint who united intelligence and compassion as no other member of the family could, setting for all a standard of performance which they try to recapture, Holden seems intolerant, perhaps even harsh. The controlling mood of the novel—and it is so consistent as to be a principle of unity—is one of acute depression always on the point of breaking loose. But despair and depression are kept, throughout, in check by Holden's remarkable lack of self-interest, a quality of self-heedlessness which is nearly saintly, and by his capacity to invoke his adolescent imagination, to "horse around," when he is most likely to go to pot. These contrary pressures keep the actions of the novel in tension and keep the theme of sentimental disenchantment on the stretch; and they are sustained by a style of versatile humor.[272]

The action begins at a prep school from which Holden has flunked out, and continues in various parts of Manhattan; it covers some three days of the Christmas season. The big city, decked out in holiday splendor and gaudiness, is nevertheless unprepared for Holden's naked vision, and it seldom yields any occasions of peace, charity, or even genuine merriment. From the moment Holden leaves Pencey behind, leaves its Stradlaters and Ackleys, its oafs, creeps, and hypocrites, and dons his red hunting cap—why not, it's a mad world, isn't it?—we know that we are on to an adventure of pure self-expression, if not self-discovery.

In New York, it is once again the same story of creeps and hypocrites revealed in larger perspective. We hardly need to recapitulate the crowded incidents of the novel to see that Holden is motivated by a compelling desire to commune and communicate, a desire constantly thwarted by the phoniness, indifference, and vulgarity that surround him. He resents the conditions which force upon him the burden of rejection. In protest against these conditions, he has devised a curious game of play-acting, of harmless and gratuitous lying, which is his way of coming to terms with a blistered sensibility, and of affirming his values of truth and imagination. But above all, he is continually performing the quixotic gesture. Thus he socks Stradlater, who is twice his weight, because he suspects the latter of having seduced Jane Gallagher, without any consideration of the fact that she is the kind of girl to keep all her kings, at checkers, in the back row. He gives money away to nuns. He can read a child's notebook all day and night. He furiously rubs out obscenities from the walls of schools. And when Phoebe asks him very seriously what he would like to be, he muses on Robert Burns's song, "If a body meet a body coming through the rye," which he had heard a kid hum in the street, and answers back: "...I keep picturing all these kids playing some game in this big field of rye and all. Thousands of little kids, and nobody's around—nobody big, I mean[273]—except me. And I'm standing on the edge of some crazy cliff.... That's all I'd do all day. I'd just be the catcher in the rye and all. I know it's crazy...."[2]

A closer look at *The Catcher in the Rye* might allow us to separate its real from imaginary failings. Mr. Aldridge, for instance, taking his cue perhaps from Phoebe's comment to her brother, "You don't like *any*thing that's happening," has recently observed—Maxwell Geismar makes exactly the same point—that Holden "has objects for his contempt but no objects other than his sister for his love."[3] It is true that Holden has *more* objects for his contempt than his love—this is the expense of his idealism and the price of his rebellion. But it is impossible to overlook his various degrees of affection for Allie, his dead brother, for James Castle, the boy who was killed because he wouldn't retract a statement he thought true, for the kettle drummer at Radio City, the nuns at the lunch counter, the kid humming the title song, or even the ducks in the park, without missing something of Holden's principal commitments. And his answer to Phoebe, "People never think anything is anything *really*. I'm getting goddam sick of it," may do for those who find these commitments rather slim.[4] Nor can we disallow the feeling of pity which often modifies Holden's scorn, his pity for Ackley and the girls in the Lavender Room, or his confession to Antolini that he can hate people only part of the time, and that he quickly misses those whom he may have once hated. Holden, of course, is not in the least cynical; nor is he blind except to part of the truth which he can otherwise entertain so steadily. Still, there are those who feel that the novel accords no recognition to its hero, and that it fails to enlist our sense of tragedy. The lack of recognition, the

---

[2] J. D. Salinger, *The Catcher in the Rye* (New York, 1953), p. 130.
[3] John W. Aldridge, *In Search of Heresy* (New York, 1956), p. 130.
[4] *The Catcher in the Rye*, p. 129.

avoidance of conversion and initiation, is almost as inherent in the structure of the novel as it is consonant with the bias of the American novel of adolescence. The action of the book is recollected by Holden who is out West recuperating from his illness, and Holden only chooses to tell us "about this[274] madman stuff that happened to me around last Christmas"—nothing more.[5] He refuses to relate incidents to his past or to his character, and he refuses to draw any conclusions from his experience: "If you want to know the truth, I don't *know* what I think about it.... About all I know is, I sort of miss everybody I told about. Even old Stradlater and Ackley, for instance.... Don't ever tell anybody anything. If you do, you start missing everybody."[6] This is an embarrassed testament of love, full of unresolved ambiguities, the only lyrical and undramatic recognition the novel can afford. The partial blindness of Holden, which has been correctly attributed to Holden's juvenile impatience with the reality of compromise, is made more serious by Salinger's failure to modify Holden's point of view by any other. In *Joseph Andrews,* for instance, the innocence of Adams is constantly criticized by the tone of the book and the nature of its comic incidents. There is also some danger that we may be too easily disarmed by the confessional candor of Salinger's novel. When Holden says time and time again, "I swear to God I'm crazy," the danger is equally great in taking Holden at his word as in totally discounting his claim. Holden does succeed in making us perceive that the world is crazy, but his vision is also a function of his own adolescent instability, and the vision, we must admit, is more narrow and biased than that of Huck Finn, Parson Adams, or Don Quixote. It is this narrowness that limits the comic effects of the work. Funny it is without any doubt, and in a fashion that has been long absent from American fiction. But we must recall that true comedy is informed by the spirit of compromise, not intransigence. Huck Finn and Augie March are both, in this sense, closer to the assumptions of comedy than Holden Caulfield. This once understood, we can see how *The Catcher in the Rye* is *both* a funny and terrifying work—traditional distinctions of modes have broken down in our time—a work full of pathos in the original sense of the word. But suffering is a subjective thing, and the novel's sly insistence on suffering makes it a[275] more subjective work than the two novels which relate the adventures of Huck Finn and Augie March. Adventure is precisely what Holden does not endure; his sallies into the world are feigned; his sacrificial burden, carried with whimsey and sardonic defiance, determines his fate. The fate is that of the American rebel-victim.[276]

---

[5] *Ibid.,* p. 7.

[6] *Ibid.,* p. 159.

MAXWELL GEISMAR

. . . *Nine Stories,* in 1953, was a collection of the *New Yorker* stories which had already established Salinger's reputation with an elite group of magazine readers. Among these tales, "A Perfect Day for Bananafish" was notable for the unpleasant suicide of a disturbed war veteran.

Seymour Glass has shot himself, seated on the bed next to his sleeping wife. Shortly before this, while carrying on a whimsical conversation with one of Salinger's innocent little girls, he has pushed the child ever deeper into the Florida ocean. There are intimations of a murder before the suicide: and similarly in another well-known story in the collection called "Teddy," a jealous sister pushes a child prodigy into an empty swimming pool. Here the little genius has anticipated and even welcomed his own death, however, while here indeed the morbid, the more than[199] neurotic emotions which are implicit in Salinger's first novel take a more prominent place in his writing. The obsessive affection for little children has usually been accompanied, in the major writers, by other untoward elements of the psyche (child seduction, child rape), as witness Dostoevski, Dreiser, or Nabokov. But like the post-Freudian and revisionist psychologists of the Fifties, Salinger has also attempted to deny or reject the darker urges that are present in the idyl of pure childhood.

One of the best tales in the volume describes the drunken binge of an unhappy exurbanite wife, whose lonely little daughter kills her imaginary playmate, Jimmy Jimmereeno. Two other stories deal with the comfortable bourgeois New York Jewish society in which, again, the leading figures are called Ginie, Selena, Franklin, Eric, etc. That is to say, Jewish and not Jewish: this "assimilated" German-Jewish urban group, not wishing any longer to be identified with their religious and cultural minority group, whose bright children now attend the fashionable American Christian schools like "Miss Basehoar's." If Salinger has primarily been concerned with the pure, the isolated, the *causeless* child, one sees that he can describe the milieu of their origin very well indeed when he chooses to, even under its pseudonymic and self-protective coloring.

Or at least, up to a point. In "Down at the Dinghy," Boo Boo Tannenbaum, who, we are told, is "a stunning and final girl," dis-

121

covers that her son believes a "Kike" to be something that flies in the sky: a tricky little bit of anti-anti-Semitism. (Boo Boo and Seymour Glass are to be heard from again.) "For Esmé—with Love and Squalor" concerns a beautiful, dignified, precocious upper-class English maiden of thirteen who saves an American soldier from a nervous breakdown. There is no doubt of Esmé's grace and charm (or of her social standing), but only whether, in this case, an adolescent's romantic affection can replace the need for mental therapy. The young hero of "De Daumier-Smith's Blue Period" has a similar background: disturbed and Continental. The mother, divorced, remarried, has died in Europe. Back in New York, the second husband and the lonesome son have gradually discovered "that we were both in love with the same deceased woman."

What was curious about Holden Caulfield's chronicle, besides[200] the shadowy mother, was the absence of any father relationship at all. Perhaps here, through the device of the second husband or the "false father," the writer can express humorously and even gaily what was more difficult to describe seriously. At nineteen, at any rate, the present hero invents a "deceased wife," a false name, a small estate in the south of France, a kinship with Daumier and "poor Picasso," and goes off to teach art at an obscure correspondence school in Canada. The school and its inscrutable Japanese owners, and the types of students who use it, are all brilliantly described in the story; the young hero is engagingly and wildly adolescent, and falls in love, by mail, with a certain Sister Irma of St. Joseph's whose portraits of Christ have caught his fancy.

On a walk through the provincial town he is also fascinated by the window display of the local orthopedic appliances shop:

> Then something altogether hideous happened. The thought was forced on me that no matter how coolly or sensibly or gracefully I might one day learn to live my life, I would always at best be a visitor in a garden of enamel urinals and bedpans, with a sightless wooden dummy-deity standing by in a marked down rupture truss.

This is engaging and illuminating imagery; and perhaps the rupture-truss deity, before whom the hero has his moment of mystic insight, leads directly to the Eastern *gurus* who are invoked in Salinger's later and more famous short story "Franny," which took up considerable space in the *New Yorker* of January 29, 1955, and caused another minor sensation in the undergraduate (feminine) academic world. The central question was whether the story's heroine was pregnant, or insane, or both—or neither.

As in any good Scott Fitzgerald tale, it is the week end of the Yale game. The young men are waiting on the station platform for their dates. In his Burberry raincoat, Lane Coutell is reading Franny's passionate love letter and thinking that station-platform kisses are "rather inhibited in the follow-through." (The collegiate atmosphere is done very well.) Yet their dinner at Sickler's—a symbolic name—turns into a catastrophe. Lane is talking about his paper on Flaubert's concern for the *mot juste*. Franny, listening to him "with a special semblance of absorption," is overcome by her distaste for his vanity, his complacency. He is indeed a dreadful portrait of a college intellectual, who will become[201] a typical graduate student in English, a "section man," and then perhaps a minor contributor to the *Partisan Review*.

That is what Franny tells him in effect, as she feels her "destructive" impulses coming to the fore, with the disloyalty and guilt "which seemed to be the order of the day." (She has had to strain to write him her last [false] love letter.) Lane's self-absorbed egoism can't stand criticism; the conversation becomes a controversy. Up to this point the story is sharp and sensitive. Then comes the mysterious scene in Sickler's ladies' room, where Franny collapses:

> Without any apparent regard to the suchness of her environ-
> ment, she sat down. She brought her knees together very
> firmly, as if to make herself a smaller, more compact unit.
> Then she placed her hands, vertically, over her eyes and
> pressed the heels hard, as though to paralyze the optic nerve
> and drown all images in a voidlike black.... She held that
> tense, almost fetal position for a suspensory moment—then
> broke down. She cried for fully five minutes. She cried with-
> out trying to suppress any of the noisier manifestation of
> grief and confusion, with all the convulsive throat sounds
> that a hysterical child makes when the breath is trying to
> get up through a partly closed epiglottis. And yet, when fi-
> nally she stopped, she merely stopped, without the painful,
> knifeless intakes of breath that usually follow a violent out-
> burst-inburst. When she stopped, it was as though some
> momentous change of polarity had taken place inside her
> mind, one that had an immediate, pacifying effect on her
> body. Her face tear-streaked but quite expressionless, almost
> vacuous, she picked up her handbag from the floor, opened
> it, and took out the small pea-green clothbound book.

And, armed with this mysterious weapon of spiritual guidance, but periodically overcome by other symptoms of nervous collapse, she proceeds to tell her lover off.

It is not only him, it is his whole life of habits, values, standards that she cannot bear. She ends up not only with an indictment of upper-class American society, but almost of Western culture itself. "It's *ev*erybody, I mean. Everything everybody does is so—I don't know

—not *wrong*.... But just so tiny and meaningless and—sad-making." She thinks she is going crazy, she says; she is sick of "ego, ego, ego." While her teeth chatter, she explains that her little green book, *The Way of a Pilgrim,* is the story of a Russian peasant's attempt to find salvation through prayer. "Lord Jesus Christ have mercy on me," is the prayer[202] that Franny herself keeps repeating incessantly, while Lane, not impressed by her religious conversion, reeking of garlic from his frogs' legs, discusses his psychoanalytic paper on Flaubert, i.e., his own literary ego.

Here is the central conflict, in collegiate terms, of the life of re-nunciation versus—just what? For Lane is certainly not an artist (which also implies a form of self-renunciation) but closer to a boor. There are references in Franny's hysterical outbursts (she is more learned than one might suspect) to the Nembutsu sects of Buddhism and the Indian meditation on the "Om." "You get to see God. Something happens in some absolutely nonphysical part of the heart—where the Hindus say that Atman resides, if you ever took any Religion—and you see God, that's all." But Lane says it is really a matter of the most ele-mentary psy*chology,* and adds that she should take a rest in the room he has reserved for them. "When was that Friday night? Way the hell early last month, wasn't it?" And that maybe Franny's real trouble comes from another source. "Too long between drinks, to put it coarsely." Left alone, while he goes off to make the necessary arrange-ments, Franny begins to pray. "Her lips began to move, forming sound-less words, and they continued to move." It is the Jesus prayer she is saying, to keep herself from fainting again; but then why does the story also leave such an unpleasant or disagreeable impression?

It is mainly, of course, the trickiness. After Lane's parting words we are still left wondering whether the painful description of Franny's "fetal" position was the opening of pregnancy or of mystical incanta-tion. The descriptions both of Western materialism and Eastern spiritualism in Franny's adolescent terminology are hardly convincing, and her insistent tone finally loses her the original sympathy she had gained in the story. Both the central characters become almost equally unpleasant toward the close; and there are still more personal ele-ments of Salinger's own philosophic conflicts involved here. For the remaining obscurities in "Franny" were developed, if not entirely clarified, in its sequel, "Zooey," to which the *New Yorker* devoted even more space—almost the entire issue—about two years later, on May 4, 1957.[203]1

---

1 "Raise High the Roof Beam, Carpenters," in the *New Yorker* of November 19, 1955, tells the story of Seymour Glass's disastrous marriage to the girl, whose name is difficult to locate, on the other bed in "Bananafish,"—his wife, I mean, when he commits suicide. This is in fictional terms the best story in the series, because Salinger's philosophical and mystic preoccupations had not

"Zooey" is an interminable, an appallingly bad story. Like the latter part of "Franny," it lends itself so easily to burlesque that one wonders what the *New Yorker* wits were thinking of when they published it with such fanfare—or what they might not have done with it, were it published elsewhere. Yet in terms of Salinger's career, and of the fashionable school of writing which he represents, it is also a very illuminating story. One notices, first of all, the uneasy tone of the prose. The writer's artistic conscience is at war with the apparent urgency of his message. What is here offered, we are told, isn't really a short story at all, "but a sort of prose home movie, and those who have seen the footage have strongly advised me against nurturing any elaborate distribution plans for it."

True enough, and the tale is full of these uneasy insights, or with a kind of Woukian ambiguity, where the artist both is and is not responsible for what he is saying. For the narrator of the "prose home movie" turns out to be Buddy Glass (at least Salinger won't say he isn't), a brother of the late Seymour Glass and of Boo Boo Tannenbaum, both of whom we have met.

Risking the "aesthetic evil" of a footnote, Salinger indeed gives us a detailed chronology of the entire Glass family, including the dead twin Walt, and Waker, a Roman Catholic priest. One begins to realize that this is a sort of Yoknapatawpha County on Park Avenue. All of the Glass children have starred on the famous radio program "It's a Wise Child." They are all, apparently, prodigies (like the deceased and also famous Teddy, who should be related). And just as we remember that Boo Boo was "a stunning and final girl," so the present "hero" of the new story, Zooey, is "surpassingly handsome, even spectacularly so." Boo Boo has in fact described Zooey as "the blue-eyed Jewish-Irish Mohican scout"—an odd bit of childhood romance.

The Glass children all seem to admire each other no end. Zooey is indeed in the bathtub, reading Buddy's four-year-old letter, when the story finally begins to move (in its own static way), and when Mrs. Glass herself slips into the bathroom to[204] have a family conference with her handsome, talented, and naked son. (There is a shower curtain drawn between them, which apparently obviates both the oedipal and the pornographic factors here.) Franny Glass is still pursuing her nervous breakdown in the living room, and Zooey now repeats, in greater detail, the nature of her spiritual conflict, and the meaning of her quest for what is now a clear case of Zen Buddhism.

While Bessie Glass would appear to have all the anxious, doting traits of a Jewish matriarch, she turns out in fact to be a sort of mystic

---

yet got the better of his craftsmanship. But it is simply an entertaining tale, with rather morbid undertones, comment on which is omitted here since most of the material in it is repeated with far more emphasis in "Zooey."

Irish druidess. She is indeed the Ideal Mother, understanding, perceptive, wise in her eccentric way, hiding her grief for her two dead
sons, and crossing and uncrossing her remarkable legs throughout this
whole scene. But there are really only two people talking—or one—in
any given area of "Zooey," and now the camera moves on to the prone
and ailing Franny. Zooey has already dissuaded his mother from calling in a psychoanalyst ("Just think of what analysis did for Seymour.").[2] Now he instructs his sick sister that what is totally wrong
in her personal revolt against the Western ego is her inadequate view
of Buddha, the Indian Japam, and the Bible itself. (During this scene
Franny continues to fondle the altered tomcat Bloomberg, who is apparently the only honest Jewish character in the tale.)

Zooey proceeds to explain that she has never understood Jesus
himself from the time she was a child. "Your age has nothing to do with
what I'm talking about. There are no big *changes* between ten and
twenty—or ten and eighty, for that matter"—an interesting rationaliza-
tion for the perennial world of childhood. "You keep talking about
ego," he adds. "My God, it would take Christ himself to decide what's
ego and what isn't. This is *God's* universe, buddy, not yours, and he
has the final say about what's ego and what isn't." Moreover, Jesus was
far superior to[205] earlier prophets. Moses "was a nice man, and he
kept in beautiful touch with his God and all that—but that's exactly
the point. He had to keep in touch. Jesus realized there *is* no separa-
tion from God."

This is again an odd synthesis of Eastern and Western thought
which might not have the approval of Christian or Jewish scholars;
and yet Zooey's own final picture of Christ is closer to the religious
fantasies of a John Steinbeck or a Bruce Barton. "Jesus was a supreme
adept, by God, on a terribly important mission," he says:

> This was no St. Francis, with enough time to knock out a
> few canticles, or to preach to the *birds,* or to do any of the
> other endearing things so close to Franny Glass's heart. I'm
> being serious now, God damn it. How can you miss seeing
> that? If God had wanted somebody with St. Francis's consist-
> ently winning personality for the job in the New Testament,

---

[2] Salinger's description of a "good" analyst is couched, alas, in about the same
terms that Graham Greene uses for the Catholic analyst (another servant of
God) in *The Potting Shed*. But isn't this revisionist concept of psychoanalysis
contrary to Freud's whole scientific and antireligious orientation—as is the
modern fusion of depth psychology and Eastern mysticism in the disciples of
Jung, or even the recent Zen Buddhism itself of the Erich Fromm school?
But perhaps the primary historical function of psychoanalysis (to cut through
all these forms of supernatural myths, fantasies, illusions and prejudices) was
too ruthless, too cruel, for the civilizations which live on such illusions.

he'd have picked him, you can be sure. As it was, he picked
the best, the smartest, the most loving, the least sentimental,
the most un*imi*tative master, he could possibly have picked.
And when you miss seeing that, I swear to you, you're missing the whole point of the Jesus Prayer.

Isn't it odd, too, in Salinger's synthesis of Eastern and Western reli-
gions, that only the Jewish faith, like the Jewish father of the family,
should be barely mentioned, and in effect is omitted? Nevertheless
Franny, under the spell of this therapeutic magic, or that of Buddy's
continuous, insistent, repetitious, sermonizing lecture, somehow
achieves her peace of mind, and falls asleep.

There is no doubt also that Salinger is deadly serious about all
this, and that his continual use of collegiate phrases is no longer for
the purposes of satire, but of persuasion of his mainly collegiate
audience. Yet to read "Zooey" seriously is indeed like being in a
lunatic asylum, as the heroine says about the Glass family, where it is
difficult to distinguish between the doctors and the patients, as these
self-appointed spiritual saviors play out their dubious roles. What is
obvious of course is that these roles are all identical; and the literary
"personages" in the narrative are merely the splintered parts of the
same literary ego, persuading, opposing, convincing and arguing with
itself. Thus there is the almost deliberately static effect of the story:
the lack of all inner or outer action, the monotonous and repetitious
use of the same trite and paralyzed gestures—as though, finally, we
were hearing[206] one voice speaking endlessly in an empty room. This
is close to a catatonic tale.

And perhaps those buried monsters and horrors, always hinted at in
Salinger's work, are having their say here. *"Yes. Yes. Yes. All right.
Let me tell you something now, buddy ... Are you listening ... I'll tell
you a terrible secret. Are you listening to me?"* And yet "Zooey" is
also the logical climax of Salinger's career to this point. We have
noticed the narrow range of his literary orbit, its uneasy base, its super-
structure of sham. This predominantly Jewish middle-class urban
circle, which ends up with its exotic Irish and druidic thespians! This
inner psychological world of highly confused parental images, of ef-
fusive, sentimental and false sibling affection, which arrives at a Super
Mother and a whole clan of brilliant child prodigies! The family name
of Glass could hardly be better as a symbol of the pervading narcissism
of all these identical "characters"—their ego-bound armor of self-
vanity which is so illusory and so fragile.

Nowhere in this whole literary scene is there a genuine parent, or
perhaps a genuine child. The true existence of the "glass" family is
indeed on the perennial radio program of the Wise Child. And perhaps the almost compulsive naturalism of "things" in "Zooey" is the
writer's unconscious attempt to substitute a material solidity of fur-

nishings for the missing social, economic, and psychological bases of his craft. Very likely these stories represent the writer's search, too, for his lost origins. Yet this family is still so evasive in its origins, so histrionic in its nature, so unnaturally handsome, talented, beautiful, wise, and sensitive in all its component parts (parents, children, furnishings, atmosphere), and so brilliantly artificial in the end! It also represents the failure of the writer really to understand his own, true, life experience and to fulfill himself.

Is this indeed the "terrible secret" that is contained and never revealed in the tormented latest story of Salinger's? For a serious writer it could be. The buried depths of the past, which are the core, the source, the dark and ever-fresh quarry of his work, have failed. Thus, too, the satiric study of formal American education, with which Salinger opened his career, has its own limited focus. It is not really concerned with all those jerks, morons, and queers that Holden Caulfield feels sorry for. It is directed at the failure of this educational system to understand the solitary "creative"[207] rebel who protests against it. And Salinger's scathing references to the "normalcy" of those people who read the *Times,* care about the H-bomb, join the Westport or Oyster Bay Parent-Teachers' Association (not Bronx, Brooklyn, or Manhattan) proceeds from the same source. This is an Exurbanite Radical Party of One.

We might say much the same thing about Salinger's disdain for the mass entertainment of Broadway and Hollywood from the superior vantage point of the *New Yorker* school of entertainment. Gifted, sensitive, perceptive, such high verbal talents as, say, John Cheever, Irwin Shaw or Edward Newhouse, among the *New Yorker* Impressionists exist in a cultivated and most knowledgeable void. Maybe Salinger's real trouble is simply to be the brightest of all these bright children. "Always, always, referring every goddam thing that happens right back to our lousy little egos," says Zooey, in sober truth. But what a perfect solution Salinger's mode of Zen Buddhism offers for this uneasy and unresolved conflict. In favor of a higher ego renunciation, it "transcends" all the solid material facts of environment and personality which this writer has ignored or evaded in his own literary career. In behalf of a kind of oceanic moral grandeur, it dispenses with any attempt at self-knowledge.

In a desperate spiritual revulsion against a devouring infantile egoism, is the answer really to repudiate our whole notion of Western individuality? Is there really no such thing (as Zooey tells Franny) as time or change or growth in our concept of human personality? In the Zen quest for "No-Knowledge" (as Buddy Glass tells his split-half Zooey) is it true that all legitimate religious study must lead to unlearning "the illusory differences between boys and girls, animals and stones, day and night, heat and cold"? Then indeed Lord Jesus Christ have mercy on us—and perhaps we should also invoke the practical, hard-headed, wrathful Jehovah whom Salinger has always repudiated. For the universe surely has a final transcendent unity. But meanwhile, here on earth, it is the legitimate business of the writer, in his mortal and un-Zenish career, to make clear just what those "illusory" differences are between boys and girls, day and night, animals and stones.

"Cleverness was his permanent affliction," the latter part of Salinger's literary personality (whom we might call Zen Buddy)[208] has also announced, in another of those brilliant half-insights which never make an artistic whole. And we may remember that little Teddy himself, the first of these precocious Eastern mystics, was attracted to Oriental philosophy just because it negated the "mind" which had distinguished him in favor of the pure and primary world of childhood sensation. That lost world of childhood indeed to which somehow or other, Salinger, like the rest of the *New Yorker* school, always returns! That pre-Edenite community of yearned-for bliss, where knowledge is again the serpent of all evil: but a false and precocious show of knowledge, to be sure, which elevated without emancipating its innocent and often touching little victims.... The root of the matter is surely here, and perhaps all these wise children may yet emerge from the nursery of life and art.[209]

MICHAEL WALZER

"In Place of a Hero," *Dissent*, VII (Spring 1960), 156–162. Reprinted by permission of *Dissent*.

Young people today have no spokesmen. The day of the youth league and its ideology seems to be over. Today we have the club again, and the gang, and perhaps the family. It might even be wrong to say that the young have heroes—models of courage, skill, commitment or self-sacrifice. Bright middle-class teenagers often have a developed sensitivity to each other's problems, but are very unlikely to require heroic activity from their friends. Young people do sometimes have *successes:* short-run Horatio Algers of the entertainment industry, eighteen year old novelists, precocious females demure and impure. These are even sought out, by men who know the market. But among the young themselves, they are usually the objects of a very cynical admiration; they have "made it"—which is to say: they have been made.

Ideology, heroism, success: none of these seems sufficiently compelling. For the young today, the importance and excitement of the adult world have become somewhat problematic. On the one hand this can lead to that odd combination of indifference and professionalism which one sometimes encounters in college students. On the other hand, it produces an earnest confusion, less often critical than nostalgic, which contemplates without enthusiasm or alternatives its possible maturity.

Some sense of this confusion and of the painful sincerity that goes with it is necessary in order to understand the phenomenon of J. D. Salinger, the writer most admired and read by many young people today. In one sense, Salinger represents the indulgence of a mood; but he is also the confidant of those who indulge the mood. Affectionate and tender, he speaks to the adolescent soul with urgent but reassuring intimacy. Yet he is also full of advice. He understands the ways in which growing up is a misfortune, a process of compromise and surrender. Reconciliation, however, and not resistance is his eventual concern: he is whimsical, all right, but not absurd. His opening theme is childhood lost, his conclusion is a half-mystic, half-sentimental resignation—with an ultimate glimpse of childhood regained. Finally, he is successful, appealing and comforting because he suggests a kind of reconciliation with the adult world which is at the same time an evasion of worldliness.

It is in grateful recognition of this evasion that many young people have accepted Salinger's characters, Holden Caulfield as a brother and Seymour Glass as a private and sainted memory. Holden, it should be remembered, had his last fling at sixteen; Seymour committed suicide[156] at thirty-one. The two events have the very moderate virtues of aimlessness and failure—we don't after all want moral lessons—but in their retelling, Salinger slips into sentimentality, contrived whimsy and a cagey, esoteric piety. So the academic critics, committed as they are to the surface seriousness of things, call Holden a pilgrim, and undoubtedly one of them will shortly grasp the somber truth that Seymour is a martyr and a saint.

This portentousness is Salinger's own fault—perhaps his intention— and it surely misrepresents the young; it even misrepresents Holden and Seymour. For precocious piety and innocent goodness are not yet wisdom, resourcefulness, or moral conduct; they cannot motivate martyrdom or, by themselves, make pilgrimage significant. They are qualities which remain to be tested, to be embodied and sharpened by worldly encounter. Salinger, however, turns them into the standardized equipment of a cautious, wistful rebel. When the earnest and uncertain young men identify with Holden Caulfield, they are expressing a deeply felt discontent. But it is a discontent devoid of all appetite for adult satisfaction. It seems on the one hand to lack purpose and on the other hand to be free from all anxiety about purposelessness. It lacks, above all, just that moral irascibility which was once thought the truest sign of youth. This vague rebelliousness is Salinger's material —what he both truly expresses and badly exploits. He cultivates a sense for its style, and he adds to its gentle ineptitude an engaging piety, at once sentimental and exotic. He does not, of course, suggest any actual confrontation between the discontented and the world of their discontent.

II

Salinger's characters are not heroic in part because they are members of the family. They are members, almost, of a Victorian clan— the patriarch vague or missing, the clan more of a fraternal coterie— and it is familial feeling which provides the background for the affection, honesty, and love which he seeks to describe. The gang would not do, for the gang exists in the jungle, its energy is already worldly. Salinger's family is an alternative to worldliness, a place of dependence and protection, a safe foundation for fantasy. Out in the world, Holden is a delightful and an inventive liar; he resembles at moments the characters in some recent English comic novels. Like them, he has nothing to tell the truth about. But to his ten year old sister, he can explain—at length and with *sincerity*—how he really feels. Holden, that is, has someone to tell the truth to; in this sense, at least, Salinger may well be a prophet. The English have not yet advanced so far that they can recognize the family as a retreat.

But Holden explains himself also to us—the painful readers—and it is to us that Buddy Glass addresses his tense and emotional reminiscence. "If you really want to hear about it... What I mean... If you want to know the truth..." Salinger's artfulness is best revealed in his ability to reconstruct the circumstances and sentiments of teenage revelation: sit down a minute, I want to tell you everything.[157] He tirelessly reads us his family mail, prints fragments from the diaries of the dead Seymour, relates the unassorted jottings of his brothers and sisters. He gathers his stories through a presumably random (but he assures us, total) recall, and pays a public price for the remembering. He drags us into his living room for "home movies"—I think of Salinger as the only modern writer with a living room—and there we sit, silent members. He is insistently intimate, urgently garrulous, wordily familiar. For Salinger this familiarity has a moral (as well as a literary) motive, and that motive is affection. He seeks to draw us into the clan, to bind us by the somewhat tendentious (not to say, onesided) heatedness of his intimate, utterly candid communications. There is not a drop of cold blood in his veins.

Outside the family "people never believe you," as Holden says. He means adults and he is right enough; adults are suspicious, and children, if they have a native honesty, have also a native gullibility. Salinger is incapable even of suggesting the virtues of the wary, artful adult. In the past Americans discovered a kind of heroism in the tight-lipped, middle-aged man who combined reticence, competence and secret goodness. He was a "tough guy," and his toughness paid awkward tribute to experience; one was not born resourceful and independent. But today, Salinger seems to say, the only contrast to the innocence and fervor of the child is the affectation, the cruel conventionality, the phoniness of the adult world. The adult is not "real"; he lives amidst sham.

But not sham at all: that is what one would like, for it is at least the proper opposite of innocence and sincerity. If children are candid, then let adults be hypocrites and the war of generations rage. But neither Holden's complaint, nor that of Franny Glass, is about hypocrisy; they are not really concerned with the lie, nor with actual cruelty. It requires something like moral firmness to resent hypocrisy, and though Holden has, as do all of Salinger's children and, I would guess, many of his readers, a natural sense of the sweet and the good, Holden is no moralist. His true concern is with foible, affectation, minor pomposity, casual carelessness—all of which combine to make this a jungle of fallible (but not ferocious) animals. The jungle itself, however, is no part of Holden's experience. Nor of Franny's; and when her brother tells her that every fat woman is Jesus Christ (and hence not to be resented), it is a counsel of imperfection which bears little relationship to the real imperfections of the world. Love, he tells her, can transcend foible and fatness alike: *it certainly had better.*

So the professor who goes into the men's room to muss up his hair before class is after all no villain. Nor is the Ivy Leaguer in the theater lobby who "said the play *itself* was no masterpiece, but that the Lunts, of course, were absolute angels." With them, one can make emotional peace. But surely the hypocrite and the moralist have another difficulty, and a fairly simple one: they are permanently at odds, irreconcilable. This occurs to none of Salinger's characters, and for that reason I don't believe it is fair to say that they are simply unspoiled; I think they are untouched.[158]

At the same time as the child approaches the adult world, he escapes into fantasy. Holden's fantasies are relatively modest, though they bear a close relationship to the religious aspirations of Salinger's later characters: Holden dreams of being a "catcher in the rye," the defender of children at play, or a gas station attendent in the west, deaf, dumb and solitary. Now these are obviously not alternatives to his inevitable fate; his older brother, a writer, is already "out in Hollywood...being a prostitute." Still, if fantasies were alternatives, they would not be fantasies. It would surely be foolish to wish that Holden dream instead of a better social order, or of revolutionary heroism. His own dreams are attractive enough: childlike, comfortless, intransigent. What is disturbing, however, is that his dreams do not lead him to any kind of adventure, not to anything at all but casual encounter and sensitive recoil. As Seymour's mother-in-law says, he doesn't relate. Salinger's characters can't like or even know anyone they don't love—*who isn't in the family, for chrissake*.

If this is really true, then why doesn't Holden set out for that gas station in the west? He might be a beat traveller. That, I suppose, is the real alternative and it is not especially interesting. Holden, instead, goes home to his ten year old sister; he doesn't want adventure, any more than do most of Salinger's readers; he wants affection. He will become an adult gently, carrying with him in the phony world only a single moral image, the image of childlike simplicity.

One of Salinger's most enthusiastic critics, Arthur Mizener, with a revealing inability to imitate that simplicity, has suggested that the writer's search is for the Good American. I'm inclined to agree, despite the capital letters. The concept is worth examining. The Good American wears short pants, preferably; he's not too tough ("I'm a pacifist, if you want to know the truth"); he's a little precocious and entirely inexperienced and he goes under as soon as he encounters America. "I mean it's very hard to meditate and live a spiritual life in America." A rebel in a world he scarcely saw.

III

Since Holden's last fling, Salinger has written almost entirely of the Glass family, a clan of seven precocious children, of Irish-Jewish stock and distinctly Buddhist tendencies. The main theme of these stories has been love. Love is the bond which holds the seven children together—and love, along with a touch of friendly condescension, is what binds them even to their parents. The family here is a mythical gang, truly fraternal, truly affectionate; it is as if, remembering Holden's loneliness, Salinger is determined never again to permit one of his characters to be alone.

The precocity of Salinger's children takes many forms: they learn foreign languages with amazing ease and write poetry in Japanese. But the most important form is an extraordinary religious and mystical insight. I think it fair to say that love for Salinger is either familial or Christlike; it is the love of brothers and sisters—or of brethren. The [159] last of these is obviously the more difficult, and Salinger sensibly recommends but does not describe it. He writes of erotic love not at all, and it is worth at least entertaining the idea—though it contradicts many of the operative assumptions of our culture—that his young readers are really not interested in it, that they are entirely satisfied with the love of Holden and his sister or of Zooey and Franny.

Marriage in Salinger's stories is a sorry affair; it takes place only after childlike love is finished or surrendered. Seymour marries in what seems to have been a burst of purely private ecstasy and mystic condescension. He needed, he thought, the "undiscriminating mind" of his wife; she would represent and embody his commitment to the ordinary. His wife Muriel married out of "a primordial urge to play house permanently." Seymour's suicide, in one sense at least, was an escape from a woman he had neglected to meet. Towards her Salinger is pitiless, even (or especially) when he is being kind, and yet, except for Sister, Muriel is his only woman. Poor thing, she has neither mystery nor wisdom; neither innocence nor whimsy. She is at home in the world, the phoney world, and therefore no part of Salinger's fervent household.

But reconciliation with the ordinary world there must be, else Salinger's affection would have curdled long before now, and his readers, who can have little taste for bitterness, moved on. Seymour's marriage was an apparently unsuccessful rehearsal for this reconciliation. But his suicide was less a confession of failure than a whimsical withdrawal from the commitment. His brothers and sisters continue the effort to invest the conventional world with a spiritual value they know to be peculiarly their own. If only they can believe it, the fat woman *is* Jesus Christ—though it is not, after all, necessary to marry her. Commitment can happily take less physical forms (and withdrawal less drastic ones); characteristically, these forms are occupational. Zooey Glass becomes a television actor; Buddy Glass, Salinger's favorite narrator and the writer of the family, teaches English at a small, upstate New York girls' college. His withdrawal is signified by his unelectrified, unwinterized cottage, on the other side of the mountain. At the very end of Salinger's last story, Buddy describes, in an amazingly pretentious paragraph, the true nature of reconciliation:

> I have an impulse...to say something mildly caustic about the twenty-four young ladies, just back from big weekends at Cambridge or Hanover or New Haven, who will be waiting for me in Room 307, but I can't finish writing a description of Seymour...without being conscious of the good, the real. This is too grand to be said (so I'm just the man to say it), but I can't be my brother's brother for nothing, and I know—not always, but I *know*—there is no single thing I do that is more important than going into that awful Room 307. There isn't one girl in there, including the terrible Miss Zabel, who is not as much my sister as Boo-Boo or Franny. They may shine with the misinformation of the ages, but they shine. This thought manages to stun me: There's no place I'd really rather go right now than into Room 307. Seymour once said that all we do our whole lives is go from

one little piece of Holy Ground to the next. Is he *never*
wrong?

Yes, he is wrong. There is a great deal of ground that is not
holy,[160] acres of it—if you will just look. What is most objectionable
in the passage above is its terrible inclusiveness. I don't doubt that
every good teacher, when he goes into Room 307, must—sometimes—
feel something of what Salinger has described; but if he begins to
imagine that every girl in class is his sister I can only suggest resistance.
But Salinger is wholehearted; Room 307 undoubtedly represents the
whole world; it must be indiscriminately "awful" and indiscriminately
"holy." In a similar way, Buddy is terribly superior and infinitely
condescending, and his embrace must be all the more total for the emotional distance from which it is undertaken.

Love at a distance, whimsical appreciation ("the terrible Miss
Zabel"), manages to combine commitment and withdrawal; I would
guess that it makes both marriage and suicide unnecessary. But what
does it do to the quality of love? In Salinger's stories love, familial and
Christlike together, is primarily the habit and the wisdom of precocious children. It is almost inevitably, given Salinger's style and his
subject matter, a bit precious. It is also indiscriminate and uninvolved.
"They don't seem able to love us," Teddy says of his parents, "unless
they can keep changing us a little bit." He loves them, on the other
hand, with no such demands. Preciousness is even more revealing. As a
small boy, Buddy glows to tell us, Seymour refused to go to the barber-
shop when he thought his neck was dirty, for fear of hurting the
barber's feelings. Holden is a little bit in love with "old Jane" because
when they play checkers she won't move her kings out of the back row.

Love is also made a matter of mystic feeling and insight, but of
this I will offer no examples. Salinger has announced that he is holding oriental cards—in footnotes and occasional esoteric references he
has specified, presumably for the learned, which cards those are—but
he has not yet played his hand. Holding exotic cards is something like
refusing to move one's kings from the back row. It's a testimony to
one's unusual self, but it has little to do with other people.

IV

Whimsy and religion are Salinger's ploys. He does not mean them
to indicate willfulness, that is too harsh, nor mere childishness, that is
too unimportant; nor morality, that is too difficult, and not pure
contemplation, that would be farfetched. He means them to indicate
superiority. Whimsy is the caprice of the precocious; religion, their
secret insight. For such people does Salinger write: gentle, unconventional people, who find themselves behaving exactly like everyone else,
but who know that they are different, if only because they remember

that once they were young. But is that really such a precious or exclusive memory? Perhaps it is, and perhaps that moment of uncertainty before a young man surrenders himself to higher education and total organization is as important as Salinger's prose suggests. But I doubt that the moment is adequately represented by whimsy, or that it can survive in reminiscence, or be resurrected in esoteric piety.

The numerous silent members of the Glass family, Salinger's ardent[161] readers, share a kind of emotional superiority, which, one must admit, has little that is worldly in it. They pursue their careers with a sense of grace, that is, with an assurance of style. They are reckless, but only in imagination; after all, they were rebels once. They are painfully sincere, which is to say, loquacious; and—their truest mark—they are whimsically discontented, that is, they complain only about unimportant things.

Membership in this fervent household, however, is for the good alone. And here I think Salinger and his admirers must be taken seriously. Goodness for many of us has always implied activity, vigor, commitment. Good men—let me put it strongly—are energizing centers of ethical action. This is simply not so for Salinger, and presumably it is not so for most of his readers. Goodness for them seems rather a matter of personal style and impulse; its quality is unpretentious, naive (indeed, willfully so), sincere, whimsical. It imitates the child because he presumably has these qualities naturally and indulges them freely; he represents the absence of convention and corruption. That is not, of course, because he is corruptible. But what is for him a merely temporary condition can easily become a permanent posture. The posture is not entirely incompatible with world activity, but questions of ambition, work and conflict are evaded; the engaging precocity of the *wunderkind* makes them all seem irrelevant.

Salinger's idea of goodness is another version of disaffiliation, but it is the happiest version, and the easiest, because it makes disaffiliation a secret. Who, indeed, would guess that S. never moves his kings out of the back row? So far as society is concerned, the earnest, uncertain young man goes underground. But not to cultivate the resources of the rebel, not to test his capacity for silence or for patience. The underground is his irregular home, a unique realm of security and affection, sharply contrasted with the worlds of Hollywood, advertising, the organization. Up above, the young man may lie, it is a bit of whimsy; he may prove querulous, it is an indulgence; he may be a success, it doesn't matter; but he will not be active, involved, driving, lustful. He is the first among the disaffiliated to give up cult of experience, and therefore he is permanently untried. But for his readers, perhaps, that is Salinger's greatest appeal. I said above that he is seemingly incapable of cold-bloodedness; surely his readers understand this and appreciate it. Their lack of ambition is also an absence of taste for danger, even for the simple dangers of everyday human encounter. But what will their love come to, and what their goodness, if they do not calculate and take risks?[162]

DAVID L. STEVENSON

From "J. D. Salinger: The Mirror of Crisis," *The Nation*, CLXXXIV (March 9, 1957), 215–217. Reprinted by permission of the author and *The Nation*.

. . .

Salinger is surely one of the most skillful practitioners of the *New Yorker* short story or sketch. And, invidious critics aside, his sketches show it to be, at its best, one of the truly distinctive and definable fictional types of mid-century American letters. This kind of story contains no more than two or three characters, seen always at a moment of crisis in one of their lives. The concentration is on the crisis: the relationships which have led to it are indistinct, only suggested by the tone of the dialogue, by characters' momentary actions and gestures. The Salinger-*New Yorker* story is always a kind of closet scene between Hamlet and his mother with the rest of the play left out. It accomplishes its shock of surprise, and it evokes our emotions, by a frugal underplaying of plot and event, by its very minimizing of narrative. The reader is usually not projected into the problems of its characters because he is not given enough of the fabric of their lives to make such projection possible.

What a Salinger story *does* involve the reader in is something quite different. It is his awareness that the crisis of the sketch is a generic one of our time and place. The crisis of the usual *New Yorker* story may be fairly casual, and we have come to expect a Salinger story to be more stern in its implications because its roots are stronger and probe more deeply. But its crisis runs true to form. Salinger does not take you out of yourself into a living, substantial world of fiction. He throws you back into your own problems, or into an awareness of them in your contemporaries. His characters do not exist in a rich narrative, in a detailed setting, so that they become wholly separable, fictional beings. Rather they give us a feeling of our own sensitivity to compensate for their lack of created density.

One can best illustrate this quality of a Salinger story by comparing his *New Yorker* sketch "Pretty Mouth and Green My Eyes" with
Hemingway's "The Short Happy Life of Francis Macomber." The two
stories offer the same basic character relationships: passively suffering
husband, aggressively lustful wife, and casual, opportunistic lover. In
Hemingway's version, however, the characters are embedded in a full,
complex plot in which motive and event are made inexorably overt.
The tensions of the characters are in open balance for the reader, and
the husband's declared failure of nerve is what provokes his wife's
ruthless retaliation in taking a lover. The Macombers exist in the
round as "created" individuals in a self-contained narrative which
could be translated into mandarin and remain comprehensible.

Part of the virtue of "Pretty Mouth and Green My Eyes," on the
other hand, is that it is not a self-contained narrative. We know of
the characters only that they are apartment dwellers in New York. They
exist as voices on a telephone to illustrate the desperate irony of a
husband calling his wife's latest lover, after a party the three of them
have attended, at the moment when the lover is in bed with the wife.
The tearing crisis of the story is the husband's slow realization, as he
complains in hideously maudlin, drunken terms of his wife's infideli-
ties, that he has put his own self-respect beyond the point of sal-
vage.[215] Salinger's characters, here, come alive *New Yorker* fashion
through the skillful verisimilitude of their conversation. But, like E. B.
White's famous figure in "The Door" (also untranslatable into mandarin), they have social rather than narrative roots. They are important
to us in direct proportion to our recognition of them as generic sketches
of our urban, childless, apartmented men and women, alienated by
the hectic nature of their lives from all quiet interflow of love and
affection.

One significant element in the structure of a Salinger story, then,
and a source of his power over us, is that his characters come alive in
our recognition of them. In complementary fashion, an equally significant element is the effect on us of the special kind of crisis he asks
us to identify. As in "Pretty Mouth and Green My Eyes," it is a crisis in
a character's life that results from an erosion of personality peculiar to
upper middle-class, mid-century America. It is related to our sense of
the heightened vulnerability of men and women to emotional disaster.

I am not prepared to argue that the Salinger species of crisis is
unique, and that other ages did not feel themselves alienated from
inner security and outward affection. *Hamlet* alone would suffice. I
should only assert that in our time and place the individual estranged
from his fellows seems peculiarly understandable and therefore touching to us. If one needs outside documentation, I cite the fact that no
age but our own has found a partial picture of itself in such a sociological study of estrangement as David Riesman's *The Lonely Crowd*. It

is not that we, as a generation, are defeated, or without will. Perhaps it is merely that our religion, our family ties, our cultural traditions now give us a lighter armor than our predecessors wore.

At any rate, Salinger's fiction convicts us, as readers, of being deeply aware of a haunting inconclusiveness in our own, and in contemporary, emotional relationships—members all of the lonely crowd. His characters exist outside the charmed circle of the well-adjusted, and their thin cries for love and understanding go unheard. They are men, women and adolescents, not trapped by outside fate, but by their own frightened, and sometimes tragi-comic, awareness of the uncrossable gulf between their need for love and the futility of trying to achieve it on any foreseeable terms.

Salinger's short stories are all variations on the theme of emotional estrangement. In "Down at the Dinghy," a small boy runs away when he overhears his father referred to as a "kike." In "Uncle Wiggily in Connecticut," two women, unsuccessful adventurers in love, let a Connecticut afternoon drift away on highballs and reminiscences, while the timid child of one of them retreats farther and farther into compensatory fantasy as the two women get progressively more sodden. In "A Perfect Day for Banana Fish," a young soldier released from an army hospital confronts his wife's complicated indifference during their first reunion. When he is forced to weigh a small child's warm, intuitive sympathy against his wife's society prettiness, he shoots himself. The actions of the characters in all these stories could seem arbitrary, judged by the sketchiness of Salinger's narrative. In fact, however, the actions seem real and shocking because they are the kind of thing we can anticipate from the needs and stresses we share at least in part with the characters.

Salinger's most ambitious presentation of aspects of contemporary alienation, and his most successful capture of an American audience, is in his novel *The Catcher in the Rye*. It is the brief chronicle of Holden Caulfield, a sixteen-year-old boy who escapes to New York after flunking out of his third prep school. The novel is written as the boy's comment, half-humorous, half-agonizing, concerning his attempt to recapture his identity and his hopes for belonging by playing a man-about-town for a lost, partially tragic, certainly frenetic weekend. *The Catcher in the Rye* is a full-length novel, and yet gives much the effect of his shorter pieces. Its dimensional depth is extrinsic to the narrative, and is measured by the reader's response to the dialogue, and the background of city America. It is supplied by one's recognition that Holden Caulfield, sensitive, perceptive, is too aware of the discrepancies between the surface intentions and the submerged motives of himself and of his acquaintances to feel at ease in any world. Through him, Salinger has evoked the reader's consciousness[216] of indefinable rejections and rebellions that are part of the malaise of our times.

As we have come to expect from Salinger's other work, the main devices of characterization in *The Catcher in the Rye* are an apparently effortless verisimilitude of dialogue and an unerring sense of the appropriate in details of gesture, of bodily movement. There is a further fictional device, used elsewhere in his short stories, but of paramount importance in his novel in creating a hold on the reader. It is his use of almost Chaplin-like incidents and dialogue, half-amusing, half-desperate, to keep his story always hovering in ambivalence between comedy and tragedy. Whenever a character approaches hopelessness in a Salinger sketch, he is getting there by the route of the comic. It is usually both the character's way of holding on for a moment longer (as when the husband in "A Perfect Day for Banana Fish" goes out of his way to insult a proper dowager just before he kills himself) and, at its sharpest, a way of dramatic irony, a way of heightening the intensity of a character's predicament (as when Holden attempts to be bored with sex to get rid of a prostitute). But no single scene from his novel completely demonstrates this peculiar strain of comedy in Salinger: it pervades, seeps into, almost every incident.

When one is reading Salinger, one accepts his carefully placed "New Yorkerish" style and tone, and surrenders one's mind almost completely. It is only when you put the story aside and turn to other contemporary writers and to other fictional methods and techniques that you begin to wonder whether the immediacy and vividness of Salinger might be limited in power. Nowhere in Salinger do we find ourselves plunged into the emotional coiling and recoiling provoked by passages from Styron's novel, *Lie Down in Darkness*. Nowhere in Salinger is a character moved against the murky intensity-in-depth of a Nelson Algren Chicago scene, in *The Man with the Golden Arm*. Nowhere is a character revealed by the great clots of heterogeneous detail yoked together in single crowded sentences, as by Saul Bellow in *The Adventures of Augie March*.

But despite the temptations of comparison there remains one's conviction that Salinger is deeply and seriously committed in his fiction. Further, a little research into the Salinger canon reveals that two of his major creations, Holden Caulfield and Seymour Glass, the young husband of "A Perfect Day for Banana Fish," have deep roots in Salinger's own imagination. His novel, in its way, is as much a final version of "work in progress" as are the novels of his more literary contemporaries, pulled together from fragmentary excursions as short stories in *Partisan Review*, in *Hudson Review*, in *New World Writing*. Only with Salinger, the professional, early sketches of Holden Caulfield occur in a series of stories published in *The Saturday Evening Post, Collier's*, and in *The New Yorker*, in the years 1944–1946. And Seymour Glass turns out to have rich inter-connections in Salinger's mind with the uncle of the runaway boy of "Down at the Dinghy," with the older brother of the heroine in a sketch "Franny" (*New Yorker,* January 29, 1955), and with the bridegroom in a novelette *Raise High the Roofbeam, Carpenters* (*New Yorker,* November 19, 1955).

This extrinsic information helps verify one's feeling that there is actually more weight to his explorations of human alienation than his bright dialogue and his frugal use of background and event might suggest. Moreover, Salinger's non-literary status leaves him, as a serious writer, almost unique as a wholly free agent, unhampered by the commitments of his more dedicated contemporaries to one or another school of critics. One might guess that this is Salinger's most precious asset. Rather than wishing quarterly significance or "greatness" on him, we can be content to take him for what he is: a beautifully deft, professional performer who gives us a chance to catch quick, half-amused, half-frightened glimpses of ourselves and our contemporaries, as he confronts us with his brilliant mirror images.[217]

FREDERICK L. GWYNN and JOSEPH L. BLOTNER

From *The Fiction of J. D. Salinger.* Pittsburgh: University of Pittsburgh Press, 1958. Reprinted by permission of the publisher.

"A Perfect Day for Bananafish" (1948)

To turn to the period of Salinger's major esthetic successes is to enter a world of psychically underprivileged persons occasionally saved by love. Sicker than Holden Caulfield and Sergeant X, Seymour Glass of "A Perfect Day for Bananafish" is destroyed by his own hypersensitivity pathetically heightened by lack of love. Released from an Army hospital, he is unable to adjust to life with his crass wife Muriel amidst the lavish and vulgar atmosphere of their post-war second honeymoon, in the Miami Beach which Philip Wylie once called "the loveless tunnel of love." Oblivious to poetry but responsive to expensive clothes and tabloid-magazine sex, Muriel seems to be incapable of giving Seymour the love that will make him whole. The attention he does receive, from a four- or five-year-old child, serves ultimately only to reveal further to him the impossibility of his situation.

Everything is compact and organic in this story, despite its division into two separate scenes. The first part of the tale renders the characters of Muriel (to Seymour, "Miss Spiritual Tramp of 1948") and her mother and a part of Seymour's case history[19] in one long telephone call; and the second part reveals Seymour's needs and emotional state in a scene culminating with his suicide. Salinger skillfully manipulates the images which suggest an underlying motif: Seymour's sexual inadequacy. There is his obsession with trees, his story of the engorged bananafish trapped in the banana hole, his paranoiac suspicion that a woman is staring critically at his bare feet, and his choice of the pistol as the suicide weapon. Like Holden Caulfield and Sergeant X, Seymour Glass (he sees more than others and he shatters like glass) forms his most satisfying relationship with a sexually immature female child, but this girl's fateful name is Sybil, and she prophetically *sees* not only a bananafish but a doomed one with six bananas in his mouth; earlier she has been concerned with the six tigers of *Little Black Sambo,* who, we may recall, destroyed themselves through gluttony and vanity. In the water he kisses the arch of her foot, which she has recently stuck "in a soggy, collapsed castle" of sand. She too suffers from lack of affection: her mother sends her off to play while she goes for a midday martini ("I'll bring you the olive"). And even Sybil's affection has its blemish—her jealousy of three-and-a-half-year-old Sharon Lipschutz.

The situation and its meaning are reinforced, in part ironically, by a seemingly casual reference of Muriel's to a volume of German poems by a man Seymour had called *"the only great poet of the century."* This can only be Rainer Maria Rilke, the sensitive and frustrated spirit who, like Seymour, was unable to adjust to the military and to the bourgeois worlds, failed in his marriage, and was emotionally involved with young girls.[1]

Two other Salinger hallmarks are here—realistic[20] dialogue and functional sarcasm—but the real success of "A Perfect Day for Bananafish" rests upon the way that the disturbed young man, deprived of love, recognizes symbolically the inevitability of his destruction. Yet unlike Sergeant X, whose suffering and compassion take him outside himself, Seymour's concerns succeed only in turning him wholly inward. For example, his quixotic gesture of kissing Sybil's foot seems to have only a personal and pathological rationale; if he had possessed an aware-

---

[1] There is an interesting cluster of associations in Salinger's work progressing from Seymour's Rilke to Rilke's admiration of Picasso's *Les Saltimbanques,* the painting appropriately mentioned in Salinger's "De Daumier-Smith's Blue Period," and thence to Seymour's Glass Family, vaudevillians and public performers who bear some resemblance to Picasso's saltimbanques as described by Rilke in the Fifth Duino Elegy.

ness of the compassion often seen in Dostoevskian characters such as the one Sergeant X remembers, Seymour's story might have been different. Indeed, one of the most universalizing gestures in *Crime and Punishment* comes when Raskolnikov kisses Sonia's foot and says, " 'I did not bow down to you, I bowed down to all the suffering of humanity' " (Garnett translation). Because Seymour Glass and Sybil Carpenter are so preoccupied with their own feet, the story falls below the heights of "For Esmé," but it still has a power beyond melodrama.[21]

The High Point of Salinger's Art:
"For Esmé—With Love and Squalor"

At the outset, it might be well to consider Salinger's major fictional victory—the victories being the only reason for considering any of the failures that punctuate his unique career. The high point of his art, the moment at which particular narrative and general truth are identified most successfully with one another, comes in his most famous story, "For Esmé—With Love and Squalor," when Sergeant X, stationed in Bavaria after V-E Day, reads a German inscription in a German book and caps it with a Russian quotation written in English. The four agents in this process are perfectly chosen, and three of them are presented simply and at top speed. The reader is told that the book is *Die Zeit ohne Beispiel* by[4] Joseph Goebbels, that one inscription is by a 38-year-old unmarried woman, "a low official in the Nazi Party," and that the other inscription is from Dostoevsky. The fourth agent, Sergeant X, whose gesture of quotation sounds the depths of the human condition, thereby prepares himself and the reader for the salvation he receives from someone else's gesture later in the story.

What Goebbels represents should be obvious to anyone over thirty, but surely the range of this evil cannot be fully registered on the generation that adores Salinger, and it may even have dimmed in the more timeworn mind. To make any kind of contact with Joseph Goebbels is to be overwhelmed by the very type of psychotic hatred for everything weaker or more human than itself. His diaries show him to be "the unflagging motive force behind the vicious anti-Semitism of the Nazi regime," as Hugh Gibson says, whose "aim was the extermination of all Jews"; an ex-Catholic, he planned to "deal with the churches after the war and reduce them to impotence." It was this man, the holder of a *bona fide* doctorate, who in 1933 personally selected and had burned thousands of printed pages in which man had communicated with man. Less known than the genocide and the book-burning is Goebbels's hatred for humanity itself. In 1925 he wrote in his diary: "I have learned to despise the human being from the bottom of my soul. He makes me sick in my stomach." A year later he concluded that "The human being is a *canaille*."

But as Louis Lochner says, "Nobody who has not lived under Nazism can grasp how absolute was Goebbels's control of the German mind." It is this irresistible influence that (we may guess) had stimulated the second agent in the Salinger situation[5] first to her Nazi Party activities and later to the revulsion that she expressed by penning in the Goebbels book that X finds:

" 'Dear God, life is hell.' " To X, "the words appeared to have the stature of an uncontestable, even classic indictment," and he impulsively writes a comment underneath, one of Father Zossima's exhortations in *The Brothers Karamazov*: " 'Fathers and teachers, I ponder 'What is hell?' I maintain that it is the suffering of being unable to love.' "

The woman's substitution of the Christian God for Hitler and Goebbels is paralleled by the Sergeant's reference to Russian Christianity, and her implicit recognition of *Die Zeit ohne Beispiel*—The Unprecedented Era—as unprecedented hell is paralleled by Zossima's and X's awareness of the non-love that brings about disintegration and war; together these form not only a "classic indictment" but a profound objective correlative for the love and "squalor" experienced by Sergeant X—and the reader—in the rest of the story. (It is the young girl Esmé who asks Sergeant X to write her an "extremely squalid and moving" story, adding the question, " 'Are you at all acquainted with squalor?' " The Sergeant's answer is typically ironic but correct: "I said not exactly but that I was getting better acquainted with it, in one form or another, all the time....") We may now see exactly what is correlated.

The conflict of "Esmé" places the protagonist, Sergeant X, against four "squalid" forces in the four chronological sections of the story. (1) In 1950, the present, he is set off against his wife, "a breathtakingly levelheaded girl," and his mother-in-law. (2) Back in April 1944, he is set off against the dullness of pre-Invasion training and the incommunicativeness[6] of his sixty male mates, as well as against his wife and his mother-in-law, the women who write selfish civilian letters to this soldier about to be landed in France. (3) In the long year from D-Day in 1944 to V-E Day in 1945 (referred to only briefly in the story), the protagonist is set off against war itself (which has resulted in his nervous breakdown) as well as against his jeep-mate, Corporal Clay. (4) In May 1945, Sergeant X's combat fatigue is set off against the insensitivity of the loutish Clay, as well as against the selfish civilian triviality of his brother (who writes asking for souvenirs) and Clay's girl Loretta (who sits at home callously and amateurishly derogating X's psyche).

To balance these "squalid" antagonists there are four demonstrations of "love." (1) In 1950, exactly six years after X met Esmé, and apparently without any communication between them during this period, he receives an invitation to her wedding that makes him want to fly to it, "expenses be hanged." (2) In 1944, he has met Esmé, a brave English orphan of thirteen, who, nervous like X ("her nails were bitten down to the quick, her hand, as I'd suspected, was a nervous hand, damp at the palm"), is also precociously sensitive to artistic, intellectual, and emotional values. (3) Set opposite X's shattering experience in the war against Germany is the simple inscription in the book that communicates to him the shattering experience of a German in the war against the Allies. In answering the *cri de coeur* of an enemy whom he has actually just arrested as a criminal, Sergeant X equates himself with her simply as human beings against the total war they have suffered in—"a method of existence that is ridiculous to say the least," as Esmé naively but perceptively describes[7] World War II. (4) Finally, in 1945, X receives the wrist watch which Esmé mailed to him the day after D-Day, almost a year before. It is a stunning gesture for a titled gentlewoman who is "Usually not terribly gregarious" thus to give her father's watch to a G.I., a foreigner casually and briefly met, a man who had countered almost every one of her statements with an ironic answer. The gift, which belonged to a British nobleman "s-l-a-i-n" in war (in her younger brother's hearing she spells out crucial words), helps restore the possibility of life ("f-a-c-u-l-t-i-e-s") for the American Staff Seargeant X.[8]

. . .

JOHN HERMANN

"J. D. Salinger: Hello Hello Hello," *College English*, XXII (January 1961), 262–264. Reprinted with the permission of the National Council of Teachers of English and John Hermann.

Salinger's story, "For Esmé—with Love and Squalor," has been anthologized, selected as his best story,[1] and in general accorded the high point of his as yet beginning career. And the attention that has been given to Esmé is warranted, for it juxtaposes in one story two of

---

[1] Frederick L. Gwynn and Joseph L. Blotner, *The Fiction of J. D. Salinger* (Pittsburgh, 1958), p. 4.

Salinger's major theses, love and squalor, in one of his favorite subjects, children: Esmé, the distillation of squalor, of people who are, according to the choir director in the story, "silly-billy parrots" if they sing without knowing the meaning of the words; and Charles, Esmé's five year old brother, the epitome of love. Not all critics agree, but I should like to suggest, contrary to some recent interpretations, that it is Charles, rather than Esmé, who is the key to the story. It is his riddle of what one wall says to another: "Meetcha at the corner," which is the nexus between Sergeant X and the world, and it is Charles's final, spontaneous, and insistent Hello, Hello, Hello, Hello, Hello, affixed to the end of Esmé's letter, that brings Sergeant X's F-A-C-U-L-T-I-E-S back together.

The contrast between Charles and Esmé[262] is the burden of the first half of the story. The second half, in which the *I* point-of-view is shifted to Sergeant X "so cunningly that even the cleverest reader will fail to recognize me," is the squalid or moving part of the story, and shows a projection of Esmé's squalor (lack of compassion, of affection) in Corporal Clay, his girl friend, Loretta in the States, her psychology professor, Sergeant X's older brother—the same squalor, magnified further, which war itself shows in the punishment of a German girl who has been a minor Nazi official. It is the extension of this squalor, that war engenders, that has driven Sergeant X to the brink of disintegration, of faculties shattered. Esmé's letter, with Charles's P.S. at the end, brings the worlds of *I* and Sergeant X together at the conclusion of the story.

In the first half, the character of the narrator has been well established by the time he meets Esmé, Charles, and their governess, Miss Megley, in a tea-room in England during the war. From an introductory two paragraphs, we know that it is six years after the end of the war, that the narrator is married to "a breath-takingly levelheaded girl" in the States, that he has been invited to Esmé's wedding, that with the help of his mother-in-law they have decided he is not going, and that instead he is jotting down a few notes for Esmé's groom: "And if they give him an uneasy moment or two, all the better. Nobody's aiming to please here. More really, to edify, to instruct." The notes that give not only Esmé's groom but everyone an uneasy moment or two follow, based on experiences during the war.

The narrator has been undergoing commando training at a small town in England in preparation for D-Day. Finished with the training, waiting for orders and the chance to liberate Europe, he looks out the window of his quonset hut, "his trigger finger itching imperceptibly, if at all." It is our first indication of what he thinks training to kill other people is worth—nothing. We know that he also synchronizes his over-the-top watch by the clock in the latrine (what he thinks of their regulations), and wears his overseas cap (Two fingers above the left eye, soldier) jammed straight down over both ears. His gas mask long ago has been chucked out the window of the ship coming overseas and its case used as a convenient knapsack. The *esprit de corps* of his outfit manifests itself in isolated heads bent over V-mail letters home, in the thoughtless whack-whack of a ping-pong ball back and forth across the net "an axe length away" from where he sits. Except for the two introductory paragraphs, the tone has been wry, jocular—a man making fun not only of the army but of himself.

Later, wandering the streets in the rain, he hears children singing in church and enters. They are practicing. One of the singers is a young girl "whose eyes seemed to be counting the house." Even in a church. It is the first intimation we have of Esmé's character, and it is given by the narrator half in admiration, half in amazement.

After the practice, they meet by accident again at a nearby tea-room, where Esmé comes with Charles and their governess. Before the narrator quite realizes how, Esmé is standing with "enviable poise" beside his table. Invited, she sits down, a "truth lover or a statistics lover" of thirteen. He is the eleventh American she has met. She sits beautifully straight on her chair so that he too must come out of his army slouch. Her conversation with the narrator is that of a census taker—"Are you deeply in love with you wife?" "How were you employed before entering the army?"—or has the tone of an almanac dispensing facts—"To be quite candid Father really needed more of an intellectual companion than Mother was" (her parents become case histories in psychology); her wet hair, now straight, is when dry "not actually curly but quite wavy" (she is meticulously exact even in a situation in which a young girl might normally be tempted to alter truth a trifle, claiming curls rather than waves).

She finally asks the narrator, even though she is somewhat disappointed that he is not a published writer, to write her a story about squalor. "About what?" he says, incredulous, for he is confronted with a girl who believes everything can be learned by statistics, by so many notes taken, by so[263] many Americans kept count of, by so many figures put together. "Silly-billy parrots" the choir director had said of those who mouth words without knowing their meanings. She is talking about Esmés.

In contrast is Charles, disdainful of appearances like wet hair, of the facts that his sister cherishes ("He certainly has green eyes. Haven't you, Charles?" the narrator asks him. "They're orange," Charles says); enjoying his game of riddles; arching his back across the chair in contrast to Esmé's perfectly achieved poise; covering up his face with his napkin; giving a Bronx cheer at one point of the conversation between his sister and the narrator; engulfed with laughter at his own jokes; and furiously disappointed when the Sergeant tells him the answer to the riddle when asked the second time. He is everything his sister is not (She takes his wet cap from his head when they enter the tea-room "by lifting it off his head with two fingers, as if it were a laboratory specimen"). The last image that we have of the two of them in this part of the story is the picture that remains: Charles, blushing but determined, comes back to kiss the Sergeant good-bye. Asked the answer to the riddle, his face lights up. He shrieks: "Meet you at the corner," (and he does at the end of the story, saying at the corner of sanity and insanity to the Sergeant, Hello, Hello, Hello) and races out of the room "possibly in hysterics." Esmé leaves too, "slowly, reflectively, testing the ends of her hair for dryness"; one risking embarrassment to show his friendship; the other, worried about her own appearance.

The second, or squalid part of the story, extends Esmé's attitude to other people, etching the dilettantism into callousness, into stupidity, into destruction. For what does it mean to know squalor without love? It means a Corporal Clay who uses Sergeant X to write letters home to impress his girl, Loretta. It means a Loretta who uses the war experiences of men overseas as case histories in her psychology class (Esmé's treatment of her father and mother's relationship). It means a psychology professor explaining what war is about to soldiers who have suffered in it and have made other people suffer. It means an older brother, stateside, who writes: "Now that the g.d. war is over, how about sending the kids a couple of bayonets or swastikas." It means Goebbels's book, *Diet Zeit Ohne Beispiel,* and on the fly-leaf the words of the thirty-eight year old, unmarried German daughter of the household where Sergeant X is staying and whom he has had to arrest: "Dear God, life is hell." It means finally the last protest of Sergeant X, scribbled almost illegibly underneath: "Fathers and teachers, I ponder 'What is hell?' I maintain it is the suffering of being unable to love," which are the words of Father Zossima in *The Brothers Karamazov.* (Esmé: "My Aunt says that I'm a terribly cold person." "I am training myself to be more compassionate.") And Sergeant X's faculties under these pressures begin to disintegrate.

On his desk is a pile of packages, letters, books, that he has left unopened for days. He pushes them aside to use his typewriter to write a letter connecting him to someone, somewhere. But he cannot. He collapses on the typewriter. When he opens his eyes again, he sees a green package ("He certainly has green eyes, haven't you, Charles?" "They're orange," Charles says). Unconsciously Sergeant X moves to open the package.

It is a present and a note from Esmé—her father's watch (broken), and the notation that it was an extremely pleasant afternoon that they had spent "in each other's company on April 30, 1944, between 3:45 and 4:15 P.M. in case it slipped your mind."

But appended to the note is a message from Charles, of one wall saying to another, without thought, without knowledge, without statistics, but with compassion and affection: Hello Hello Hello Hello Hello. And Sergeant X's F-A-C-U-L-T-I-E-S disintegrating under squalor gradually come back together again. Much as we like Esmé's intelligence, poise, and breath-taking levelheadedness, it is her brother Charles, with the orange eyes and the arching back and the smacking kiss, who knows without counting the house, without 3:45 and 4:15 P.M.'s, the riddles of the heart.[264]

ROBERT M. BROWNE

"In Defense of Esmé," *College English*, XXII (May 1961), 584–585. Reprinted with the permission of the National Council of Teachers of English and Robert M. Browne.

I'm for critical ingenuity and latitude of interpretation and all, but there is some stuff up with which I will not put. Like Mr. John Hermann's view of Salinger's Esmé (January 1961) as a symbol of squalor, of lack of compassion and affection. Mr. Hermann gets facts wrong, as when he says that Charles, "blushing but determined...risking embarrassment to show his friendship," comes back into the tearoom to kiss Sergeant X good-bye. In context it is obvious that Esmé has to "drag" and "push" Charles to get him to kiss the sergeant.

But more important, Mr. Hermann has committed two basic errors. One is to read the story in the light of a rather romantic preconception, the other is to neglect the role of the narrator. The romantic preconception is that love of truth, including statistics, makes one unable to love people. Since Esmé is a statistic-lover, she must be unable to love people; Charles, not a truth-lover, is the real people-lover in the story. (In passing, I wonder how Mr. Hermann gets around Charles's scientific curiosity about kissing in the movies.) But Esmé's love of truth is simply part of her admirable integrity. She is still child enough not to have lost wonder and curiosity; her intelligence has not been corrupted by wishful thinking (her cool appraisal of her mother, her refusal, which Mr. Hermann thinks abnormal, to pretend that her hair is curly when it's only wavy). True enough, her literalness is a trifle comic, but it is not morally disabling, as it might be in an adult.

In the tearoom Esmé approached X in part because her aunt had told her she was "terribly cold," and she was "training herself to be more compassionate." Despite Mr. Hermann, this passage does not put her in Dostoevsky's hell of being unable to love; on the contrary, her willingness to try is enough to save her. Esmé's fidelity to truth and her acute though unseasoned intelligence do not prevent her from loving people; on the contrary they cause her to bestow her love fully on adults who, she perceives, have somehow escaped the general corruption: her father and X, whose "extremely sensitive face" attracted her in church. Though Mr. Hermann found her inattention in church objectionable, she wasn't simply counting the house, she was making an acute judgment of X, and ultimately the right response to him. For aren't we too meant to like him, and to think him worthy of love? If Esmé doesn't love him, why in the world does she write him and send him her dearest possession, the watch?

Of course her love of people, like her love of truth, has its comic side. The nervous concern about her hair, the question about X's love for his wife, the fear of seeming either too childish or too forward, these all indicate a schoolgirl's crush on a soldier. But it seems unfortunately necessary to insist on the obvious: Esmé is comic as well as admirable. Her slips when she tries to be grown-up in speech and manners, like her ignorance of Ohio and of physical squalor, are both funny and charming in X's eyes. He never tries to squelch her; he is amused, and he is also aware that her effort to act grown-up is a tribute of love to the adults she admires. Thus, after one of her polysyllabic speeches, "I said I imagined her father had had quite an extraordinary vocabulary." Throughout the story there is nothing in X's tone, explicit or implicit, which modifies the admiration for Esmé he so frequently exhibits: for her forehead, voice, smile, dress, posture, feet and ankles.

And how authoritative a narrator is X? By Mr. Hermann's own account of the preliminary section, he is wry and jocular. This sophisticated, ironic person is the most intelligent and mature observer in the story. Without discussing X's views, Mr. Hermann accepts the position of the aunt and of the choir coach with the dissonant voice, who sees Esmé and her choirmates as "silly-billy[584] parrots." (The choir coach gets the treatment she deserves from the children, "a steady, opaque look.") When Esmé asks X if he, like her aunt, finds her terribly cold, the reply of this ordinarily reserved man is "absolutely not—very much to the contrary, in fact." I will back him against the aunt, the choir coach, and Mr. Hermann.[585]

From "The Love Song of J. D. Salinger," *Harper's*, CCXVIII (February 1959), 83–90. Reprinted by permission of the author.

. . .

Because the details about the Glass family are scattered and because a reasonable knowledge of them is necessary for an understanding of Salinger's best work, it may help to set down in outline what we so far know about them. The parents, Les Glass (Jewish) and Bessie Gallagher Glass (a fat Irish Rose, her youngest son lovingly calls her), were successful Pantages Circuit vaudevillians in the 'twenties. By the 'forties Les Glass was "hustling talent for a motion picture studio in Los Angeles." In the 'fifties they are living with their two youngest children in New York, in "an old but, categorically, not unfashionable apartment house in the East Seventies." They have had seven children.

The oldest, Seymour, was born in February 1917, entered Columbia at the age of fifteen, and took a Ph.D. in English. In 1940 he and his brother Buddy reluctantly gave up the room they had shared in the Glasses' apartment since 1929 and moved into an apartment of their own near 79th and Madison. Seymour taught English for a year or two before entering the service. While he was stationed at Fort Monmouth, he met a girl named Muriel Fedder, whom he married on June 4, 1942. When he returned from the service, he was—as he had promised Muriel and her mother he would be—psychoanalyzed, presumably by what Buddy calls one of those *"summa-cum-laude* Thinker[s] and intellectual men's-room attendant[s]" so greatly admired by people like Muriel's mother. Possibly as a result, Seymour one day deliberately drove the Fedder's car into a tree, and it was decided that he and Muriel should take a vacation in Florida, at the place where they had spent their honeymoon. There, in room 507 of a fashionable beach hotel, on the afternoon of March 18, 1948, Seymour made his second, successful attempt to commit suicide, by putting a bullet from an Ortgies calibre 7.65 through his right temple.

The second child, Buddy (whose given name is, I think, Webb), was born in 1919, as was Jerome David Salinger. Buddy is the writer of the family, and it is sometimes difficult to distinguish his voice from Salinger's. *"The Great Gatsby,"* he says, "....was my 'Tom Sawyer'[85] when I was twelve." Buddy never finished college (nor did Salinger, who tried three). He entered the service early in 1942 and, when he got out, became "a writer in residence." In 1955 he was teaching "at a girls' junior college in upper New York state, where he lived alone, in a small, unwinterized, unelectrified house about a quarter of a mile away from a rather popular ski run."

The next child and first girl in the family is Boo Boo Glass. "Her joke of a name aside, her general unprettiness aside, she is—in terms of permanently memorable, immoderately perceptive, small-area faces—a stunning and final girl." She appears to be—we do not know a great deal about her yet—more successfully reconciled to the world than the rest of the Glass children. Boo Boo was a Wave, stationed in Brooklyn. During the war she met "a very resolute-looking young man" named Tannenbaum, whom she later married. The Tannenbaums live in Tuckahoe and have a summer place in New England. By 1955 they had three children, the oldest of whom is Lionel, the central character in "Down at the Dinghy," which was published in *Harper's* in 1949.

Boo Boo was followed by twins, Waker and Walt. Waker spent the war in a conscientious objectors' camp in Maryland and by 1955 had become a Catholic priest: "If you tell Waker it looks like *rain*, his eyes all fill up." Walt entered the service in the spring of 1941 and by May of 1942 was in the Pacific. In Japan, late in the autumn of 1945, a Japanese stove he was packing as a souvenir for his commanding officer exploded and killed him.

The sixth child, Zachary Martin Glass, known in the family as Zooey, was born in 1929. Zooey's face is close to being "a wholly beautiful face" or, as Boo Boo says, he looks like "the blue-eyed Jewish-Irish Mohican scout who died in your arms at the roulette table at Monte Carlo." After college he became a television actor, though his mother very much wanted him to take his Ph.D. in Mathematics or Greek, as he easily could have. By 1952 he was playing leads.

The youngest child is a girl named Frances, born in 1934. Like Zooey she is extraordinarily beautiful. In the summer of 1954, between her junior and senior years in college, she played summer stock. Zooey, an enthusiastically unrelenting critic, says she was very good, and Franny clearly loves the theater. In her junior year she became interested in a boy named Lane Coutell—interested enough to sleep with him. But in November of 1955 she was plunged into a spiritual crisis— "I'm sick of ego, ego, ego. My own and everybody else's. I'm sick of everybody that wants to get somewhere, do something distinguished and all, be somebody interesting. It's disgusting—it is, it *is*. I don't care what anybody says." After three difficult days at home, she is saved from collapse by her brother Zooey, who possibly saves himself at the same time.

Over a period of nearly eighteen years, beginning in 1927, one or more of the Glass children was performing, under the name of Black, on a famous radio quiz show known—"with perhaps typical Coast-to-

Coast irony"—as "It's a Wise Child." Their educations were paid for by these performances.

SUSPENDED EXPLANATION. This is the barest outline of what we know about the Glass family. Even so, the fullness of these details and their exactness are striking evidence of the imaginative intensity with which they have been conceived. They also make it possible for Salinger, for the first time, to use consistently the technique he is most happy with and to convey directly the feelings he cares most about.

For example, they provide the fullest opportunity for the kind of surprise an author can get from delayed or implied explanation, which writers of monologues like Salinger and Faulkner usually substitute for narrative suspense—an awkward and artificial device in a monologue. In Faulkner, one has to reconstruct the genealogy of the McCaslin family from dozens of scattered allusions before one fully understands any particular McCaslin story. In the same way one has to reconstruct the history of the Glass family.

Salinger uses suspended explanation much less extravagantly than Faulkner, but he has nonetheless confused some readers. Some of them, for instance, seem to have thought (until the matter was fully explained in "Zooey" in 1957) that the heroine of "Franny" (1955) was so badly upset during her football weekend with Lane Coutell not because she was in a spiritual crisis but because she was pregnant. There is no real reason for a careful reader to make this mistake about "Franny." In that story, Franny describes at length the idea of prayer in *The Way of a Pilgrim,* the little book she carries with her everywhere; and at the end of the story her lips are moving in the Jesus Prayer the Pilgrim recommends. Nevertheless, a good many readers apparently did misunderstand "Franny." Some even seem to have doubts about who pushed[86] whom into the empty swimming pool at the end of "Teddy," where, for much the same dramatic reasons that are at work in "Franny," Salinger depends on our understanding of Teddy's attitude to make us understand that it is Teddy who dies.

This kind of surprise is one of the most effective devices available to a writer like Salinger, and he uses it with great skill. He always plays fair; any careful reader knows what is going on. But we are frequently astonished and delighted when we catch our first glimpse of the precise connections between what had before seemed unconnected events. It must be some time, for instance, before a reader discovers that the Walt whom the drunken Eloise is talking about in "Uncle Wiggly in Connecticut" (1948) is Walt Glass, whose family connections did not begin to emerge in any detail until "Raise High the Roofbeam, Carpenters" (1955). But when the reader makes this discovery, a fascinating and important aspect of the Glass family falls into place for him.

Walt was Bessie Glass's "only truly lighthearted son"; as such he shows us an important aspect of Salinger's sense of human possibilities.

The fact that the Glass family is large and closely knit is also important to the feelings Salinger cares most about. The essential reality for him subsists in personal relations, when people, however agonizingly, love one another. "I say," remarks Buddy Glass as he begins to tell us the story "Zooey," "that my current offering isn't a mystical story, or a religiously mystifying story, at all. *I* say it is a compound, or multiple, love story, pure and complicated."

This is true of all Salinger's mature stories. Their subject is the power to love, pure and—in children and the childlike—simple, but in aware people, pure and complicated. Salinger's constant allusions to the Bhagavad Gita, Sri Ramakrishna, Chuang-tzu, and the rest are only efforts to find alternative ways of expressing what his stories are about. This power to love can be realized—and represented—most fully in complicated personal relations like those of the Glasses.

Salinger's conception of these relations is an impressive—and certainly unconscious—evidence of the way he fits into a major tradition of American literature, what might be called the effort to define The Good American. For this tradition, American experience creates a dilemma by encouraging the individual man to cultivate his perception to the limit according to his own lights and at the same time committing him to a society on which the majority has firmly imposed a well-meaning but imperceptive and uniform attitude. People in this tradition of our cultural history have a highly developed, personal sense of their experience. At the same time, they have a strong conviction—even if a bitter conviction like Henry Adams'—that no man can survive in isolation and that the only community they have to love is the American community to which they have been committed by a lifetime's involvement. Such people cannot[87] escape knowing that The Good American must be a member of a particularly demanding and not very perceptive community and simultaneously a supremely aware man, because they themselves live partly in the world of ordinary American experience and partly in what may perhaps fairly be called the transcendental world of extraordinary American experience.

The Glass children stand in this way at the center of our dilemma as, with less clarity of perception and less intensity of feeling, large numbers of Americans do. Like Thoreau and Henry Adams, Huck Finn and Ike McCaslin, Ishmael and Jay Gatsby, the Glass children are well aware of where they stand—committed, involved, torn.

"I'd enjoy [doing a movie in France], yes," says Zooey. "*God,* yes. But I'd hate like hell to leave New York. If you must know, I hate any kind of so-called creative type who gets on any kind of ship. I don't give a goddam what his reasons are. I was *born* here. I went to *school*

here. I've been *run over* here—*twice,* and on the same damned *street.*
I have no business acting in Europe, for God's sake."

This sounds like the speaker in Allen Tate's "Ode to the Con-
federate Dead," except that the voice is wholly Northern and urban
and is—for all its desperateness—less despairing.

THE EXTRA DIMENSION. It is the effort to convey their full sense of
this situation that leads the Glass children to talk the way they do. For
this extra dimension of understanding they use the everyday urban
speech Salinger has been listening to all his life. The Glass children
must speak the language of the place where they were born, went to
school, were run over; it is their native language, the only one wholly
theirs, just as the place itself is. But they need to express in this language an understanding of their experience which, if possessed to some
degree by many Americans, is wholly clear to only a few of them.

An effort to resolve a similar conflict of feelings affects most of the
writers of this tradition, with the result that they too develop odd,
brilliant styles. Salinger's style most obviously resembles those of Mark
Twain, Lardner, and Hemingway, who prided themselves on using
homely American speech with great accuracy, but were saying things
with it that few homely Americans are wholly conscious of.

Like Twain and Lardner, Salinger depends more than most prose
writers on the fine shading of his style to convey his meaning. That is
why he is at his best when one of his characters is speaking. When
Buddy Glass writes his brother Zooey about Zooey's unprofitable love
of Greek, he says, "Of course, you can go to Athens. Sunny *old*
Athens." When Zooey wants to get out of the bathtub, he says to his
mother, "I'm getting out of here in about three seconds, Bessie! I'm
giving you fair warning. Let's not wear out our welcome, buddy." Each
of these clichés is made absurd by the special quality of the Glass child's
feeling, but it is at the same time what holds him, for all his special
insight, in contact with the perception of ordinary people.

This perception is at its purest in children, whose wonderful di-
rectness fascinates Salinger. But he respects it wherever he finds it,
whether in "the very corny boy" who gave Franny the gold swizzle
stick she cannot bear to throw away, or in Zooey's producer LeSage,
who delights in scripts that are down-to-earth, simple, and untrue, but
believes with beautiful innocence that his "tired, bosomy, Persian-
looking blonde [wife is] a dead ringer [for] the late Carole Lombard, in
the movies." As Bill Gorton in *The Sun Also Rises* says of Cohn, "The
funny thing is, he's nice, too. I like him. But he's just so awful."

The Glass family's most treasured jokes hover close to this reluctant
sympathy with people like LeSage. For instance, at the end of Buddy's
trip to Florida after Seymour's suicide, when he had wept nearly all
the way, he heard a woman back of him in the plane saying, "with all

of Back Bay Boston and most of Harvard Square in her voice, '...and the next *morning,* mind you, they took a pint of pus out of that lovely young body of hers.' " As a result, when he got off the plane and Muriel "the Bereaved Widow came toward me all in Bergdorf Goodman black, I had the Wrong Expression on my face. I was grinning." It is this delicately balanced perception that gives the Glass children their special quality.

But if it makes them remarkable, it is also a quite terrible burden. "Smart men," as Dick Diver said a long time ago about Abe North in *Tender Is the Night,* "play close to the line because they have to—some of them can't stand it, so they quit." Like Abe North, Seymour, the most gifted of the Glass children, kills himself. He knows that, in spite of—because of—the unusual depth and intensity of his perception of experience, he needs to be a part of the daily life of the ordinary world. He tries, by psychoanalysis[88] and marriage, to become part of Muriel Fedder's world. This commitment is not merely an intellectual need; it is a desperate emotional necessity for him: "How I love and need her undiscriminating heart," he says of Muriel. But Seymour finds it impossible to live simultaneously the life of his own discriminating heart and Muriel's life, with its "primal urge to play house permanently,...to go up to the desk clerk in some very posh hotel and ask if her Husband has picked up the mail yet,...to shop for maternity clothes,...[to have] her own Christmas-tree ornaments to unbox annually." He is torn apart by two incompatible worlds of feeling.

This, then, is the hard thing—not to find out "what it [is] all about," which the Glass children have known from very early, but "how to live it." Knowing what it is all about, in fact, is the burden.

"Those two bastards," says Zooey of Seymour and Buddy, who had taught Franny and him what wisdom is, "got us nice and early and made us into freaks with freakish standards, that's all. We're the Tattooed Lady, and we're never going to have a minute's peace, the rest of our lives, till everybody else is tattooed, too.... The minute I'm in a room with somebody who has the usual number of ears, I either turn into a goddam *seer* or a human hatpin. The Prince of Bores."

This, Zooey knows, is not a failure of love—[89] he would not be concerned with his own freakishness if love failed—but a distortion of it. As his mother says to him:

> "If you [take to somebody] then you do all the talking and nobody can even get a word in edgewise. If you *don't* like somebody—which is most of the time—then you just sit around like death it*self* and let the person talk themselves into a hole. I've seen you do it.... You do," she said, without accusation in her voice. "Neither you nor Buddy knows how to talk to people you don't like." She thought it over. "Don't love, really," she amended.

"Which is most of the time" because, apart from children and the occasionally simple adult, the world is made up of people who are innocently imperceptive and emotionally dead.

THE POWER TO LOVE. Of the drastic limitations of such people, Salinger has a terrifying lucid perception. His stories are filled with undergraduates "giving the impression of having at least three lighted cigarettes in each hand"; young teachers "who come...in, in [their] little button-down-collar shirt[s] and striped tie[s], and start...knocking Turgenev for about half an hour...[and] if you get into an argument with them, all they do is get this terribly *benign* expression"; parents who say, "I'll exquisite day *you,* buddy, if you don't get down off that bag this minute. And I mean it." Such people, as Teddy in the story which bears his name says of his parents, "love their reasons for loving us almost as much as they love us, and most of the time more."

Nevertheless the power to love can exist in unimaginative people, and when it does, as the Glass children know they ought to know, nothing else really counts. Bessie Glass "often seem[s] to be an impenetrable mass of prejudices, clichés, and bromides"; these are a continual irritation to her children: Franny is driven nearly frantic by Bessie's insistence on nice cups of chicken soup when Franny is suffering something like a crisis of the soul. But Zooey is right when he points out to her that she is "missing out on every single goddam religious action that's going on around this house. You don't even have sense enough to *drink* when somebody brings you a cup of consecrated chicken soup—which is the only kind of chicken soup Bessie ever brings anybody around this madhouse."

Even if the acts of such people are not consecrated by love, they must not be hated. "What I don't like," Zooey says to Franny, "...is the way you talk about all these people. I mean you don't just despise what they represent—you despise them. It's too damned personal, Franny."

What Zooey knows he must learn to do in order to survive is to love even what he calls the "fishy" people—because they are all the Fat Lady for whom Seymour told him to shine his shoes before going on the air, even though the audience could not see his feet.

"This terribly clear, clear picture of the Fat Lady formed in my mind," he tells Franny. "I had her sitting on this porch all day, swatting flies, with her radio going full-blast from morning till night. I figured the heat was terrible, and she probably had cancer and—I don't know. Anyway, it seemed goddam clear why Seymour wanted me to shine my shoes when I went on the air. It made *sense.*"

It makes sense because the highest standard of performance a man's own understanding can set for him must ultimately be embodied—however mystically—in the ordinary, suffering members of the community of his fellows. Otherwise there can be no solution to the dilemma the Glass children are caught in. Zooey puts this conviction in the highest possible terms:

> I'll tell you a terrible secret...[he says to Franny]. Are you listening to me? *There isn't anyone out there who isn't Seymour's Fat Lady....* Don't you know that? Don't you know that goddam secret yet? And don't you know—*listen* to me, now—*don't you know who that Fat Lady really is?*... Ah, buddy. Ah, buddy. It's Christ Himself. Christ Himself, buddy.

What Salinger has seen in American life is the extraordinary tension it sets up between our passion to understand and evaluate our experience for ourselves, and our need to belong to a community that is unusually energetic in imposing its understanding and values on its individual members. Whatever one may think of Salinger's answer to the problem, this view of American life is important; it has a long and distinguished history. But Salinger's achievement is not that he has grasped an abstract idea of American experience, important as that idea may be in itself; it is that he has seen this idea working in the actual life of our times, in our habitual activities, in the very turns of our speech, and has found a way to make us see it there, too.[90]

ALFRED KAZIN

> "J. D. Salinger: 'Everybody's Favorite,'" *The Atlantic,* CCVIII (August 1961), 27–31. Reprinted by permission of the publisher and the author.

The publication of his two well-known stories from the *New Yorker* in book form, *Franny and Zooey* (Little, Brown), brings home the fact that, for one reason or another, J. D. Salinger now figures in American writing as a special case. After all, there are not many writers who could bring out a book composed of two stories—both of which have already been read and argued over and analyzed to death by that enormous public of sophisticated people which radiates from the *New*

Yorker to every English Department in the land. Yet Salinger's fascination for this public is so great that, although he has refused this book to every book club, it may yet sell as if it were being pushed by book clubs. Since 1953, when *The Catcher in the Rye* was reprinted as a paperback, it has become the favorite American novel on the required or suggested reading lists of American colleges and secondary schools, and it has sold well over a million and a half copies. No less unusual is the fact that the *New Yorker*—which, if it did not originate, certainly brought to perfection the kind of tight, allusive, ironic story with which Salinger's earlier stories (reprinted in *Nine Stories,* 1953) felt so much at home—published in "Zooey" (41,130 words) the longest story it had ever published, and a story for which the *New Yorker* obviously felt personal affection and some particular intellectual sympathy.

In one form or another, as a fellow novelist commented unlovingly, Salinger is "everybody's favorite." He is certainly a favorite of the *New Yorker,* which in 1959 published another long story around the Glass family called "Seymour: An Introduction" (almost 30,000 words), and thus gave the impression of stretching and remaking itself to Salinger's latest stories, which have been appearing, like visits from outer space, at two-year intervals. But above all, he is a favorite with that audience of students, student intellectuals, instructors, and generally literary, sensitive, and sophisticated young people who respond to him with a consciousness that he speaks for them and virtually *to* them, in a language that is peculiarly honest and their own, with a vision of things that captures their most secret judgments of the world. The only thing that Salinger does not do for his audience is to meet with them. Holden Caulfield said in *The Catcher in the Rye* that "What really knocks me out is a book that, when you're all done reading it, you wish the author that wrote it was a terrific friend of yours and you could call him up on the phone whenever you felt like it." It is well for him that all the people in this country who now regard J. D. Salinger as a "terrific friend" do not call him up and reach him.

A fundamental reason for Salinger's appeal (like that of Hemingway in the short stories that made *him* famous) is that he has exciting professional mastery of a peculiarly charged and dramatic[27] medium, the American short story. At a time when so much American fiction has been discursive in tone, careless in language, lacking in edge and force —when else would it have been possible for crudities like the Beat novelists to be taken seriously?—Salinger has done an honest and stimulating professional job in a medium which, when it is expertly handled, projects emotion like a cry from the stage and in form can be as intense as a lyric poem. A short story which is not handled with necessary concentration and wit is like a play which does not engage its audience; a story does not exist unless it hits its mark with terrific impact. It is a constant projection of meanings at an audience, and it is a performance minutely made up of the only possible language, as a poem is. In America, at least, where, on the whole, the best stories are the most professional stories and so are published in the most famous magazines, second-rate stories belong in the same limbo with unsuccessful musical comedies; unless you hit the bull's-eye, you don't score.

This does not mean that the best-known stories are first-rate pieces of literature any more than that so many triumphant musical comedies are additions to the world's drama; it means only that a story has communicated itself with entire vividness to its editor and its audience. The profundity that may exist in a short story by Chekhov or Tolstoy also depends upon the author's immediate success in conveying his purpose. Even in the medieval tale, which Tolstoy in his greatest stories seems to recapture in tone and spirit, the final comment on human existence follows from the deliberate artlessness of tone that the author has managed to capture like a speech in a play.

What makes Salinger's stories particularly exciting is his intense, his almost compulsive need to fill in each inch of his canvas, each moment of his scene. Many great novels owe their grandeur to a leisurely sense of suggestion, to the imitation of life as a boundless road or flowing river, to the very relaxation of that intensity which Poe thought was the aesthetic perfection of a poem or a story. But whatever the professional superficiality of the short story in American hands, which have molded and polished it so as to reach, dazzle, and on occasion deceive the reader, a writer like Salinger, by working so hard to keep his tiny scene alive, keeps everything humming.

Someday there will be learned theses on *The Use of the Ash Tray in J. D. Salinger's Stories*; no other writer has made so much of Americans lighting up, reaching for the ash tray, setting up the ash tray with one hand while with the other they reach for a ringing telephone. Ours is a society complicated with many appliances, and Salinger always tells you what his characters are doing with each of their hands. In one long stretch of "Zooey," he describes that young man sitting in a bathtub, reading a long letter from his brother, and smoking; he manages to describe every exertion made and every sensation felt in that bathtub by the young man whose knees made "dry islands." Then the young man's mother comes into the bathroom; he draws the shower curtains around the tub, she rearranges the medicine cabinet, and while they talk (in full), everything they do is described. Everything, that is, within Salinger's purpose in getting at such detail, which is not the loose, shuffling catalogue of the old-fashioned naturalists, who had the illusion of reproducing the whole world, but the tension of a dramatist or theater director making a fuss about a character's walking just so.

For Salinger, the expert performer and director (brother Buddy

Glass, who is supposed to be narrating "Zooey," speaks of "directing" it and calls the story itself a "prose home movie"), gesture is the essence of the medium. A short story does not offer room enough for the development of character; it can present only character itself, by gesture. And Salinger is remarkable, I would say he is almost frenetically proficient, in getting us, at the opening of "Franny," to *see* college boys waiting on a train platform to greet their dates arriving for a big football weekend. They rush out to the train, "most of them giving the impression of having at least three lighted cigarettes in each hand." He knows exactly how Franny Glass would be greeted by Lane Coutell: "It was a station-platform kiss—spontaneous enough to begin with, but rather inhibited in the follow-through, and with something of a forehead-bumping aspect."

And even better is his description of the boy at a good restaurant, taking a first sip of his Martini and then looking "around the room with an almost palpable sense of well-being at finding himself (he must have been sure no one could dispute) in the right place with an unimpeachably right-looking girl." Salinger knows how to prepare us with this gesture for the later insensitivity of a boy who is exactly one of those elaborately up-to-date and anxiously sophisticated people whom Franny Glass, pure in heart, must learn to tolerate, and even to love, in what she regards as an unbearably shallow culture.

But apart from this, which is the theme of *Franny and Zooey*, the gesture itself is recognized by the reader not only as a compliment to himself but as a sign that Salinger is working all the time, not merely working to get the reader to see, but[28] working to make his scene itself hum with life and creative observation. I don't know how much this appearance of intensity on the part of Salinger, of constant as well as full coverage, is due to *New Yorker* editorial nudging, since its famous alertness to repetitions of words and vagueness of diction tends to give an external look of freshness and movement to prose. Salinger not only works very hard indeed over each story, but he obviously writes to and for some particular editorial mind he identifies with the *New Yorker*; look up the stories he used to write for the *Saturday Evening Post* and *Cosmopolitan,* and you will see that just as married people get to look alike by reproducing each other's facial expressions, so a story by Salinger and a passage of commentary in the *New Yorker* now tend to resemble each other.

But whatever the enormous influence of any magazine on those who write regularly for it, Salinger's emphasis of certain words and syllables in American speech and his own compulsiveness in bearing down hard on certain details (almost as if he wanted to make the furniture, like the gestures of certain people, tell *everything* about the people who use them) do give his stories the intensity of observation that is fundamental to his success. Lane Coutell, sitting in that restaurant with

Franny and talking about a college paper on Flaubert he is horribly well satisfied with, says, "I think the emphasis I put on *why* he was so neurotically attached to the *mot juste* wasn't too bad. I mean in the light of what we know today. Not just psychoanalysis and all that crap, but certainly to a certain extent. You know what I mean. I'm no Freudian man or anything like that, but certain things you can't just pass over as capital F Freudian and let them go at that. I mean to a certain extent I think I was perfectly justified to point out that none of the really good boys—Tolstoy, Dostoevski, *Shakes*peare, for Chrissake—were such goddam word-squeezers. They just wrote. Know what I mean?" What strikes me about this mimicry is not merely that it is so clever, but that it is also so relentless. In everything that this sophisticated ass, Lane Coutell, says, one recognizes that he is and will be wrong. Salinger disapproves of him in the deepest possible way; he is a spiritual enemy.

Of course, it is a vision of things that lies behind Salinger's expert manner. There is always one behind every manner. The language of fiction, whatever it may accomplish as representation, ultimately conveys an author's intimation of things; makes us hear, not in a statement, but in the ensemble of his realized efforts, his quintessential commentary on the nature of existence. However, the more deliberate the language of the writer, as it must be in a short story, the more the writer must convey his judgment of things in one highlighted dramatic action, as is done on the stage.

At the end of "Franny," the young girl collapses in the ladies' room of the restaurant where she has been lunching with her cool boy friend. This conveys her spiritual desperation in his company, for Lane typifies a society where "Everything everybody does is so—I don't know—not *wrong*, or even mean, or even stupid necessarily. But just so tiny and meaningless and—sad-making." Her brother Zooey (Zachary Glass), at the end of the long second story, calls her up from another telephone number in the same apartment and somehow reaches to the heart of her problem and gives her peace by reminding her that the "Fat Lady" they used to picture somnolently listening to them when they were quiz kids on the radio—the ugly, lazy, even disgusting-looking Fat Lady, who more and more typifies unattractive and selfish humanity in our day—can be loved after all, for she, too, is Jesus Christ.

In each story, the climax bears a burden of meaning that it would not have to bear in a novel; besides being stagy, the stories are related in a way that connects both of them into a single chronicle. This, to quote the title of a little religious pamphlet often mentioned in it, might be called "The Way of a Pilgrim." Both Franny and Zooey Glass are, indeed, pilgrims seeking their way in a society typified by the Fat Lady, and even by Lane Coutell's meaningless patter of sophistication. No wonder Franny cries out to her unhearing escort: "I'm sick of just liking people. I wish to God I could meet somebody I could respect." The Glasses (mother Irish, father Jewish) are ex-vaudevillians whose children were all, as infant prodigies, performers on a radio quiz program called *It's a Wise Child.* Now, though engaged in normally sophisticated enterprises (Franny goes to a fashionable women's college, Zooey is a television actor, Buddy a college instructor), they have retained their intellectual precocity—and, indeed, their precocious charm—and have translated, as it were, their awareness of themselves as special beings into a conviction that they alone can do justice to their search for the true way.

The eldest and most brilliant of the children, Seymour, shot himself in 1948 while on his honeymoon in Florida; this was the climax of Salinger's perhaps most famous story, "A Perfect Day For Banana Fish." And it is from Seymour's old room in the Glass apartment that Zooey calls up his sister, Franny, on a phone that is normally never used, that is still listed in the name of Seymour[29] Glass, and that has been kept up by Buddy (who does not want a phone in his own country retreat) and by Zooey in order to perpetuate Seymour's name and to symbolize his continuing influence on them as a teacher and guide. It is from reading over again, in Seymour's old room, various religious sayings from the world's literature that Seymour had copied out on a piece of beaverboard nailed to the back of a door that Zooey is inspired to make the phone call to Franny that ends with the revelation that the horrible Fat Lady is really Jesus Christ.

This final episode, both in the cuteness of its invention and in the cuteness of speech so often attributed to Seymour, who is regarded in his own family as a kind of guru, or sage, helps us to understand Salinger's wide popularity. I am sorry to have to use the word "cute" in respect to Salinger, but there is absolutely no other word that for me so accurately typifies the self-conscious charm and prankishness of his own writing and his extraordinary cherishing of his favorite Glass characters.

Holden Caulfield is also cute in *The Catcher in the Rye,* cute in his little-boy suffering for his dead brother, Allie, and cute in his tenderness for his sister, "Old Phoebe." But we expect that boys of that age may be cute—that is, consciously appealing and consciously clever. To be these things is almost their only resource in a world where parents and schoolmasters have all the power and the experience. Cuteness, for an adolescent, is to turn the normal self-pity of children, which arises from their relative weakness, into a relative advantage vis-à-vis the adult world. It becomes a role boys can play in the absence of other advantages, and *The Catcher in the Rye* is so full of Holden's cute speech and cute innocence and cute lovingness for his own family that one must be an absolute monster not to like it.

And on a higher level, but with the same conscious winsomeness, the same conscious mournfulness and intellectual loneliness and lovingness (though not for his wife), Seymour Glass is cute when he sits on the beach with a little girl telling her a parable of "banana fish"—ordinary-looking fish when "they swim into a hole where there's a lot of bananas," but "after that they're so fat they can't get out of the hole again.... They die." His wife, meanwhile busy in their room on the long-distance phone to her mother in New York, makes it abundantly clear in the hilariously accurate cadences and substance of her conversation why her husband finds it more natural to talk to a four-year-old girl on the beach than to her. Among other things, Seymour expects not to be understood outside the Glass family. But agonizing as this situation is, the brilliantly entertaining texture of "A Perfect Day For Banana Fish" depends on Seymour Glass's conscious cleverness as well as on his conscious suffering—even his conscious cleverness *about* the suffering of "ordinary-looking" fish who get so bloated eating too many bananas in a "hole" they shouldn't have been attracted to in the first place.

In the same way, not only does the entertaining surface of *Franny and Zooey* depend on the conscious appealingness and youthfulness and generosity and sensitivity of Seymour's brother and sister, but Salinger himself, in describing these two, so obviously feels such boundless affection for them that you finally get the sense of all these child prodigies and child entertainers being tied round and round with veils of self-love in a culture which they—and Salinger—just despise. Despise, above all, for its intellectual pretentiousness. Yet this is the society, typified by the Fat Lady (symbolically, they pictured her as their audience), whom they must now force themselves to think of as Jesus Christ, and whom, as Christ Himself, they can now at last learn to love.

For myself, I must confess that the spiritual transformation that so many people associate with the very sight of the word "love" on the printed page does not move me as it should. In what has been considered Salinger's best story, "For Esmé—with Love and Squalor," Sergeant X in the American Army of Occupation in Germany is saved from a hopeless breakdown by the beautiful magnanimity and remembrance of an aristocratic young English girl. We are prepared for this climax or visitation by an earlier scene in which the sergeant comes upon a book by Goebbels in which a Nazi woman had written, "Dear God, life is hell." Under this, persuaded at last of his common suffering even with a Nazi, X writes down, from *The Brothers Karamazov:* "Fathers and teachers, I ponder 'What is hell?' I maintain that it is the suffering of being unable to love."

But the love that Father Zossima in Dostoevsky's novel speaks for is surely love for the world, for God's creation itself, for all that precedes us and supports us, that will outlast us and that alone helps us to explain ourselves to ourselves. It is the love that D. H. Lawrence, another religious novelist, spoke of as "the sympathetic bond" and that in one form or another lies behind all the great novels as a primary interest in everyone and everything alive with us on this common earth. The love that Salinger's horribly precocious Glass characters speak of is love for certain people only—forgiveness is for the rest; finally, through Seymour Glass's indoctrination of his brothers and sister in so many different (and pretentiously assembled) religious teachings, it is love of certain ideas. So what is ultimate in their love is the love of their own moral and intellectual excellence, of[30] their chastity and purity in a world full of banana fish swollen with too much food. It is the love that they have for themselves as an idea.

The worst they can say about our society is that they are too sensitive to live in it. They are the special case in whose name society is condemned. And what makes them so is that they are young, precocious, sensitive, different. In Salinger's work, the two estates—the world and the cutely sensitive young—never really touch at all. Holden Caulfield condemns parents and schools because he knows that they are incapable of understanding him; Zooey and Franny and Buddy (like Seymour before them) know that the great mass of prosperous spiritual savages in our society will never understand them.

This may be true, but to think so can lead to a violation of art. Huckleberry Finn, so often cited as a parallel to the hero of *The Catcher in the Rye*, was two years younger than Holden, but the reason he was not afraid of an adult's world is that he had respect for it. He had never even seen very much of it until he got on that raft with a runaway Negro slave he came to love and was able to save. It was still all God's creation, and inspired him with wonder. But Holden and, even more, the Glass children are beaten before they start; beaten in order not to start. They do not trust anything or anyone but themselves and their great idea. And what troubles me about this is not what it reflects of their theology but what it does to Salinger's art.

Frank O'Connor once said of this special métier, the short story, that it is "the art form that deals with the individual when there is no longer a society to absorb him, and when he is compelled to exist, as it were, by his own inner light." This is the condition on which Salinger's work rests, and I should be sorry to seem unsympathetic toward it. It is an American fact, as one can see from the relative lack in our literature of the ripe and fully developed social novel in which the individual and society are in concrete and constant relationship with each other. But whatever this lack, which in one sense is as marked in the novels of Scott Fitzgerald as it is in Salinger's emphasis upon the short story, it is a fact that when Fitzgerald describes a character's voice, it is because he really loves—in the creative sense, is fully interested in—this character. When Salinger describes a character's voice, it is to tell us that the man is a phony. He has, to borrow a phrase from his own work, a "categorical aversion" to whole classes and types of our society. The "sympathetic bond" that Lawrence spoke of has been broken. People stink in our nostrils. We are mad with captious observation of one another. As a friend of mine once said about the novels of Mary McCarthy, trying to say with absolute justice what it was that shocked her so much in them, "The heroine is always right and everyone else is wrong." Salinger is a far more accomplished and objective writer of fiction than Mary McCarthy, but I would say that in his work the Glass children alone are right and everyone else is wrong.

And it is finally this condition, not just the famous alienation of Americans from a society like our own, that explains the popularity of Salinger's work. Salinger's vast public, I am convinced, is based not merely on the vast number of young people who recognize their emotional problems in his fiction and their frustrated rebellions in the sophisticated language he manipulates so skillfully. It is based perhaps even more on the vast numbers who have been released by our society to think of themselves as endlessly sensitive, spiritually alone, gifted, and whose suffering lies in the narrowing of their consciousness to themselves, in the withdrawal of their curiosity from a society which they think they understand all too well, in the drying up of their hope, their trust, and their wonder at the great world itself. The worst of American sophistication today is that it is so bored, so full of categorical aversion to things that writers should never take for granted and never close their eyes to.

The fact that Salinger's work is particularly directed against the "well fed sun-burned" people at the summer theater, at the "section men" in colleges parroting the latest fashionable literary formulas, at the "three-martini" men—this, indeed, is what is wrong. He hates them. They are no longer people, but symbols, like the Fat Lady. No wonder that Zooey tells his sister: Love them, love them all, love them anyway! But the problem is not one of spiritual pride or of guilt; it is that in the tearing of the "sympathetic bond" it is not love that goes, but the deepest possibilities of literary art.[31]

PART THREE

SUGGESTIONS FOR STUDY AND WRITING

BIBLIOGRAPHY

SUGGESTIONS FOR STUDY AND WRITING

The Catcher in the Rye

1. Kegel points out that Holden's inability to communicate with either the adolescent or the adult world is presented symbolically by the numerous uncompleted telephone calls and undelivered verbal messages. Examine the novel, and write a paper on this subject.

2. Costello points out that some of Holden's figures of speech are original and "terribly funny." For instance, Holden says of one of his teachers, "He put my goddam paper down and looked at me like he's just beaten the hell out of me in ping-pong or something." Analyze similar figures by noting their frequency and classifying them. How appropriate are they to a person like Holden?

3. Holden has been called a snob despite his apparent detestation of snobs and phonies. If he is a snob, what form does his snobbery take? Toward whom and what is it directed?

4. Edgar Branch says that Huckleberry Finn accepts reality but that Holden rejects it in disgust. Is Branch's position borne out by other critics? Are there other critical points of view regarding Holden's rejection of reality?

5. Considering all that has been said concerning the relationship of *Huckleberry Finn* and *The Catcher in the Rye,* write a paper on the similarities and differences in the two works. (Additional essays on this subject may be found in the bibliography.)

6. Both Costello and Strauch mention Holden's use of two levels of language. Do their views correspond? Which essay contributes more to your understanding of the novel?

7. One critic, Seng, sees Antolini as understanding Holden's problems. Does he? Is he really helpful to Holden? What do the critics generally think of Antolini's role in the novel?

8. The museum scene in *The Catcher in the Rye* has been variously commented on; some critics see it as representing for Holden a kind of permanence such as Keats discussed in "Ode on a Grecian Urn." What other significance have critics seen in this part of the novel? Discuss the critical comments, and come to some conclusion about what the scene means.

9. Many of the critics included in this volume consider Phoebe's carrousel ride in *The Catcher in the Rye* a central symbol in the novel. To what extent do their opinions differ? Is there any agreement among them? What is a satisfactory explanation of this episode in the novel?

10. What does Holden admire? Do the critics in this collection agree on this matter?

11. Do the critics in this volume agree that Holden knows his own faults?

12. Defend Kermode's view that in *The Catcher in the Rye* "sex is what alters the goodness of children." Does sex alter Holden's goodness? Is sex all that Holden wants to protect children from? How does this matter relate to Holden and society, to Holden's realism, to Holden's morality? Is the evil of sex a theme in the stories? Examine the opinion of the critics.

13. Discuss childhood versus maturity in *The Catcher in the Rye.* Several critics have seen Holden's immaturity as the major cause of his anguish. Is it?

14. A number of the critics speak of Holden as a moralist. What is his code of ethics? Must one assume that Salinger subscribes to the same code? Examine this problem by considering the views expressed in this volume and by checking them against the novel.

15. It has been argued that Holden refuses to make the compromises necessary in a complex society. Which critics subscribe to this view of *The Catcher in the Rye?* What do those who take opposing views say in disagreement? How many different points of view on Holden's problems are there in this book?

16. Does Maclean say that Holden himself is a conservative, or does he say that a reader may reconcile himself to the society presented in the novel only if he subscribes to conservative maxims? Do you find anything in the novel or in other critical essays to support either of these views?

17. Branch speaks of the criticism of American life in *The Catcher in the Rye.* Does Seng believe there is any criticism of this sort? With which do you agree?

18. Seng says that "extant academic criticism" on *The Catcher in the Rye* sees the novel as reflecting a romantic view of life, but he himself sees the novel as "realistic, sensible, moral, and very hard-headed." Which of the critics printed here agree? Is there substantial disagreement?

19. How do the essayists in this volume account for the popularity of *The Catcher in the Rye?* What, to you, are the most convincing reasons?

The Stories and Matters of General Significance

1. Discuss the points of disagreement between Hermann and Browne in their essays on "For Esmé—with Love and Squalor." Are there aspects of the story which both critics have overlooked?

2. After considering the opinions expressed regarding Esmé's effect on Sergeant X, explain what her experience of evil and her lack of a sense of humor have to do with Sergeant X's story, "For Esmé—with Love and Squalor."

3. Write a paper similar to Costello's on one of Salinger's stories.

4. The language of Holden Caulfield has been discussed by most of the critics in this book. In a similar manner discuss the slang of adults in such stories as "Uncle Wiggily in Connecticut," "Pretty Mouth and Green My Eyes," and "Raise High the Roof Beam, Carpenters."

5. According to Seng, Holden wants a "world of children or children-surrogates like the nuns. He would people it with little girls whose skates need tightening. . . ." Is there evidence in *Nine Stories* that certain of Salinger's other characters desire such a world? Have other critics detected such an attitude? How many disagree, and what is the basis of their disagreement?

6. Strauch sees in *The Catcher in the Rye* a pattern of development in which Holden achieves a spiritual awakening through a child. In how many of the stories is a spiritual awakening brought about by a child? Is there any common element in the nature of such spiritual awakenings? Which critics agree with Strauch?

7. Is incommunicability a theme in Salinger's stories just as it is in *The Catcher in the Rye?*

8. Write on emotional estrangement as a major theme in *Nine Stories,* using the critical opinions published in this book to document your thesis.

9. Does the view that the movies reflect what is phony in the world find support in all the essays in this book? What differences in opinion are there?

10. Discuss Salinger's use of daydream and fantasy.

11. Discuss the critical opinions on the increasing concern with the spiritual and the mystical in Salinger's fiction.

12. According to the writer of the article in *Time,* "the predicament of the good, sensitive man in a private world of love and death" is the only theme Salinger has written about. Examine the *Nine Stories* in this light. Are there any other common themes? What do the critics suggest?

13. Salinger has become concerned with the role of the artist in society. Beginning with *The Catcher in the Rye,* trace this development. How much have critics had to say about this theme in Salinger's recent stories?

14. Some critics have seen in Salinger's stories a studied cleverness and artificiality. What is the general critical view of this matter? If you believe that Salinger is writing this *"New Yorker* type" of story, discuss *New Yorker* qualities in one of his works.

15. Hassan divides Salinger's characters into two groups, the Assertive Vulgarians and the Responsive Outsiders. How do the other critics classify Salinger's characters as types? How are these divisions useful to an understanding of Salinger's art?

16. On the basis of material in this volume, do you believe there is a character who might be called "the Salinger type"? Can you describe him?

17. How many critics represented in this volume would agree with Fowler that the "Rousseau wedge driven between good and evil" is "a falsification [which] will continue to charm the reader as long as it can command belief"? Does Fowler agree with Maclean? Is this a matter on which Salinger is explicit in either his novel or his stories?

18. Hassan states that the common charge against Salinger attacks his sentimentality. Discuss critical views of this element in Salinger's work.

19. Use *The Catcher in the Rye, Franny and Zooey,* or *Nine Stories* as a basis for discussing the theme of retreat from society. There are many scenes in Salinger's works in which characters wish to retreat from their surroundings; there are also several critical discussions of this problem.

20. Discuss causes of despair in *The Catcher in the Rye, Franny and Zooey,* or *Nine Stories.* Almost all of Salinger's major characters are, at one time or another, victims of despair. Which ones give in and which ones find a cure for this malady?

21. The subject of suicide comes up a number of times in Salinger's works. Are the reasons for his characters' suicides or contemplated suicides the same as we normally associate with actual suicides? The critics in this book discuss this problem. What conclusions do they reach?

22. In *Anatomy of Criticism,* Northrop Frye says that *tragedy* is the name given fiction in which "the hero becomes isolated from society." Can a case be made that Salinger's fiction is fundamentally tragic in this way? Do the critical opinions included in this volume support this thesis?

23. What is the importance of the theme of death in *The Catcher in the Rye?* What is its importance in the stories? Which critics contribute to your understanding of this aspect of Salinger's art?

BIBLIOGRAPHY

A Chronological Check List of Salinger's Fiction

"The Young Folks," *Story,* XVI (March–April 1940), 26–30.

"The Hang of It," *Collier's,* CVIII (July 12, 1941), 22.

"The Heart of a Broken Story," *Esquire,* XVI (September 1941), 32+.

"Personal Notes of an Infantryman," *Collier's,* CX (July 12, 1942), 96.

"The Long Debut of Lois Taggett," *Story,* XXI (September–October 1942), 28–34.

"The Varioni Brothers," *Saturday Evening Post,* CCXVI (July 17, 1943), 12–13+.

"Both Parties Concerned," *Saturday Evening Post,* CCXVI (February 26, 1944), 14+.

"Soft-Boiled Sergeant," *Saturday Evening Post,* CCXVI (April 15, 1944), 18+.

"Last Day of the Last Furlough," *Saturday Evening Post,* CCXVII (July 15, 1944), 26–27+.

"Once a Week Won't Kill You," *Story,* XXV (November–December 1944), 23–27.

"A Boy in France," *Saturday Evening Post,* CCXVII (March 31, 1945), 21+.

"Elaine," *Story,* XXV (March–April 1945), 38–47.

"This Sandwich Has No Mayonnaise," *Esquire,* XXIV (October 1945), 54–56+.

"The Stranger," *Collier's,* CXVI (December 1, 1945), 18+.

"I'm Crazy," *Collier's,* CXVI (December 22, 1945), 36+.

"Slight Rebellion off Madison," *New Yorker,* XXII (December 21, 1946), 82–86.

"A Young Girl in 1941 with No Waist at All," *Mademoiselle,* XXV (May 1947), 222–223+.

"The Inverted Forest," *Cosmopolitan,* CXIII (December 1947), 73–80+.

"A Perfect Day for Bananafish," *New Yorker,* XXIII (January 31, 1948), 21–25. Reprinted in *Nine Stories.*

"A Girl I Knew," *Good Housekeeping,* CXXVI (February 1948), 36+.

"Uncle Wiggily in Connecticut," *New Yorker,* XXIV (March 20, 1948), 30–36. Reprinted in *Nine Stories.*

"Just Before the War with the Eskimos," *New Yorker,* XXIV (June 5, 1948), 37–40. Reprinted in *Nine Stories.*

"Blue Melody," *Cosmopolitan,* CXXV (September 1948), 51+.

"The Laughing Man," *New Yorker,* XXV (March 19, 1949), 27–32. Reprinted in *Nine Stories.*

"Down at the Dinghy," *Harper's,* CXCVIII (April 1949), 87–91. Reprinted in *Nine Stories.*

"For Esmé—with Love and Squalor," *New Yorker,* XXVI (April 8, 1950), 28–36. Reprinted in *Nine Stories.*

The Catcher in the Rye. Boston: Little, Brown and Company, 1951.

"Pretty Mouth and Green My Eyes," *New Yorker,* XXVII (July 14, 1951), 20–24. Reprinted in *Nine Stories.*

"Teddy," *New Yorker,* XXVIII (January 31, 1953), 26–34+. Reprinted in *Nine Stories.*

Nine Stories. Boston: Little, Brown and Company, 1953. The only previously unpublished story in this collection is "De Daumier-Smith's Blue Period."

"Franny," *New Yorker,* XXX (January 29, 1955), 24–32+.

"Raise High the Roof Beam, Carpenters," *New Yorker,* XXX (November 19, 1955), 51–58+.

"Zooey," *New Yorker,* XXXIII (May 4, 1957), 32–42+.

"Seymour: An Introduction," *New Yorker,* XXXV (June 6, 1959), 42–52+.

Franny and Zooey. Boston: Little, Brown and Company, 1961.

Critical Studies

Material from items marked with an asterisk is included in this volume.

Anonymous. "Mysterious J. D. Salinger . . . His Woodsy, Secluded Life," *Newsweek,* LV (May 30, 1960), 92–94. Discussion of Salinger's personal isolation.

——. "The Recluse in the Rye," *Life,* LI (November 3, 1961), 130–144. An attempt by a reporter to pierce Salinger's curtain of secrecy. Largely biographical.

Aldridge, John W. "The Society of Three Novels," in his *In Search of Heresy.* New York: McGraw-Hill Book Company, 1956. Pp. 129–131. Short discussion limited to *The Catcher in the Rye.*

Barr, Donald. "Saints, Pilgrims and Artists," *Commonweal,* LXVIII (October 25, 1957), 88–90. General discussion of the work of Salinger, whom Barr considers one of the most powerful talents now practicing the short story.

——. "The Talent of J. D. Salinger," *Commonweal,* LXXI (October 30, 1959), 165. Reiteration of ideas expressed in earlier article entitled "Saints, Pilgrims and Artists."

Bode, Carl. *Wisconsin Studies in Contemporary Literature,* III (Winter 1962), 65–71. A review of *Franny and Zooey.* Proposes that "Franny" is a modern version of the debate between the body and the soul.

Bowden, Edwin T. "The Frontier Isolation," in his *The Dungeon of the Heart.* New York: The Macmillan Company, 1961. Pp. 54–65.

BIBLIOGRAPHY 175

Discussion of isolation in *The Catcher in the Rye,* with emphasis on the dissimilarities in Huckleberry Finn and Holden Caulfield.

Bowen, Robert O. "The Salinger Syndrome: Charity Against Whom?" *Ramparts,* I (May 1962), 52–60. Contends that all of Salinger's work is "catty and snide and bigoted in the most thorough sense."

*Branch, Edgar. "Mark Twain and J. D. Salinger: A Study in Literary Continuity," *American Quarterly,* IX (Summer 1957), 144–158.

*Browne, Robert M. "In Defense of Esmé," *College English,* XXII (May 1961), 584–585.

Bryan, James E. "J. D. Salinger: The Fat Lady and the Chicken Sandwich," *College English,* XXIII (December 1961), 226–229. The chicken sandwich in the story "Just Before the War with the Eskimos" may be a symbol of the Eucharist.

Bungert, Hans. "J. D. Salinger's *The Catcher in the Rye:* Isolation and Kommunikationsversuch des Jugendlichen," *Die neueren sprachen,* I (January 1960), 208–217. Incommunicability and isolation of the adolescent in Salinger's work.

Carpenter, Frederic I. "The Adolescent in American Fiction," *The English Journal,* XLVI (September 1957), 313–319. Brief discussion of *The Catcher in the Rye* and "For Esmé—with Love and Squalor." Compares Huckleberry Finn and Holden Caulfield.

*Corbett, Edward P. J. "Raise High the Barriers, Censors," *America,* CIV (January 7, 1961), 441–443.

*Costello, Donald P. "The Language of 'The Catcher in the Rye,' " *American Speech,* XXXIV (October 1959), 172–181.

*Creeger, George R. *"Treacherous Desertion": Salinger's "The Catcher in the Rye."* Middletown, Connecticut: Graduate Summer School for Teachers, 1961. A published address, delivered on August 10, 1961, to summer school students at Wesleyan University, Middletown, Connecticut.

Davis, Tom. "J. D. Salinger: A Checklist," *Papers of the Bibliographical Society of America,* LIII (January–March 1959), 69–71. A checklist of the fiction of J. D. Salinger and of criticism on his work.

———. "J. D. Salinger: 'Some Crazy Cliff' Indeed," *Western Humanities Review,* XIV (Winter 1950), 97–99. Shows that Salinger's concept of saving a child from "phoniness" comes from the bodhisattva figure of Mahayana Buddhism.

———. "J. D. Salinger: The Identity of Sergeant X," *Western Humanities Review,* XVI (Spring 1962), 181–183. Argues that Sergeant X may be Seymour Glass.

Didion, Joan. "Finally (Fashionably) Spurious," *The National Review,* XI (November 18, 1961), 341–342. Suggests that *Franny and Zooey* is spurious because it appeals to the reader's interest in trivialities.

Dodge, Stewart C. "In Search of 'The Fat Lady,' " *The English Record,* VIII (Winter 1957), 10–13. Quest motif in *The Catcher in the Rye.*

Holden makes a pilgrimage rather than a search, seeking the pure, the sincere, the divine in people.

Fiedler, Leslie. "The Eye of Innocence," in his *No! in Thunder*. Boston: Beacon Press, 1960. Pp. 251–291. Places *The Catcher in the Rye* and several of Salinger's stories in the context of modern fiction about children.

———. "Up from Adolescence," *Partisan Review*, XXIX (Winter 1962), 127–131. Proposes that the theme that has obsessed Salinger since the publication of "For Esmé—with Love and Squalor" is madness. The chief heroism possible is to reject madness and to accept sanity, achieved through a child.

*Fowler, Albert. "Alien in the Rye," *Modern Age*, I (Fall 1957), 193–197.

Gardiner, Harold C. "Words and Conscience," *America*, CIV (January 7, 1961), 444. On the morality of the language in *The Catcher in the Rye*.

*Geismar, Maxwell. "J. D. Salinger: The Wise Child and the *New Yorker* School of Fiction," in his *American Moderns*. New York: Hill & Wang, Inc., 1958. Pp. 195–209.

Giles, Barbara. "The Lonely War of J. D. Salinger," *Mainstream*, XII, ii, 2–13. Discussion of the Glass family and *The Catcher in the Rye*. The Glasses' problem is "how to love themselves excessively without feeling guilty about it."

Green, Martin. "Amis and Salinger: The Latitude of Private Conscience," *Chicago Review*, XI (Winter 1958), 20–25. Both authors concerned with the problem of finding one's place in the "ruling-class society," which is both "inadequate and dangerous."

———. "Cultural Images in England and America," in his *A Mirror for Anglo-Saxons*. New York: Harper & Brothers, 1960. Pp. 85–88. Brief discussion of Salinger's merits.

Grunwald, Henry Anatole, ed. *Salinger: A Critical and Personal Portrait*. New York: Harper and Brothers, 1962.

———. "He Touches Something Deep in Us...," *Horizon*, IV (May 1962), 100–107. A review of Salinger criticism. Proposes that Salinger is a romantic who offers delight to the halfway sympathetic reader.

*Gwynn, Frederick L., and Joseph L. Blotner. *The Fiction of J. D. Salinger*. Pittsburgh: University of Pittsburgh Press, 1958.

*Hassan, Ihab H. "J. D. Salinger: Rare Quixotic Gesture," in his *Radical Innocence: Studies in the Contemporary American Novel*. Princeton: Princeton University Press, 1961. Pp. 259–289.

———. "Rare Quixotic Gesture: The Fiction of J. D. Salinger," *The Western Review*, XXI (Summer 1957), 261–280. Substantially the same material later included in *Radical Innocence*.

*Heiserman, Arthur, and James E. Miller, Jr. "J. D. Salinger: Some Crazy Cliff," *Western Humanities Review*, X (Spring 1956), 120–137.

*Hermann, John. "J. D. Salinger: Hello Hello Hello," *College English,* XXII (January 1961), 262–264.

Hicks, Granville. "J. D. Salinger: Search for Wisdom," *Saturday Review,* XLII (July 25, 1959), 13+. Salinger has the same importance for college students today that Fitzgerald and Hemingway had for college students in the '20's.

———. "Sisters, Sons, and Lovers," *Saturday Review,* XLIV (September 16, 1961), 26, Discussion of *Franny and Zooey.*

Hinckle, Warren. "J. D. Salinger's Glass Menagerie," *Ramparts,* I (May 1962), 48–51. Discussion of the Glass family and the theme of estrangement in Salinger's fiction.

Jacobs, Robert G. "J. D. Salinger's *The Catcher in the Rye:* Holden Caulfield's 'Goddam Autobiography,' " *Iowa English Yearbook* (Fall 1959), pp. 9–14. That Holden cannot take "the step into adulthood" is his tragedy.

Jacobsen, Josephine. "The Felicity of J. D. Salinger," *Commonweal,* LXXI (February 26, 1960), 589–591. Salinger's objective pursuit of wisdom is religious at the core.

Johannson, Ernest. "Salinger's Seymour," *Carolina Quarterly,* XII (Winter 1959), 51–54. Suggests that since Buddy and Seymour had common experiences and shared a "common psyche," Buddy is unable to detach himself. Consequently Seymour cannot yet be judged.

Johnson, James William. "The Adolescent Hero: A Trend in Modern Fiction," *Twentieth Century Literature,* V (April 1959), 3–11. Comments on the differences in Holden Caulfield and Huckleberry Finn.

Kaplan, Charles. "Holden and Huck: The Odysseys of Youth," *College English,* XVIII (November 1956), 76–80. Points out similarities in *Huckleberry Finn* and *The Catcher in the Rye.*

Kapp, Isa. "Salinger's Easy Victory," *The New Leader,* XLI (January 8, 1962), 27–28. Salinger is "better at telling what personal affectations he doesn't like than locating the moral enemy."

*Kazin, Alfred. "J. D. Salinger: 'Everybody's Favorite,' " *Atlantic,* CCVIII (August 1961), 27–31.

Keating, Edward M. "Salinger: The Murky Mirror," *Ramparts,* I (May 1962), 61–66. A review of Salinger's major fiction. Concludes that Salinger presents no worthwhile adults in his fiction and proposes that all of his characters try to escape responsibility by indulgence in fantasy, by a return to childhood, or by death.

*Kegel, Charles H. "Incommunicability in Salinger's *The Catcher in the Rye,*" *Western Humanities Review,* XI (Spring 1957), 188–190.

*Kermode, Frank. "Fit Audience," *The Spectator,* CC (May 30, 1958), 705–706.

Krim, Seymour. "Surface and Substance in a Major Talent," *Commonweal,* LVIII (April 24, 1953), 78. Asserts that the reader feels that Salinger is "dodging . . . issues."

Leitch, David. "The Salinger Myth," *The Twentieth Century,* CLXVIII (November 1960), 428–435. Reprinted in *Mademoiselle,* LII (August 1961), 264+. Discussion of *The Catcher in the Rye* and the Glass family. Points out that the Salinger world is child-centered; his characters hate and fear the adult world.

Levin, Beatrice. "Everybody's Favorite: Concepts of Love in the Work of J. D. Salinger," *Motive,* XXII (October 1961), 9–11. Salinger is one of the few postwar writers to consider the relationship of man to God and of God to man.

*Levine, Paul. "J. D. Salinger: The Development of the Misfit Hero," *Twentieth Century Literature,* IV (October 1958), 92–99.

Light, James F. "Salinger's *The Catcher in the Rye,*" *Explicator,* XVIII (June 1960), Item 59. Suggests that the ducks mentioned by Holden represent mysteries beyond explanation and that Holden's questions are an attempt to understand life and death.

*Maclean, Hugh. "Conservatism in Modern American Fiction," *College English,* XV (March 1954), 315–325.

Marple, Anne. "Salinger's Oasis of Innocence," *New Republic,* CXLV (September 18, 1961), 22–23. Examines the theme of innocence in Salinger's writing. Avoidance of the sexual impedes "the free flow of Salinger's creative life."

Martin, Augustine. "A Note on J. D. Salinger," *Studies: An Irish Quarterly Review,* XLVIII (Autumn 1959), 336–345. Analysis of themes in *The Catcher in the Rye* and in *Nine Stories.* If Salinger were "never to write another line, his place in American fiction is assured in these brilliant books."

Martin, Hansford. "The American Problem of Direct Address," *The Western Review,* XVI (Winter 1952), 101–114. Considers *The Catcher in the Rye* unacceptable because it sees "inherent virtue in the culture" that almost destroys Holden Caulfield. For this reason the novel lacks logical and emotional consistency.

Matthews, James F. "J. D. Salinger: An Appraisal," *The University of Virginia Magazine,* I (Spring 1956), 52–60. Salinger is concerned with values and with the immature mind, but his cleverness sometimes taxes the reader's patience.

*Mizener, Arthur. "The Love Song of J. D. Salinger," *Harper's,* CCXVII (February 1959), 83–90.

*Oldsey, Bernard S. "The Movies in the Rye," *College English,* XXIII (December 1961), 209–215.

Peden, William. "Esthetics of the Story," *Saturday Review,* XXVI (April 11, 1953), 43–44. In *Nine Stories* Salinger presents human beings without sentimentality or condescension.

Rees, Richard. *Brave Men.* London: Victor Gollancz, Ltd., 1958. Pp. 178–187. Holden Caulfield is unique among characters in modern American fiction in his "love of reality."

Roth, Philip. "Writing American Fiction," *Commentary*, XXXI (March 1961), 223–233. There seems to be in Salinger a "spurning of life as it is lived in the world." The advice "we seem to get . . . is to be charming on the way to the loony bin."

Schrader, Allen. "Emerson to Salinger to Parker," *Saturday Review*, LXII (April 11, 1959), 52+. Since the sixteen-year-old has less to clutter his mind, he is often more likely than the adult to understand Emerson, Salinger, and Charlie Parker.

*Seng, Peter J. "The Fallen Idol: The Immature World of Holden Caulfield," *College English*, XXIII (December 1961), 203–209.

*[Skow, Jack.] "Sonny: An Introduction," *Time*, LXXVIII (September 15, 1961), 84–90.

Steiner, George. "The Salinger Industry," *Nation*, CLXXXIX (November 14, 1959), 360–363. A condemnation of the pretentiousness of much criticism of Salinger. It is possibly a disservice to Salinger to treat his work as if it were "great" literature.

*Stevenson, David L. "J. D. Salinger: The Mirror of Crisis," *Nation*, CLXXXIV (March 9, 1957), 215–217.

*Strauch, Carl F. "Kings in the Back Row: Meaning Through Structure, A Reading of Salinger's *The Catcher in the Rye*," *Wisconsin Studies in Contemporary Literature*, II (Winter 1961), 5–30.

Updike, John. "Anxious Days for the Glass Family," *The New York Times Book Review*, September 17, 1961, pp. 1+. Believes that Salinger loves the Glasses "to the detriment of artistic moderation." "Zooey" contains "too much verbal ado about not quite enough."

Wakefield, Dan. "Salinger and the Search for Love," *New World Writing*, No. 14 (December 1958), pp. 68–85. General discussion of *The Catcher in the Rye*, *Nine Stories*, "Franny," and "Zooey."

*Walzer, Michael. "In Place of a Hero," *Dissent*, VII (Spring 1960), 156–162.

Wells, Arvin R. "Huck Finn and Holden Caulfield: The Situation of the Hero," *Ohio University Review*, II (1960), 31–42. Contrasts Huckleberry Finn and Holden Caulfield.

Wiegand, William. "J. D. Salinger: Seventy-Eight Bananas," *Chicago Review*, XI (Winter 1958), 3–19. Discussion of most of Salinger's works. Salinger's heroes are spiritually ill.

———. "The Knighthood of J. D. Salinger," *New Republic*, CXLI (October 19, 1959), 19–21. Salinger is honest with his reader and will forego easy effects even at the risk of failure.

WITHDRAWN